CREDITS

EDITORS Barbara Huck, Doug Whiteway

ASSOCIATE EDITORS Peter St. John, Michael Evans-Hatch, Debbie Riley

DESIGN & LAYOUT Dawn Huck

INDEX Adrian Mather

PREPRESS & PRINTING Friesens, Manitoba

PHOTOS   Unless otherwise indicated, photos of Steven Fletcher, his family and friends are courtesy of the Fletcher family.

Photos of Steven Fletcher as a Member of Parliament, his aides, staff and campaigns are courtesy of the Office of Steven Fletcher.

Library and Archives Canada Cataloguing in Publication

McIntosh, Linda, 1943-
    What do you do if you don't die : the Steven Fletcher story / by Linda McIntosh.

Includes index.
ISBN 978-1-896150-49-9 (pbk.).--ISBN 978-1-896150-50-5 (bound)

1. Fletcher, Steven, 1972-. 2. Canada. Parliament. House of Commons--Biography. 3. Quadriplegics--Canada--Biography. 4. Politicians--Canada--Biography. 5. Politicians--Manitoba--Biography.
I. Title.

FC141.F54M35 2008   971.07'2092   C2008-900783-2

The partners at Heartland Associates wish to express our gratitude to Manitoba Culture, Heritage Tourism and Sport for its continued assistance and support.

Rolland Enviro 100 FSC recycled paper was used in this book.
For further information please see page 288.

What
Do You Do
If You Don't
Die?

THE STEVEN FLETCHER STORY

By Linda McIntosh

Heartland Associates, Inc.
Winnipeg, Canada

Printed in Manitoba, Canada

Table of Contents

Table of Contents

Dedication

This book is dedicated to
David, Joanne, Gordon and Julia

May the great love and devotion that has flowed so freely
and abundantly from each of you
be returned a thousand fold.

Acknowledgements

MY deepest thanks go to Steven Fletcher, who had the courage to bare his soul and let me tell his story. It was hard for him to go back and dig up details he had worked so diligently to bury. Much of his tale remains untold; there is only so much an essentially private man can reveal to others. Through our many long discussions I came to know Steven as I had not known him before and recognize that he is a truly extraordinary human being with a spirit that transcends the physical. I thank him most sincerely for being willing to let this project proceed.

I also extend my heartfelt gratitude to Steven's family—his mother Joanne, father David, sister Julia and brother Gordon. The cooperation and assistance they provided was beyond my expectations, and it has been a pleasure to work with them. Their boxes of records, files and documents were invaluable in researching the complex history of the decade Steven lived through after his accident. And everywhere, there was concrete evidence of their great devotion to him, then and now.

I am also grateful to those who consented to be interviewed for this book, whose comments and recollections appear in its pages. Thank you for taking the time to remember and for taking the time to tell me about those memories. I was impressed with each and every one of you. I liked the way you recalled things and the way you talked about Steven. I liked your modesty and your clear compassion.

A special thanks goes to Claire Vivier. One would not have blamed her had she decided to remove herself from this process, for it was particularly painful for her to discuss what happened to her and Steven. Yet she gave her consent, and by doing so, revealed just how devastating Steven's accident was, for the collision that damaged him damaged so many others as well. I hope Claire's courage in returning to examine the past will be a source of strength for her in the future. Thank you, Claire, for being there to allow Steven's story to be complete.

To my neighbour Liz Russell, whose support for my efforts was steady and consistent throughout, thank you for letting me store documents on your computer for safekeeping. Thank you for your wise counsel and thank you for being enthusiastic about my "work in progress".

Thank you to Barbara Huck, Doug Whiteway and Peter St. John of Heartland Associates. You polished and tightened the manuscript with skill, and kept me in the loop as you did so; for this I am truly grateful. Your experience and editorial talents made the final stages of editing this book exciting. Thank you as well to Dawn Huck, whose artistic designs have created the book's "look", which is both attractive and appropriate for the subject matter. I also want to thank Michael Evans-Hatch and Debbie Riley, who read the manuscript with such care. To all of you, my thanks. It was a wonderful experience.

My husband, Don McIntosh, has been a great source of support as this book has developed. In ways too numerous to count, he has been there to assist me, to console me, to humour me and to help me keep things in perspective. For all that he has done to smooth my way, I can't say thank you enough.

And finally, I wish to acknowledge Squadron Leader Hugh McKay Laughlin, Royal Canadian Air Force (retired), my father, for teaching me to recognize heroism in its many forms. As the child of a career military officer, I grew up with the RCAF motto firmly planted in my consciousness. In Latin it is *per ardua ad astra* and in English, "through adversity to the stars". This motto springs to mind frequently when I watch Steven Fletcher in action. To live each day as he does, to continue reaching for the stars through unparalleled adversity, makes him a hero of tremendous and incomparable stature. He sets an example that people of all abilities can strive to emulate. Steven's story is one of incredible courage and determination, a triumph of the human spirit, and it is my fervent hope that the telling of it will inspire others to seek Life Abundant, regardless of their circumstances.

Introduction

STEVEN Fletcher always had a zest for politics and an interest in governments at all levels. As a young man, he was intrigued by the way in which decisions made by elected representatives eventually played out in the public domain and, like many other Canadians, he was not always happy with the results. As he grew to adulthood, Steven watched with interest, absorbing what worked and what didn't in the tumultuous and adversarial culture of partisan politics. Whether or not he would have decided to enter the fray had a moose not stepped in front of his vehicle and changed his life forever will never be known.

As a young engineer, working for a mining company in northern Manitoba, Steven was talented, ambitious and hard working. He was proud to wear the iron ring worn by Canadian engineers and enjoyed his work and the financial security the profession afforded him.

A champion athlete and an avid outdoorsman, he was strong, healthy and energetic. Many felt that Steven Fletcher had it all. Six-foot-four, dark and handsome, he was not only superbly fit, but blessed with a razor sharp mind and a friendly, pleasing personality. Had he been told on New Years' Eve, 1995, that the coming year would start him on a journey that would lead to his becoming a role model and an inspiration for the severely disabled, Steven would have found the notion impossible to fathom.

To imagine descending into the depths of hell—facing terrors that can never be accurately described—and emerging to discover that he was trapped in a body that could not move, would have been inconceivable. But fate can deliver the inconceivable. On January 11, 1996, Steven's neck was broken, resulting in a C4 level injury, and he became a quadriplegic, paralysed from the neck down. To understand the battles he had to wage to be restored to meaningful life is to open one's eyes and heart to the true meaning of what life is all about.

Refusing to be placed in a personal care home, to be tended to as a hopeless and useless invalid for the rest of his life, he fought authorities and bureaucrats, experts and naysayers, insurance adjusters and politicians. And in the end he made it back into the world.

Somewhere along the way, he became an activist. Somewhere along the way he became seriously political. Somewhere along the way others who were physically disabled took note of him and, seeing his successes, gained renewed hope that their own potential could be realized. Steven Fletcher did not set out to become a role model and an inspiration, but he understands that things happen along the way. If his story helps others to focus on their abilities rather than their disabilities, if it educates and improves the Canadian health care system, or helps eliminate prejudice and discrimination against severely disabled people, then he accepts and rejoices in that consequence.

Some things, once survived, are difficult to contemplate later. Returning to consider those things is almost unendurable. One becomes torn, as are many Holocaust survivors, between wanting the world to understand, and wanting to erase the memory from one's mind forever.

I am immensely grateful to Steven Fletcher, for he has allowed me to tell his tale. I know what it cost him to recount it in detail, and together we hope that it will help others to understand and to take both courage and comfort from its telling.

Here, then, is Steven's story, a story of incredible courage and determination, truly a triumph of the human spirit.

I

Before

Claire met him at the airport.

On this cold winter night she was wrapped in a brightly coloured parka, her face fresh and reddened from the icy air, her green eyes peeking from beneath the woollen toque that fitted tightly over her hair. He pulled her into his arms in a secure hug, as glad to see her as she was to see him. For a moment there was nothing else in the world but her—her warmth and fresh fragrance, her laugh, and her embrace—the rest of the world had faded into nothingness. Holding Claire filled him with a sense of well-being that completed the happiness of the last few days.

Claire shared his happiness. It was a natural feeling to be cradled in his arms, sheltered and protected from the rest of the world, just the two of them alone in the crowd of travellers milling about the baggage carousel. She laughed with delight as, still clasping her closely, he leaned back and lifted her feet off the floor. They were young and in love, but as they would soon discover, star-crossed.

The day before, Claire had been struck with a surge of intense feeling for Steven. Perhaps it was the foreign film she'd watched, a story of ill-fated and repressed love, that had affected her in such an unusually profound manner. The movie left her with lingering emotions she couldn't easily identify and she was overcome with an overwhelming desire to find Steven and hold him as tightly as she could. Not one to give in ordinarily to such irrational impulses, Claire felt compelled on this occasion to act on these thoughts. She had contacted Steven's mother at his family home and asked if she could meet

Steven when his plane landed the next day. Seeing him now filled her with joy and she was glad she'd acted on her impulse.

When he'd left Winnipeg to fly to Kirkland Lake, she had given him her winter mitts because he had forgotten his. "Northern Ontario in January is no place to be without mittens," she had said, and when he hesitated, she had added, "Think of it this way—you'll have my hands wrapped around yours while you're away." He had laughed and agreed to take them if it meant that he would always be holding her hand. She smiled at the recollection. Things were always so easy and comfortable between them. Driving to the airport, she realized how deeply they had become attached to each other, and how tenuous the future could be for them as their opportunities and circumstances changed.

"I was so anxious to talk to him, to be near him and to hold him," Claire later recalled, "that when we got to my car, instead of driving off, we just sat there under the street lights and a pink winter sky and talked. Steven was getting ready to take the next steps in his life and we would soon be coming to a defining moment for us."

Reclining with his head in her lap, Steven listened to Claire, and together they shared thoughts and feelings and wondered about the adventures and the mysteries of the future that lay before them. Steven believed that, while making allowances for the uncontrollable circumstances of their lives, people could mostly control their own destinies. Claire didn't necessarily disagree, but she believed that fate played a stronger role in people's lives than Steven did. Neither of them knew that their beliefs and philosophies would influence them in ways yet to be discovered in the year to come.

Later, at his parents' home, he and Claire sat at the kitchen table with his mother and siblings, sharing in the pleasure of Steven's good fortune and exciting prospects for the future. As Steven told them about the extensive job interviews he had just come through, and the incredible new position he had been offered as a result of them, his enthusiasm rose. Waving his arms while talking, he would frequently hit his hands on the table, causing the iron ring on his right small finger to clang against the tabletop. His sister noted the sound and it stayed in her memory as a special pleasure, for it was made by the ring that only Canadian engineers are entitled to wear. She was proud of her brother and hoped some day to wear the iron ring herself. The evening was a happy one.

After the family gathering, Steven and Claire curled up on the sofa in the family room, talking and anticipating good times to come.

He was eager to share the details of his new job with her. Steven was on the cusp of the next phase of his life, which ultimately could become their next phase of life. He was anxious to accelerate his career path and attain his goal of becoming manager of a large mine. The new job, and the geographical distance that would separate him from Claire, would be a challenge for them both. But they were young and confident, and each of them was certain that, whatever tomorrow would bring, tomorrow would always be better than today. Claire was happy for him and supportive of his move. Trying things on their own would be a real litmus test for them, and healthy in the long run.

Reluctant to end the evening, they discussed the possibility of Claire's driving north to Bissett with Steven the next morning. She was in the midst of an enforced break from her engineering studies at the University of Manitoba, for a strike by university professors had led to cancelled classes. She had time, therefore, to accompany Steven on his trip, but getting back to Winnipeg presented a logistical problem they didn't have time to solve. In the end, they decided it would be better for Claire to stay in Winnipeg. They would be together when Steven was next in town and, in the meantime, they could talk or write.

As Claire was getting ready to go home that evening, Steven knelt down and pulled up the zippers on her winter boots. She was touched by his attentiveness, and ever after that, whenever she put on those particular boots, she would see him kneeling there, his black hair shining in the hallway light and his strong hands adjusting her footwear. It became one of many bittersweet memories, this last gesture that he made for her, so full of grace, humility and generosity. It is one she will never forget.

Steven got up at five a.m. the next day to make the three-hour drive north from Winnipeg to Bissett. Though early January had been brutally cold, on the morning of the 11th, the temperature hovered around 0° Celsius, unusually warm for the season. The crunch of snow under his feet, the scent of moisture-laden winter air, and the stillness of the sky all signalled the promise of a beautiful day ahead.

Steven headed out of the city on Highway 59. Because the weather was mild, the roads were slush-covered in places, but otherwise normal. Steven was a careful and cautious driver. He respected the rules of the road and understood the perils of Manitoba's northern highways. On this trip, as on others he had made throughout Canada's wilderness areas, his seat belt was securely fastened and

Claire and Steven, Christmas 1994.

his car's headlights were on. He was travelling ten kilometers under the posted speed limit and had his eyes on the road, alert for anything unusual.

Each increment of his journey north would take him into locations more and more remote. His ultimate destination, Bissett, is a small Manitoba community of some 200 permanent residents. Located on Rice Lake, 240 kilometres northeast of Winnipeg, the town sits on the Canadian Shield, a vast expanse of Precambrian rock that surrounds Hudson Bay and stretches across Canada's northland from Labrador to the Northwest Territories. As it is in many places across Canada's northland, the Shield in northeastern Manitoba is a landscape of rivers, rapids, falls, lakes and valleys carved by forces of nature—glaciers, water, ice and wind—over hundreds of millions of years. The soil is shallow and sparse, encouraging the growth of pine, spruce and other conifers, as well as soft mosses and lichens that cling to rocks and trees.

The Canadian Shield offers a unique northern landscape— wild, magnificent, and still pristine in many places. Its rugged terrain is one with which Steven was intimately familiar; he had grown up paddling the rivers and lakes in this wilderness with family and friends. By the age of twenty-three, he had logged more than 5,000 kilometers in his canoe on the cold waters of many of the wild rivers of eastern Manitoba and Northwestern Ontario, including the Bloodvein and Manigotagan.

Steven had travelled to Bissett countless times. Each turn and twist of the road was familiar. Not long after passing Brokenhead, he would leave Highway 59 and drive for a couple of hours up a paved road, finally turning east at Manigotagan. From there he would travel north on a gravel road for about an hour until he saw the mine headframe silhouetted on the skyline. The mine stood over the small community of Bissett as a tangible marker of the town's *raison d'être*.

The Canadian Shield contains a wealth of metals and ores, including gold, which has been mined at Bissett since the 1930s. Here, at Bissett's San Antonio gold mine, Steven was employed by the Rea Gold Corporation as a mining engineer-in-training. For a young geological engineer, it had been an ideal job to begin a career and he had gained great experience. He lived in a large white house provided by the mining company. The tenancy of the dwelling had varied over the time he had been there, for the working population was fairly transient and the prosperity of the mine depended on the ebb and flow of the stock market. During Steven's tenure, gold was trading at a respectable $400 an ounce.

The mine was conventional, with a main shaft and three internal shafts called winces. These vertical shafts were connected by horizontal hallways called drifts, through which ran narrow old-fashioned rail tracks. The ore body itself lay at an angle of about forty-five degrees, so the shafts had a series of winces or internal shafts joining them, which followed the slant of the ore deep underground. By the time miners reached the end of this zigzag staircase-like passage to the rock face where the actual ore was being worked, they had travelled nearly two kilometres down and the same distance away from the entrance of the mine.

Steven was often down at the working face of the mine and in the recovery operations in its upper parts. The elevator, called the cage, that carried miners to their various destinations was ancient. It shook, creaked and rattled noisily as it strained under its load, but it had served the San Antonio well throughout its history. Descending in the cage through the dark rock shafts, Steven often imagined that he was going back in time, to the 1930s, when the mine was in its heyday. (It was, in fact, in the '30s that the one of the largest nuggets ever found in simple mines in Canada was dug out of the mine at Bissett. Many years later, when visiting the Natural History Museum in Ottawa as a Member of Parliament, Steven was delighted to see a replica of this great nugget displayed for museum visitors.)

Part of Steven's job in 1996, however, included tasks that had not existed—at least not formally—in the 1930s. He was responsible, for example, for examining the environmental aspects of the mine, working on environmental assessments and making certain that the mine's waste water met government regulations. As an environmentalist whose love of and respect for nature was a powerful and determining part of his being, Steven valued the opportunity to contribute to the mining operations in this way.

He also enjoyed the challenge of using his engineering knowledge to help increase the mine's productivity. To improve efficiency and speed up the time it took to descend to the mine's ore body, a decision was made to extend some of the underground hallways that connected the vertical shafts. To accomplish this, Steven was working with the head engineer to survey a thousand-metre extension to a lower-level wince.

Deep in the mine people lose their sense of direction. They rely on maps, and it is imperative that those maps be correct. Digging an extension from an existing horizontal tunnel to connect it with a downward tunnel a thousand metres away requires absolutely accurate surveyors' work. The openings of the two tunnels must meet, or the effort is wasted. Being even a metre off in direction translates into big trouble for an engineer.

Steven loved all this activity. He never wanted to sit at a desk in an office, have a sedentary lifestyle or spend the majority of his time indoors. He loved to climb around on hills, looking at rock faces, conquering difficult outcrops, stretching and pushing himself to the limit. But he was a sensible adventurist, always careful in his planning and preparation.

Similarly, he found great satisfaction in intellectual stimulation. Spirited debate and philosophical discussions delighted him, and his reputation as a skilled debater and lover of a good argument was well-known and appreciated. He enjoyed a good laugh and had that rare ability to see the funny side in bizarre situations as they actually occurred, rather than after the fact.

Steven's jokes and one-liners were often dry and his personal values and standards were evident in whatever laughter-provoking circumstances he happened to find himself. He understood how to use biting wit to put people in their place when required, and he also knew how to use the gentle warmth of humour to put a person at ease.

He loved playing with words that referenced aspects of mining and geology. "Bed rock is not where rocks sleep," he once told me as he launched into a series of one-liners about mining, including such gems as "I dig Mother Earth" or "I don't mind classical music, but I prefer rock." And "mines aren't perfect—one can discover faults in them." He was quick to pick up on unintended humour in everyday situations, though he sometimes regretted this ability as he struggled to keep a straight face when someone made a verbal *faux pas*.

While happy in his job and pleased with the direction of his life, Steven was ambitious. He was eager to progress and seek bigger challenges. So in December 1995 he had read the ads for engineers in the *Northern Miner* magazine with enthusiasm. He particularly noted two positions in the Kirkland Lake Gold Mine, north of North Bay, Ontario. The Kirkland Lake mine seemed a viable career move for him. One of the ads was for an engineer with a master's degree in rock mechanics, a degree that Steven had not yet acquired. Steven always said that his university studies were ongoing, because he never felt that he could learn enough to say his education was complete. He had begun the admission process for the Masters of Business

Administration program at the University of Manitoba, which was to have been his first postgraduate degree. As a result, feeling that he was not qualified for the job outlined in the first ad, he turned his attention to the other one.

Finding the second, less challenging, job description also appealing, Steven had sent off his resume and a letter of application. In short order, he'd received an invitation to fly to Kirkland Lake, for a series of interviews with the executives of the Kinross Gold Corporation.

It was thus that Steven had ended up in Kirkland Lake, just south of Timmins, Ontario, in early January 1996. Containing his nervousness and excitement during the three days of interviews, he had so impressed the Kinross executives that they had offered him a position of higher responsibility and salary than he had expected. He had, in fact, been hired, not for the job for which he had applied, but for the first, more complex job that he had seen described in the *Northern Miner*. He was to begin his duties at the Macassa Mine at Kirkland Lake after giving notice to his employers at Rea Gold.

The Macassa Mine was much larger than the mine at Bissett. Touring the mine with a Kinross engineer, Steven was keenly interested in all that he'd seen. The deepest operating mine in North America, the Macassa was almost 2,500 metres deep. Steven was impressed with its unique character; he could actually see the stresses in the rock where excavations had been done and identify where circular shapes in the rock had become ovals as the rocks compressed.

Anyone suffering from claustrophobia would have had a difficult time in the Macassa. The cage descending into the mine was often used for hauling material from the production sites under-ground, which meant that it was not always available for passengers. Each level of the mine, however, could be reached by way of a "raise", a vertical crawl space one metre in diameter that contained narrow metal ladders for climbing up and down. The crawl spaces, which extended up to 1.6 kilometres underground, were lined and enclosed by sleeves of mesh to catch loose tumbling rocks.

A natural teacher who loved to explain things, Steven described the tunnels in the mine to me like this: "Imagine," he said, "a piece of loose-leaf paper. The blue lines on the paper are like the horizontal drifts in the mine. The red line going down is like the main vertical shaft. There would be a raise from one of the blue lines to the next all the way to the top. Miners could climb these raises instead of using the cage to move up and down."(My doodles on loose-leaf paper thereafter included tiny miners climbing all over the pages.)

Large chambers, called "stopes", are located off the shaft and it is in these chambers that the ore is extracted. Because of the high stresses, mini-earthquakes, rock bursts and cave-ins occur, dangerous realities that mining companies work diligently to avoid. Part of Steven's new job would be to operate advanced computers in the office above ground to keep the miners safe from these potential hazard. It was exacting, stimulating work, right up Steven's alley.

Kirkland Lake, home to approximately 10,000 people, was also a much larger settlement than Bissett and Steven had liked what he'd seen in both the mine and the community. His last requirement before leaving Kirkland Lake to return to Bissett was a compulsory physical examination, an understandable necessity for employment at the Macassa Mine. On January 10, 1996, he easily passed the physical.

Steven knew that his father, an engineer whose scientific interests were shared by all his children, would be keenly interested in his new job and he looked forward to discussing all the details. Like his father, grandfather and great-grandfather before him, Steven took great pride in being an engineer. It was an honourable and challenging profession, immensely satisfying and financially rewarding. His younger sister, Julia, had also indicated her intention to become an engineer, and his younger brother, Gordon, was already a student in the University of Manitoba's Faculty of Engineering, where Claire, too, was a student.

A love of engineering was not the only thing the members of the Fletcher family had in common. An intense passion for wilderness spaces surpassed all other interests, aside from family. His father, David Fletcher, says that when he took Steven, as a young boy, on wilderness camping trips, he always elected to sleep on the rocks (weather and mosquitoes permitting) rather than in a tent, so that he could gaze at the night sky before drifting off to sleep. Canoeing, hiking, camping—all were a regular part of the Fletcher lifestyle.

As soon as they could manage a portage, David Fletcher had made a practice of taking his three children on annual week-long canoe trips. On these trips, David, whose professional work takes him all over the world, had discussions with his children about history, world politics and current affairs. In addition to honing his paddling skills and learning about nature, these canoe trips helped Steven gain an understanding of the world beyond Manitoba and Canada and an appreciation of what it was to be Canadian.

Among other outdoor activities, the thrill of competitive flat-water kayaking had captured Steven's imagination. With his

Top, from left: Gordon, Steven and Julia, in the Shield. Above: Though he enjoyed kayaking and other wilderness pursuits, canoeing was Steven's true love.

encouragement, his siblings also became kayaking devotees whose expertise in the sport was soon well-known. Steven became the 1988 and 1989 Manitoba kayak champion, competing in the 1989 Canada Games in the K1, K2, K4, 500-metre, 1,000-metre and 6,000-metre events. Julia became a renowned kayak champion and was, among other things, Manitoba women's kayaking champion for three consecutive years (1995–97); she also represented Canada at the World

Marathon Kayak Championships, winning two bronze medals. And under Steven's tutelage, Gordon became the Canadian marathon kayak champion when he was just sixteen. The Fletcher family was admired by flat-water and white-water canoeists, flat-water Olympic style paddlers, and white-water riders from coast to coast.

At sixteen, Steven joined the Manitoba Naturalists Society and was known to be a dedicated and enthusiastic outdoorsman. He believed in challenging his physical limits and constantly sought to surpass his achievements. In the wilderness, he says, he understood spirituality.

There is a place on the Bloodvein River called Manitou Falls, where the water spills over a high cliff into a large clear pool. The sound of the falls echoes off a high granite cliff opposite, greatly amplifying the power of the river. Mist and spray dance up from the pool as the waterfall splashes into it, and the sight and the sound of water meeting water is so incredibly beautiful that one's breath is momentarily taken away when coming upon the scene.

Manitou Falls never failed to fill Steven with wonder. There, sitting quietly on a windless lake, floating on cool silver water, he would gaze up at rocks billions of years old. He would see ancient, moss-covered evergreens clinging perilously to crevices and cracks, while delicate new pines and cedars started their own stretch to the skies in unexpected places that seemed to have no soil at all. In the forests by the falls, dead and decaying trees lay on the ground, providing a variety of services to other life forms as they sank softly into the earth. He could see the cycle of life and death and rebirth in everything, from ferns and wildflowers to birds and quick scampering creatures.

"I would listen to the water and waves lap against rocky shores or the rush of the water through a rapid or falls," he recalls. "I realized my vulnerability in such a place where living things are seen to exist for only a short time before returning to the Earth. It's not a bad feeling to be part of all this, to be in tune with the elements and weather and to feel part of the universe. There is a sense of eternity in the wild, where there are no clocks and no artificial barriers between a person and the natural world to which we all belong. Science talks about infinity, time, mass, energy. As a naturalist I would add wonder and mystery to this good list."

Everyone who knew him understood exactly why Steven Fletcher was sublimely happy working as a geological engineer in Canada's rugged north. There he could climb around in rocky caverns and tunnels all day, and glide through fresh, cold, clear water during his free time. Mind and body were constantly stretching, reaching for excellence. Photographs of him during this period show a rugged young man, tall and tanned, exuding confidence and well-being.

As he drove to Bissett that clear January morning, he felt that sense of well-being. A modest man, he was nonetheless aware of his many blessings and gifts. He was eager to get on with his opportunities, to grow and achieve and prosper. He would marry and have children and he would share with them the wonder of wilderness, just as his parents had done with him. Life was bright and his expectations were high.

Then something happened.

II

Meeting the Moose

He lay in a frozen ditch. The top of his car was mangled and partly missing and he could see the winter sky above him. As a scientist, he knew the composition of air and he wondered briefly how the air could look icy when it wasn't solid. He couldn't see the body of the great beast that had shaved off the roof of his car because it lay outside of his field of vision and he couldn't move to look around him. He wasn't certain of the time that had passed before he heard voices and met the men who had stopped their car to help. Gasping for breath and drawing on his knowledge of emergency assistance, he had the wherewithal and strength to ask, "Can you help me?"

Steven doesn't know whether he said the words aloud or only mouthed them. "Don't move me. I think my neck is broken. Get an ambulance." He has some memory gaps about the details of the accident, but those fragmented memories, along with other information provided by those who tended to his broken body, have helped piece together the event.

At about 6:30 a.m. on that cold winter morning, when he was twenty-three years old and full of hope and happiness, a calf moose stepped in front of Steven's car. Swerving to avoid it, he collided with the giant moose coming up behind. The massive animal hit the hood and flew over the car, peeling back the roof as it went, partly impaling itself on the shredded metal and landing heavily on the trunk. The vehicle was propelled across the road and into the steep highway ditch on the opposite bank. As the car descended, the moose reversed its flight and crashed from the trunk to the front of the car, slamming the roof back down, sheering part of it off and snapping Steven's neck forward. The huge creature was thrown forward faster than the car was moving and it landed hard in front of the vehicle, so the car again made contact with the moose, coming to an abrupt halt atop part of its body. What was left of the vehicle, with Steven strapped inside it, lay shattered in the deep, cold ditch.

About a half-hour after the collision, Duncan McIvor and John Stroet, travelling to Manigotagan on an assignment for the Manitoba Telephone System, passed the accident site. The wreckage in the ditch wasn't visible from the road, but as they drove past, they noticed a light beaming skyward. It was one of the headlights from Steven's car, the only visible sign that something was out of order, the only clue that someone might be in peril. Without that headlight shining to the heavens, no one would have suspected that anything unusual had occurred. But the light did shine. The two men stopped their car and got out for a closer look.

Climbing down the bank, they saw the steaming body of the moose, and in the tangled metal that was twisted behind and above it, the body of a man.

They heard the faintest of sounds, a choked voice attempting to be heard, and they moved closer to see what they could do to help. They found Steven alive, but motionless and semiconscious, his face bleeding from deep lacerations, his left ear almost completely severed. He was slouched in a sitting position in the ruined front seat with his head hanging over toward the console, the remnants of the steering wheel pressing tightly on his chest. They could see the huge cut that had sliced open the side of his head and pieces of glass shimmering through the thick dark blood. There was blood everywhere, and Duncan's first concern was that the injured man would bleed to death. Closer inspection showed that the blood was coagulating, thickening, perhaps from the cold, perhaps because he had been lying there for a long time.

Most alarmingly, they could see the clear outline of a bone pressed up in an unnatural position beneath the skin of his neck, a bone where no bone should be seen, a bone not quite protruding through the skin, but so tightly pressed against its inner wall that it was as visible as if it were lying outside the flesh. They spoke gently to him. Steven recalls their voices coming at him as from a great distance, "Can you hear me? Can you hear me? Hear me? Hear me?" Yes, he could hear them. He was unable to move but he could hear them and he could speak. He tried to tell them not to move him, but

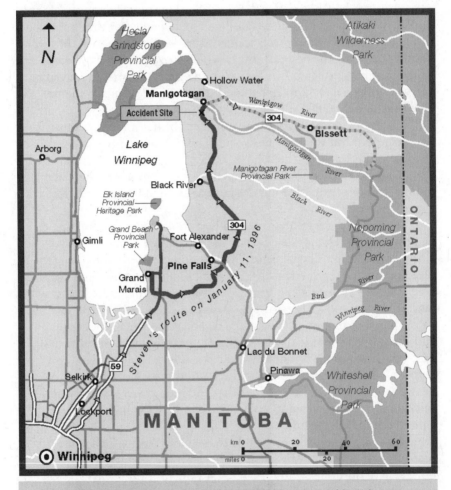

Though less than two hours northeast of Winnipeg, the accident site was well into the Shield, a wild land populated by black bears, white-tailed deer and North America's largest ungulate, moose.

they had already looked closely at him and understood why he must be left to lie still.

They asked him, "Are you in pain?" He replied hoarsely, "My neck." He could feel nothing else.

The steering column was exerting too much pressure on his chest. He was solidly pinned on it and it was crushing him. They didn't dare touch Steven himself, but McIvor and Stroet instead tied the steering wheel to a corner post of the car and the column eased off him slightly, enough to release some of the pressure so that he could breathe more easily.

They opened the trunk and found blankets, which they draped over him to keep him warm. During the previous weeks the temperature had hovered consistently around minus thirty degrees Celsius, but on this day, they were fortunate. While cold, the temperature this January morning was not punishing. At only minus three degrees, with blankets and other warm coverings, they could keep him from freezing.

In the Manigotagan area, as in other isolated parts of the Canadian Shield, there is no cell phone service. Duncan McIvor climbed to the edge of the road and flagged down a truck with two men in it. The truck driver had a cell phone, and McIvor, explaining that it was a matter of life and death, asked him to call 911 as soon as he was able to pick up a signal. The trucker promised to do so. Just to be on the safe side, McIvor flagged down another vehicle ten minutes later and repeated his plea for help, again being assured that the 911 call would be placed as quickly as possible. McIvor and Stroet knew that the young man trapped in the frozen ditch would surely die if help did not come quickly. McIvor remained by Steven's side, comforting him and reassuring him that the Pine Falls Hospital ambulance was on its way and that help would soon arrive. They understood that "soon" would be at least a half-hour, since Pine Falls was a long drive away. Meanwhile, Stroet began to dig a path through the deep snow from the highway to the spot where Steven lay, to provide easier access for the paramedics to reach and transport Steven when they arrived.

Brenda Boulette, who was at the time the mayor of Manigotagan, was scheduled to attend classes that January morning for an administrator's course she was taking in Pine Falls. The course was nearing its conclusion, and the classmates had decided to meet in Pine Falls for a friendly early morning visit at Clarke's Corner, a popular travellers' stop that provided gasoline, food services and a convenience store. Though she enjoyed the course and was looking forward to the coffee and conversation, Boulette was reluctant that morning to leave home. However, she couldn't identify the cause for her desire for delay. She just had, as she confided to her husband, "an uneasy, ugly sort of feeling" that "something was wrong".

Boulette's husband couldn't understand why she didn't want to go to school, and persuaded her to keep her scheduled commitments. "You're not sick," he told her, "there is nothing wrong, and there's no logical reason for you not to go to Pine Falls today." Recognizing rationally that there was indeed no logical reason for her to stay home, the mayor shook off her feelings, pulled herself together and left for Pine Falls. Her hesitation, however, had cost her time. She was twenty minutes late leaving Manigotagan.

A few miles out of town, Boulette saw the car parked by the side of the road with its hazard lights on. As is customary in the north, she stopped to see what had happened and to offer help if it was required. Climbing over the top of the ditch, she witnessed the carnage below.

"What I saw was awful," she recalls, "The impact of the car and the moose colliding was enormous. The roof of the car was twisted like a sardine can and squashed beyond recognition. The moose itself was lying mangled and bloody, jammed up in front of the car. It was the biggest moose I have ever seen in my life. I took one look at the moose's head and turned away. I didn't want to see the rest of it."

Brenda Boulette's heart jumped a beat when Steven came into full view. "I felt so bad for him," she remembers, choking on her words. "He had this big slash across his ear, a gash that was open and spread apart as wide as it could be."

McIvor and Stroet, who were tending to Steven in the ditch, told Boulette that they had sent for an ambulance, and that they would stay until it arrived. Continuing on to Pine Falls was now out of the question for Boulette. She turned back to Manigotagan, where she picked up blankets and clean water from the local store. Returning to the accident site, she decided to remain with the men from MTS and wait for the emergency response team. "I couldn't leave," she said. "I had to stay and do what I could to help."

There was nothing that could be done for Steven until the ambulance arrived. The three people at the scene knew they couldn't touch him, so they focused their energy on keeping him warm and awake. Afraid that he would lapse into a coma if he fell asleep, his rescuers would talk to Steven every time his eyelids started to droop.

"We told him the ambulance was coming and that help was on the way," recalls Boulette. "Still he kept falling asleep, going under. Steven was strapped into the seat belt and his body was held in place. I will always remember his beautiful eyes. Whenever he looked up at me, I would think how wonderful they were and how everyone who knew him must have always admired his eyes."

The Good Samaritans took turns monitoring Steven and shovelling out a pathway for the medics. Boulette looked in the trunk of Steven's car and noted that he had a large emergency survival kit with everything a stranded driver would need to safely wait out a long stint in sub-zero weather. Sadly, Steven was enduring a roadside wait caused by something far more sinister than merely being stranded, and the large emergency kit could not begin to address his circumstances.

Forty-five minutes after McIvor and Stroet spotted the light in the ditch, the ambulance arrived from Pine Falls. Looking the scene over, the attendants knew they faced a serious challenge. Getting Steven out of the car would be exceedingly difficult. The rescuers had helped immensely by preparing passage through the deep drifts of snow and clearing a working area around the car, but extracting Steven from the car itself was another matter. The passenger door would have to be removed somehow to safely move him, but no sophisticated Jaws of Life was available. There were only two strong men, one willing woman and two ambulance attendants, all of whom were very concerned about keeping Steven's head immobile through whatever action they would need to take to release him from his prison. Ultimately, McIvor and Stroet had to use sheer brute strength to bend the passenger door around to the front of the car. They had to nearly pull it off its hinges, which they would gladly have done if they could have. Then, discovering that the corner post and the roof were also blocking a clear route out of the vehicle, they had to bend them away as well. That McIvor and Stroet were both big men, with strength in their limbs and muscles, was a blessing.

The attendants then moved carefully to rescue Steven from his trapped position in the car. To do this safely was no easy task. They first had to brace his neck to immobilize it; then they had to strap him on a stretcher board and render him immobile for the trip to Pine Falls. Eventually, after much effort, they were able to maneuver the board into position and lift Steven out of the car. It took all five able-bodied people to carry him up the snowy side of the ditch to the ambulance. Steven was so tall and muscular that he took up the whole board.

McIvor went back to the wreckage and retrieved Steven's suitcase. The attendants told him they weren't supposed to take it, but they did anyway. "The young man," they all agreed, "would want to have it."

McIvor and Stroet had been in the ditch for more than two hours. They estimated that Steven had been lying there for at least a half-hour before they arrived, and that the ambulance, slowing for unusually bumpy stretches on the road to Pine Falls, would have to take close to forty minutes to get to hospital. By their calculations, approximately three-and-a-half hours would have elapsed from the time of the accident until a doctor could see Steven. They could do nothing more to help. Hoping that the young man would pull through, the two MTS employees climbed back into their car and carried on to their assignments.

Following the ambulance's departure, Brenda Boulette resumed her journey to Pine Falls. Still shaken by the morning's events, she arrived at Clarke's Corner and was met by a classmate who immediately noted that she was soaking wet to her knees and that her hair was plastered to her forehead. Boulette hadn't noticed the melted snow. It was good to have a friend to talk to, and good to have a friend with her when she took out the phone number she had found in Steven's car and dialed it. Her call was answered by the Fletchers' voice mail. Carefully she worded a message to the household. After identifying herself, she said that Steven Fletcher had been in a car accident, had been taken to the Pine Falls Hospital, and that they should phone the hospital for more information. She then phoned the RCMP to report her observations.

Then, having made her phone calls, Boulette was suddenly weak in her wet knees and abruptly sat down. It was time to have a late coffee with her friend.

By this time Steven had lapsed into a semi-conscious state and was unaware of the events unfolding around him. He vaguely recalls being in the ambulance, and remembers tremendous pain—pain so overwhelming and all-encompassing that its source was unclear. He couldn't tell where the pain was coming from, but the force and fury of it sent him deeper and deeper into unconsciousness, where the agony of the world fades away. He remembers gasping for air and an oxygen mask being put over his face. He remembers the many bumps on the road that caused the ambulance to jar and bounce as it travelled.

He doesn't remember when the frantic ride to the Pine Falls Hospital ended and the subsequent ambulance trip to the Health

Sciences Centre in Winnipeg began. When he roused momentarily from his stupor and asked where they were, he was told they were on McPhillips Street in Winnipeg, on their way to Manitoba's largest hospital. Most of the details of that day have been filed away in the deepest recesses of his mind and to this day he cannot bring them forward, nor does he ever want to. The bits and pieces of memory that have drifted through are enough to persuade him that forgetting can, on occasion, be the gift of a merciful God.

To this day, though, when he goes out on a cold and humid January day and smells the winter wetness in the air or hears the sound of snow crunching underfoot, Steven is instantly transported to the accident. On a ride to the St. Boniface Hospital for tests in April 1996, the day's conditions were similar to those of January 11th. To his horror Steven felt the sensations of the terrible day come crashing in on him. He remembered clearly hearing the snow cracking under the wheels of that earlier ambulance ride and the smell of the air. Memories of walking out to the car from his parents' driveway that morning, memories of the snow creaking under his boots, of the journey up the highway, of being in the ditch and in the ambulance all vividly returned. He tried to purge these from his mind as quickly as they had entered because he couldn't bear to re-experience them. He knows, however, that certain sounds and sensations will always recall them, and that they will haunt him forever.

Brenda Boulette, who still lives in Manigotagan and regularly drives past the accident site, experiences similar distressing recollections whenever the winter weather conditions at the site are similar to those of January 11, 1996. She is instantly transported to the horror of that morning and to the broken body and beautiful eyes of a young man lying in a blood-spattered snowy ditch. She ponders the knowledge that had she not had an uneasy feeling that something was wrong, she wouldn't have been late heading out of town that day and she wouldn't have been able to help Steven. "Life is full of puzzling things," she concludes, "and we are often left asking why things happen as they do."

Steven has been told that after his assessment at the Pine Falls Hospital, the medical staff ordered him to be rushed to Winnipeg for emergency care. A surgical team was required that could reconnect Steven's skull to his spinal column. His neck was completely broken, and if not restrained in a vise-like grip, his head would wobble uncontrollably, causing further damage to the blood vessels, ligaments, muscles and skin that were still connected and keeping him alive. Doctors said later that it was Steven's superb physical condition that saved his life. Years of paddling and physical activity had strengthened his shoulders and upper body, including his neck muscles. It was his incredible strength that protected Steven from the consequence that one might normally expect from an injury as severe as the one he sustained. He did not die.

What do you do if you don't die?

III

Ties that Bind Us

Julia Fletcher idolized her big brother Steven. Seven years her senior, Steven in his turn adored his little sister and made a point of looking out for her. (This protective attitude was still evident several years after his accident when one of Steven's election campaign volunteers remarked to Steven that his sister Julia was "one hot-looking babe". "That," Steven responded with a scowl, "will be enough of that kind of talk.")

The eldest of the Fletcher children, Steven was four years older than his brother Gordon, and both boys delighted in Julia's presence in the family. Julia was always a natural beauty, graceful and fun-loving. She tagged along with her brothers whenever she could.

Looking out for her didn't mean treating her with kid gloves. Steven led the way in sports, and he didn't choose the gentle ones. Whatever he did, Gordon did too and whatever Steven and Gordon did, Julia did as well.

"I always followed Steven," Julia says, "I thought everything he did was pretty cool. Steven always made a point of making sure that I was included, even if the other kids groaned about it. Steven always took a special interest in any activity I was involved in. I was always so excited to show Steven my latest figure-skating medal or track-and-field ribbon and hear his encouraging or praising words. When I was older and job-hunting, he gave me his resume template to use and I really only had to change a few details and the first name on the resume because I had followed him so closely in all the things he had done. When I hear other people complain about their older siblings, I can never relate to their complaints, because my experience with both my brothers was so positive."

On January 11, 1996, Julia was in her eleventh-grade classroom at Shaftesbury High School in Winnipeg when an announcement came over the PA system, bidding her to the principal's office right away. As Julia rose, the announcement was repeated, and within the minute repeated once again. She knew before she got to the office that something terrible had happened. Her thoughts flew to the dangers of travel. Her dad was flying to Washington, DC, and her brother Steven was driving north to Bissett. Had there been an accident?

"I remember grabbing my coat as I headed for the door," she says, when school staff told her to get home as quickly as possible.

For Julia, Steven was more than a big brother; he was her inspiration, her role model, her protector.

"But I didn't put it on 'til I was nearly home and even then I put it on while I was still running. I knew something really bad was happening."

She ran three blocks. Her mother met her at the door of their home. "Steven," Joanne blurted out, "has been in a car accident. They are bringing him in from Pine Falls and he might die." Julia's knees buckled and turned to water. She fell down on the floor, but didn't pass out. *He might die*, echoed in her ears. "My legs just became weak," she recalls, "and my knees wouldn't hold me up."

Joanne also slipped to the floor and, lying there in the hall beside Julia, she wept. "My beautiful boy ... my beautiful boy ..."

The Pine Falls Hospital staff, they later learned, had found David Fletcher's business card in Steven's wallet. They had called David's office and were told that he was in Washington at a World Bank meeting. After getting a Washington contact number, the Pine Falls Ambulance Service called David there. Breaking into the meeting and interrupting the discussions, a clerk told David he had an urgent phone message from Manitoba that his son had been critically injured in a vehicle accident.

Trembling and badly shaken, David took the call, spoke to the Pine Falls medical people and gave them Joanne's number at Arctic Co-Op, where she worked with Canadian Arctic Producers and wholesale Inuit art dealers, asking to have someone from the hospital call her while he rushed to get home.

Joanne received the call at work around nine o'clock that morning. "The nurse, Susan Dyck, said that Steven had been in a car accident," Joanne recalls. "I asked her how serious it was. She said, 'Very serious. Are you alone?' She asked me to find a private place and sit down, which I did. I had the call transferred to a private room. Then she told me that Steven had hit a moose and could die and that he would be coming by ambulance back to Winnipeg, driving slowly because his neck was unstable and they didn't want to disturb it. They didn't tell me too many details on the phone. They just told me to go to Health Sciences Centre and wait for Steven's ambulance to arrive there.

"I learned later that moving him had been really risky. The Pine Falls doctor gave Steven steroids right away, because of the swelling of the spinal cord. He was on oxygen and gasping for breath."

David immediately left Washington to return to Winnipeg. Unable to communicate with Winnipeg until he landed, he spent the trip sick with dread and cold with terror. Though he had taken the first flight out, he wasn't able to get to the hospital until 7:30 that night.

Self-controlled and disciplined, David was normally reserved. But his demeanor was shattered by the thought that his son might be dying. The son of a British engineer who had suffered as a prisoner of war during World War II and been forced by his captors to work as a slave on the notorious Burmese railway, David had spent his youth in a New Zealand boarding school. Having enjoyed very little time with his family as a child, he had pledged that he would spend as much time as he possibly could with his own children. That his son might be taken away was beyond imagining.

Meanwhile, as David was preparing to leave Washington, Joanne drove home alone. Once there, she immediately called Claire and Julia's school.

Rob Burton was a fellow engineer who not only worked with David Fletcher at Teshmont Engineering, but also shared David's passion for the wilderness, as well as his love of canoeing and his determination to provide outdoor experiences for his children. The Fletchers and the Burtons often took wilderness canoe trips together. Just two weeks before Steven's accident, the two families had shared Christmas dinner together.

When the call from Pine Falls Hospital came to the Teshmont offices that January morning, asking to connect with David Fletcher, Rob's antennae went up. When he was told that Steven had been in a terrible—potentially fatal—accident, Rob immediately called Joanne at home, reaching her before she had had a chance to call him.

Joanne told Rob that she was going to drive downtown to the Health Sciences Centre emergency ward to wait for the ambulance. Concerned that her mental state would impair her driving ability and knowing how distraught she was, Rob told her to stay right where she was. She remembers him saying, "I am on my way to get you."

"The last thing Joanne needed to worry about," Rob said later, "was maneuvering through all those one-way streets and then trying to find a place to park. She was so emotional I was afraid for her safety if she tried to get there by herself."

On the way to the hospital, Joanne was coherent, but badly shaken. Julia had managed to find a reserve of strength from somewhere deep within and Rob was impressed with her control under such stress. As she quietly comforted her mother, it struck Rob that Julia had slipped automatically into the kind of role reversal that often comes to mothers and daughters much later in life. Julia was no longer the child, and he wondered if she would ever be able to be one again.

At the hospital, Rob called home. One of his twin sons answered and Rob told him what had happened. To this day he can't remember which boy—Robert or David—he spoke to. He asked his sons to look for Gordon Fletcher at the University of Manitoba Engineering Building, with the instruction to "tell him to meet us here in the emergency ward."

That morning, Jean Burton, a registered nurse, was on a

community home visit. Calling from the hospital, Rob had contacted Jean's office and had asked a colleague to track her down. Her colleague reached Jean at her patient's residence and told her that she had to call home right away—but not to worry because "her kids were okay". The message, with its air of urgency, was ominous. Jean wasted no time getting to the phone and dialing her house number. The news she received was about as bad as it could be. With her medical background, Jean had a pretty good idea of what might lie ahead for Steven and his family. With cold dread, she turned to complete her visit with her patient, and prepared herself mentally to help her best friend through what was sure to be a devastating ordeal.

Jean arrived at the hospital in the early afternoon to join Rob, Joanne and Julia in the hospital's family room waiting for Steven to arrive. Seeing Jean, Joanne broke down and fell into her friend's arms, sobbing, "This is a horrible nightmare, my worst nightmare." Joanne's crying had left her eyes red and swollen and she had a terrible headache. She kept trying to hold herself together, trying to compose herself, but the wait seemed endless.

IV

Birds on Frozen Branches

C laire was next to arrive at the hospital, where she sat stunned, pale and silent with the others through the long hours until the ambulance finally arrived from Pine Falls.

Steven Fletcher and Claire Vivier met through the Manitoba Naturalists Society (MNS), a non-profit organization offering educational and recreational activities for Manitobans of all ages. They had been dating for over two years, having known each other since Claire's mother had registered herself and Claire, then sixteen, for a wilderness canoe trip to Mantario Lake in the Canadian Shield five years before. Outdoor adventures with her mother were not unusual for Claire, since they took part in many MNS events. As a single parent, her mother "is all things family to me," says Claire. "She fills the role of mother, father, sister, brother, close friend and confidant. Going on canoe trips and having outdoor adventures were great times for us."

Mother and daughter travelled to Manitoba's Whiteshell region and stayed there in a cabin made available for paddlers travelling with the MNS. Steven Fletcher was one of two trip leaders assigned to guide them through the rigours of the trip they faced. Claire was impressed with him from their first encounter.

"His personality sparkled," she recalls. "Any woman, no matter the age, would be captivated by his charm. I should have known he was destined to be a politician." At the time, however, what struck Claire most was his ability to enable others to try things they never thought they could do. "I found myself swinging an axe, carrying heavy backpacks over portages, and finding physical strength and confidence I didn't know I had," she remembers. "Steven has an instinctive ability to lead others without effort. Participants didn't even know they were being led. It's a true sign of his natural talent."

Most memorably, Steven introduced Claire to the heady and terrifying exhilaration of cliff jumping. He encouraged the trip participants to scramble up to the edge of a high pink granite cliff, which stood over deep cold water. He talked about the way one could jump into the water, and how to relax and enjoy the cool refreshing plunge. Then he invited the paddlers to jump into the lake and experience for themselves the immense pleasure of splashing into the depths.

Claire was torn between her desire to leap into the water and her fear of stepping out into thin air. Understanding her nervousness, Steven reached out his arm and said, "Here, take my hand, and we'll jump together." Falling through the air holding Steven's hand was a thrill Claire ranks as one of her life's most memorable moments.

Steven's engaging personality not only won Claire's admiration, but her mother's as well. "He exuded confidence. He had strength, ease and authenticity," Claire says. "He seemed to be able to pull groups of people together, and he went out of his way to make everyone feel comfortable and to be themselves. He was always interested in group dynamics, observing and facilitating group interaction. Bringing people together towards a common goal was something he really enjoyed, a talent that has probably helped him to become such an effective politician. I didn't think of such things. I just enjoyed the adventure Mum and I were on, and Steven's plans for the group."

Steven was an avid reader, with a penchant for learning about history, world politics and early civilizations like those of the Greeks and the Romans. One of the books he was reading the summer he met Claire was *I, Claudius*. The book was tucked into his backpack during the Mantario trip. While such literary tastes might seem incongruous for a man of Steven's interests and activities, Claire felt they were quite in keeping with his eclectic and wide-ranging exploration of the world.

Steven's enthusiastic interest about everything he encountered inspired those in the canoeing group to try to match it—"try" being the operative word. One night there was a particularly spectacular sunset and Steven led the group members, in their canoes, over to a cliff where he knew the view would be "breathtaking". Everyone raced as fast as they could, but no one could keep up with Steven. They recognized then that he had been holding back during their daily runs, so that the group wouldn't fall behind its leader.

"Steven always had a reason or a strategy for doing things," Claire says. "When we were hiking that summer, he always whistled as he walked. I liked the sound of it. It was so cheerful and friendly and it seemed that he was really happy and having a great time. Well, maybe he was, but he told me later that whistling or making other sounds kept the bears away. Some people carry jingle bells when in the woods for the same reason, and Steven jokingly told us that if you ever saw bear droppings with jingle bells in them you should get out of the woods fast."

Claire was Steven's canoeing partner on the journey back from Mantario Lake to Big Whiteshell Lake. She was thrilled to travel in the same canoe with him and before the trip was over she was smitten. "But," she says, "he was entering second-year engineering and I was still in high school, so socially and culturally we moved in different worlds." Time would have to pass before the two would begin to date.

At the end of the summer, a reunion of all the season's canoeists took place. Claire and her mother saw Steven again, and met his family, which had come to join in the festivities. Claire recalls, "We could see instantly where Steven had gained many of his character traits. His mom, his dad, his sister and brother were all so friendly and engaging, genuine, natural, intelligent people. They made us feel at ease and it was clear how devoted they all were to one another. What was so great in thinking back was that my Mum got to meet Steven and his family under the same circumstances as I did, and she could see how he got on with every age group. She liked what she saw and that was important to me."

Time passed. Claire and Steven continued on their individual paths and didn't see each other again for more than a year, until they ran into each other at a Winnipeg shopping mall on Boxing Day. Claire was shopping with her mother when she heard a deep voice behind them say, "Hello, Vivier gals." She remembers with absolute clarity how her heart nearly stopped and butterflies began to flutter in her stomach when she recognized the voice. It was Steven. He had already been cross-country skiing that morning and he was wearing a backpack full of textbooks. He wasn't reading the textbooks. He was using them as weights to prepare for an upcoming cross-country wilderness ski trip back into the Mantario region they had travelled during their canoe trip with him.

"Engineering textbooks are heavy in more ways than one,"

he kidded. Claire was quite overwhelmed by her emotional reaction to running into him. She couldn't stop thinking about him and realized she was still smitten.

At the time, Claire was completing Grade 12 and preparing to enter the University of Manitoba to obtain a science degree. As a final high school project, she was required to do a paper on what a student could expect to experience during the transition from high school to university. For this project, among other things, it would be necessary to interview university students. Steven Fletcher, with his experience and his ability to communicate, would be ideal. If he agreed to be interviewed, it would give them a chance to become better acquainted. It was a chance Claire believed was worth taking, so she screwed up her courage and phoned the Fletcher household. When the phone was answered, however, and it wasn't Steven on the other end of the line, she panicked and hung up. She was too nervous to complete the call.

Eventually, she did manage to get through to Steven and he cheerfully agreed to be interviewed. She should have been embarrassed when he told her that their house phone had call display and her earlier aborted call had been registered, but he was so casual and relaxed that she found it easy to confess her earlier speechlessness. Steven was astonished that anyone would be nervous to talk to him and started to laugh. In fact he laughed so hard that Claire thought her line was breaking up. There was such good will in his voice that before she knew it she was laughing too, and after that her nervousness disappeared.

Steven invited her to follow him around campus for a whole day with a video camera. Everywhere he went he knew somebody; he stopped professors, introduced them to Claire and asked them to answer questions on camera. Having faculty members on the video helped both her project and her personal understanding of campus life. Steven had no false façade, belonged to no clique and treated everyone he met with good-humoured respect. Claire received a good mark for her project. And to this day, she has the video.

The two began to stay in touch. When Claire was chosen as a valedictorian for her graduating class, she asked if she could make use of some of the witticisms he had used in one of his speeches as school president, because she'd heard it contained superb humour. Instead of mailing or reading her the excerpts, he drove to her house early in the morning with his old speech and offered to help her prepare hers. It seemed that Claire wasn't the only one smitten.

Claire and Steven had their first official date on November 14, 1993. By that time, she was studying in the Faculty of Science and he was in his third year of geological engineering. Claire remembers his attire earlier that day because "He wasn't preoccupied with fashion. He was just himself." Himself wore a bright aqua T-shirt with "Mantario" emblazoned across the chest, equally bright maroon sweat pants, a black stitched leather engineering jacket and heavy socks with sneakers. He was carrying a bright yellow shopping bag filled with school notes.

"He looked, well, very bright," recalls Claire, "and quite splendid."

Thus began a period of the best of times for them both. They were relaxed and comfortable with one another; there was no tension, no self-consciousness. They talked endlessly about everything and anything. Their values were much alike and their relationship became richer as they came to know each other better. He was her first real boyfriend, her first love, her first soul mate and the world was fresh and glowing.

When Steven reintroduced Claire to his father (the brief meeting at the canoeists' reunion years before having faded from memory) and informed David that Claire was working towards a bachelor's degree in science, David grinned. Teasing her, he said he hoped she would marry well. It was his way of indicating that a general non-professional undergraduate degree was not of much benefit in landing a rewarding, well-paid job. Like Steven, David believed people should strive toward their greatest potential. Steven persuaded Claire that she did indeed have great potential, inspiring her to "push out her thinking" and go for a career that would give her definition and direction.

Claire thought she would like to become an engineer, but didn't originally believe that she had the skill set to handle the rigours of the program. "I don't think I have the right mind-set to become a professional engineer," she remembers telling Steven. Steven assured her that she would pass with flying colours if she made the attempt, and after much encouragement, Claire switched faculties and obtained her mineral engineering degree. Today she works for a global mining company.

In the fall of 1995, Claire transferred to the University of Manitoba engineering program. Steven, having graduated the spring before, was already working as a mining engineer at Bissett and theirs became a long-distance relationship. Ironically, this added to their growing understanding of each other. Distance allowed them to communicate thoughts and ideas, hopes and aspirations and dreams for the future. She knew that the northern life, while rewarding in many ways, could become lonely, so she sent him care packages. He knew that the heavy course load she was carrying could be exhausting, so he sent her messages designed to refresh and revitalize her. They both kept each other's letters.

On January 11, 1996, having decided not to accompany Steven on his trip to Bissett, and taking advantage of the free time afforded her because of the faculty strike, Claire was at home. She had been relieved to learn that morning that she had passed her physics exam. It was not one of her favourites and she had been worried about it.

When the phone rang and she heard Joanne Fletcher's voice at the other end of the line she knew something terrible had happened. Joanne managed to get the information about the accident out, and Claire understood immediately how serious it was. She remembers sitting at the kitchen table holding the phone and looking at some little birds sitting on a shrub outside the window. It was winter, and yet the birds sat chirping on the frozen branches, enduring the cold and the icy blasts of wind. The phone call lasted only a few minutes, but Claire knew instinctively that those few minutes signalled the beginning of a long journey.

There is chaos in the world, she thought, *and horrid, foreign things are happening. I have to endure like the winter birds. There must be a reason, a lesson in this. But why Steven, a tender soul who contributes so much and loves so deeply?*

Pacing from room to room, she kept saying to herself that Steven was important to the world; he was too good a person to be taken away. It became a litany, almost lyrical in its refrain. *He doesn't deserve this. He doesn't deserve this.*

She phoned her mother at work and listened to her cry, fearing for Steven, for his family and for Claire. Steadying herself, Claire responded calmly, hoping by doing so to create strength for others. At very least she would remain calm.

She changed into a blouse that was Steven's favorite and put on a pair of silver earrings, two tiny shimmering canoes that Steven had given her as a gift. She imagined that he might be frightened, and that seeing her wearing these familiar items might help him feel connected to something good.

She ran to the car, started it and pulled away without warming the engine, forgetting in her haste to unplug the car from its block heater, pulling the plug and its socket right out of the garage wall.

Jumping out of the car, she yanked out the still-attached portion, threw it on the ground and took off. It occurred to her that she might be in shock, and she concentrated all her attention on just getting to the hospital safely. The haunting refrain—he doesn't deserve this— echoed in her head until she arrived at the emergency ward. Then, seeing Joanne, Julia and the Burtons, things became horribly real. Steven didn't deserve it, but it was nonetheless happening.

V

Gathering

Though he knew that Steven's injuries must be bad if the whole family was gathering to wait for him, Gordon didn't fully comprehend the severity of the situation as he left for the hospital. Steven was so strong and healthy that whatever his injuries, Gordon believed Steven would soon be up and around, as good as new. He had the family car that day, so he took the time to drive a friend home and then decided to pick up Julia at school. Learning that she had already left gave him a sudden flash of fear. Just how bad were things? Suddenly, he knew he had to get to the hospital as quickly as he could.

While Gordon was en route, the others sat in the emergency room anxiously waiting for the ambulance bearing Steven. Many ambulances arrived at the emergency entrance and each time the family thought it must be Steven. They rushed as a group to one particular stretcher, thinking it was from Pine Falls, only to see the startled face of a complete stranger looking up at them as though they were all crazy.

David phoned the hospital from the Toronto airport on his way back to Winnipeg. Joanne tried to talk to him, but she was so distressed she was unable to speak, and had to hand the phone over to Jean to speak for her. Jean recalls David asking, "Can he walk?" and telling him, "No", before he had to say goodbye to continue his flight to Winnipeg.

At that point, they had been told almost nothing at the emergency room about the details of Steven's condition. They didn't know exactly what had happened to him, except that he would not likely survive. When the Pine Falls ambulance finally arrived, they rushed to greet it with great trepidation. Reading the words—"Pine Falls"—written backwards along its side, they were almost afraid to believe it was really there.

Steven was wrapped as if in swaddling or in an odd-looking sleeping bag. His head was held immobile in a casing of some sort. His dark hair was wet with blood and sugared with fragments of glass. The blood had caused the hair to clump and thicken, pasting it like *papier-mâché* to his forehead and cheekbones. His left ear hung, partially severed, from under the hair, black with dried blood, which continued to ooze periodically and sluggishly from the great gash on the side of his head.

It was as if Death, hovering about, swept in with the winter wind, riding on the wheels of the stretcher. They knew now with a terrible certainty that Steven might not be saved. They ran to him, knowing they couldn't interrupt the medical team as it raced the clock to save him, but his eyes were open. He looked at them and saw them. "We're here," they cried, "and we love you. We love you, Steven. We're here." The words followed him into the hospital.

The waiting room was grungy, run-down, depressing and poorly maintained. It was not an uplifting environment, but that seemed irrelevant in the face of Steven's ordeal. The plastic surgery required to reattach his ear and close the wound on his face and neck, the necessity of fixing a broken collar bone, and the minor treatment of lacerations and cuts all paled in comparison to what would be needed to reattach his skull to his spinal column.

Gordon had arrived just in time see his brother arrive in the emergency room. He recalls, "Steven looked scared. The atmosphere was tense. Everybody was upset. The staff members looked very serious. They were kind to the family. The doctor was incredibly nice, incredibly kind. I realized then that Steven really was in serious trouble. From the way everyone looked and the way they acted, I knew this was not routine."

The emergency room doctor took them into a private room and told them that Steven had broken his neck, that he might live, but that he was paralysed from the neck down. Emergency care was all about keeping him alive. The doctors said the fact that Steven didn't smoke, didn't drink and was extremely athletic had saved his life.

They were told that if he lived he might be able to gain some limited movement in his shoulders. Julia remembers hearing the doctor use the word "quadriplegic" and not understanding what that meant. She thought, *That's something they can fix, right? They can do something about that.* As her understanding grew, Julia was to learn that paralysis was not something that was "fixable". It was a hard truth to absorb.

The wait in emergency seemed interminable. They stayed in the ER waiting room until Steven was taken to the intensive care unit, and then moved to the waiting room outside the ICU. There, Claire saw Steven for a few minutes. She stroked his forehead because she wanted to impart some sense of touch to him and to connect with him somehow. She loved him deeply, as he did her. Because of his injuries, she was nervous about touching him anywhere else except on his forehead. She remembers thinking that there were so many strangers around, and that he had no privacy.

Rob Burton was waiting when David's plane landed at Winnipeg International Airport. He was told that Steven was paralysed from the neck down. Hoping against all odds that this would be a temporary thing and that his son would recover fully, David was nonetheless filled with apprehension. At the hospital, he saw that his apprehension was justified. Things were not good, not good at all.

Once David arrived and they had wept together, Jean and Rob Burton went to a nearby grocery and bought food, drinks, oranges and grapes for the family, knowing that they would not leave for a meal.

Jean suggested to David that he should begin a journal and write down everything that happened, in case it became important to remember later on. David did this, and it proved to be good advice. Not only did the journal provide a personal medical record for Steven, it also helped the family trace the days and overcome the peculiar feeling that they were somehow living in warped time.

Later that first evening, while he could still speak, Steven asked to see Rob and Jean Burton. The doctors allowed them only a few minutes with him and when they went in and stood by his stretcher, he managed to get out the words, "Thank you for being there for Mom."

Jean said later, "It was hard to believe. His concern for his family was so strong, and his graciousness in expressing thanks for their comfort while suffering under his own terrible circumstances, was good manners beyond all I know. I wept. I said stupidly, 'How are you doing?' and he replied, as only Steven could, 'I've had better days.' We had to leave, but I still can see him lying there, unable to move, facing dangerous life-threatening surgery and expressing gratitude to us for giving his mother comfort."

That first night, the members of the Fletcher family all slept together in the ER waiting room. "The nurses in emergency were kind, compassionate," says Joanne. "They let us stay all night and they gave us blankets." It was the beginning of what would become an intimate acquaintance with hospital waiting rooms.

Claire drove home from the hospital around 10 p.m. and told her mother what she could about Steven's condition. They tried to comfort one another and make some sense of all that was happening.

Then she crawled into bed and lay as still as she could. She tried to be motionless, immobile, imagining that she was robbed of all independence. She tried to understand what he was going through, what it must be like. It occurred to her that she was the last one to see Steven before the accident—*in his natural state*, she thought—realizing that he might never revert to his natural state. Her heart ached. What would have happened if fate had seen fit to send her on the trip with him? Would the accident have been averted, or would it have doubled in tragic consequences? To this day, she thinks, "If only there had been a second pair of eyes with him on the highway."

She lay there thinking, and remembered a letter he had written to her recently, in which he had described the northern lights, pondering the histories of people and times gone by, and the wonder of the stars and the sky, which seemed to stay forever and never go away. She rose, found the letter and put it under her pillow. Then she lay very still again, sleepless and motionless until morning.

> September 11, 1995
>
> Dear Claire
>
> I have been gone just a day and already I miss you. I enjoyed our Saturday evening walk and canoe video evening and of course our intimate Sunday Afternoon — I felt really close to you this weekend, I hope we MAKE Time in our busy schedules to continue our closeness & intimacy.
>
> When I was driving up to Bissett last night I saw the most spectacular sight. Out of my Right window was a full moon (harvest moon) and on my left was an amazing show of Northern Lights. They swayed, trembled and swam across the sky like angels. I felt

Claire rose from her stillness at five in the morning. Unable to sleep and with hospital visiting time still hours away, she did the household laundry. By seven a.m., she was back at the hospital sitting with Joanne and David. Determined to think positively, to provide hope and to quell anxiety, Claire began to speak optimistically about Steven's future. To her dismay, she realized that her words were increasing Joanne's pain and adding to her anguish. Joanne, who had been told that her son, if he lived, would be completely paralysed for the rest of his life, could see no positive future for Steven. Claire's words, rather than giving comfort, felt like salt being rubbed into an open wound. Claire saw the fear and grief rising in Joanne's eyes and wished she could take the words back. They all sat there in abject misery, waiting for they knew not what.

Grief is intensely personal. We each feel it in different ways at different times. People cannot experience exactly what other people experience, no matter how they try. Despite being bound by their mutual grief, all of those who cared for Steven agonized in their own lonely, tortured ways.

The thought of her healthy, athletic, twenty-three-year-old son being turned into a quadriplegic in the blink of an eye was incomprehensible to Steven's mother. The shock was incredible. The hospital waiting room was stuffy and noisy. Things flashed through her consciousness, disjointed thoughts that she had trouble organizing; she and David taking turns sleeping on a little sofa in the hospital waiting room; not washing or eating properly; hearing other people crying and sometimes shouting or screaming; so many people weeping. It was a kaleidoscope of images: a boy, also named Steve, badly burned and in agony; someone feeding Julia and Gordon. Things flashed by, noted in passing, but not absorbed.

Joanne was sick to her stomach, throwing up acid and bile because she couldn't eat. Once, in the car weeks later, she had to pull over to the side of a road to vomit. All she could do was retch and heave violently until she thought her insides would come up.

David, in his own personal torment, wept continually.

David and Joanne made the difficult phone calls to family members who lived in far away places, in New Zealand, in British Columbia, in Ontario, in Québec. With each telling of the tragedy, the task became harder and more devastating.

Their family and friends also felt this sense of unreality. It was hard to conceive of an active man like Steven suddenly being robbed of the ability to move, literally stopped in his tracks.

Living down the street from the Fletchers, David and Marilyn Jones had watched Steven grow up. The two families had moved onto the street at about the same time—the Fletchers fresh from a five-year stint in Brazil and the Jones family from another part of Winnipeg.

The Joneses' son, Bill, was close in age to Steven and Gordon. As their boys grew, the Fletchers and the Joneses had become special friends. Like David Fletcher, David Jones was an engineer and Joanne and Marilyn were both friendly, outgoing women who delighted in knowing that their sons had good companions living nearby. Each of the families came to know the other's children well, and all cared deeply for each of them.

"When you see kids start school together, and play together all year round, you get to know all those little familiar details about them that endear them to you," says Marilyn. "I remember taking Bill and Steven somewhere in the car that first year on Stanford Bay, when it started to snow. Steven, having lived all his life in Brazil, had never seen snow. He was awestruck. I pulled over and stopped the car, and let the boys out. They ran around in the snow, turning circles, raising their hands and trying to catch snowflakes. Steven held out his tongue to taste the snow as it came down, and lay down on the ground to watch it falling straight on to his face. His wonder and delight at this new experience made an exciting addition to the first snow of the season for Bill. It was a magical event.

"When I remember that joyful little boy getting so much pleasure from lying in his first snow, and then I think of the last time he lay in the snow so many years later in that lonely frozen ditch, my heart breaks. The comparison between the first and last experience is hard to bear."

When Jean Burton phoned the Jones household, Marilyn and David were devastated. In horrified disbelief, they dressed in the early dawn and prepared to go over to the Fletcher house to be there when family members came home from the hospital.

Meanwhile, Joanne Fletcher's younger brother, John Hobbs, was driving to Winnipeg from Regina where he practises law. Conditions were terrible; ice and snow, which races over the TransCanada Highway and blows sideways—always sideways—across the road, blew in gusts in front of the car, obscuring his vision and making it hard to navigate.

John was not only worried about his nephew's chances of survival, but what the future might hold for him if he did survive. It was clear that his sister Joanne was totally devastated, and John knew that his brother-in-law would be just as deeply affected. Knowing David's character, John was concerned that, like so many men of British descent, he would feel the added pressure to be stoic, to "keep a stiff upper lip". For Gordon and Julia, Steven's accident would be a trauma unparalleled in their lives. His sister and her family were in crisis, and John's need to go to them kept him driving through the winter wind.

John, a Queen's Counsel or QC, felt that his knowledge and legal expertise might help the family cope with the problems they were bound to encounter, as they worked their way through the frightening days that lay ahead. Nothing in their lives had prepared them for the experience they were about to undergo. It would be worse, he knew, than anything they could have imagined in their darkest nightmares. He could help hold things together until they could recover, get into some sort of a routine and adjust to their new shared reality. At the moment, they had no one to act as backstop for them. He wanted desperately to strengthen them for their own comfort, and he was conscious as well that it would not be good for Steven if his family began to break down.

By the time John arrived at the Health Sciences Centre, Steven was out of the emergency room and had been moved off the stretcher onto a hospital bed. Looking at his nephew lying there, he felt a lump grow in his throat. Steven himself was barely visible through the many pieces of medical equipment that engulfed him. The web of wires, tubes and mechanical things beeped and blinked and buzzed. Odd-looking metal contraptions dangled in front of him; liquids dripped into his body through needles inserted in his arms; machines that somehow deciphered his body's vital signs whirred and spit out data.

"He was so wrapped in gauze bandages," John said, "that he looked like a Hollywood version of a mummy. I choked just looking at him and I couldn't say a word. Steven was conscious, and he looked up at me and tried to grin. 'Uncle John,' he kidded, 'You should see the moose.' I couldn't believe it. It was a really funny line. There he was making a joke, trying to relax me. Whatever he had going against him, he still had retained his sense of humour and he knew how to use it to fight against the dark. It was a moment I will never forget. I knew then, as I smiled at his small joke, that no matter how bad things would get—and I knew they would get much worse—my nephew Steven would prevail. He would come through this tragedy changed in many ways, but still be himself way down deep inside. His spirit was indomitable."

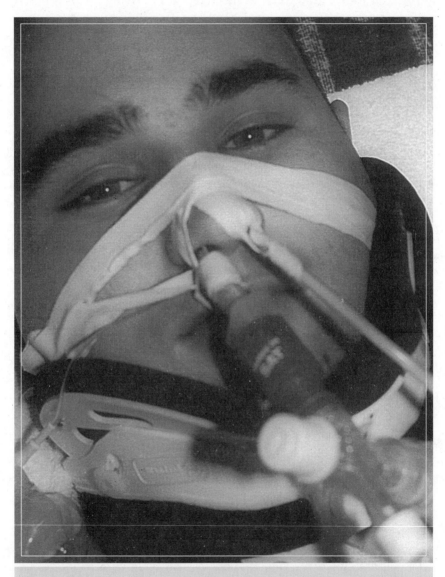

His breathing assisted with a web of tubes, his head thickly bandaged and stabilized with an unyielding neck brace, even in the first days following the accident Steven's gaze portrays the inner courage and determination that would make him an inspiration for disabled and able-bodied Canadians alike.

VI

Becoming Aware

As Steven became more aware of his surroundings and the fact that he had been in a very bad accident, he remembers feeling that all this was highly inconvenient. He'd had these job interviews and had to prepare for his new job. He was slated to give a speech to the Manitoba Recreational Canoe Association the following week. He had to study for his GMAT (the entrance exam for the Masters of Business Administration program), which was coming up later in the month. He had dates with Claire and commitments at work. He was worried about not showing up as scheduled in Bissett, or later on, at the Kirkland Lake mine.

As soon as he was able, and while he could still speak, Steven asked his father to contact the manager at the mine in Kirkland Lake and tell them that he would be delayed in starting his new job. He also asked his father to telephone the mine in Bissett and let his superior there know that he would be late in completing a particular report. "Tell them," he said, "that I will be out of commission for a while, maybe even for a few months, but I'll be back on the job just as soon as I'm better."

The knowledge that a moose had caused the accident both relieved and dismayed him. He was thankful that the accident had not been his fault, but distressed because in all his years of driving that road, he had never before seen a moose. "It's hard to believe that all this has happened because a moose decided to cross the road at that particular time and in that particular place," he said.

"Steven's time in the hospital," says David with characteristic

British understatement, "was not a happy time. There were, however, a few humorous moments." He tells the story of Jennie, one of the nurses in the intensive care unit. As part of an initial check to determine whether or not Steven exhibited signs of brain damage, she asked him a series of standard questions designed to reveal the functioning of certain parts of the brain. "What day it is today?" she asked Steven. He gave her what he believed to be the correct answer and she gently corrected him, explaining that his response was a day off.

Steven, in turn, gently suggested that Jennie go and check the calendar because he was certain that *her* response was a day off. To placate him, she went to check the calendar, and returned red-faced and chagrined, to admit he was right. Pleased with the knowledge that her patient was obviously alert and aware, Jennie good-naturedly accepted the teasing Steven gave her. Small victories like this were good for him. Through them he recognized that if he could use his brain to triumph in small things, he could surely triumph in bigger challenges as well. Not all his experiences would prove to be as satisfying as simply knowing the correct date, however.

On January 12th, the day after his accident, Steven was moved from the ICU to the recovery room on Ward D2. A window was open and he felt cold as doctors undertook various tests to assess exactly how far his paralysis extended. Simple tests such as pricking his neck with a pin to determine where he could feel sensation, or asking him to move his toes or lift his arms, were undertaken by medical personnel.

In order to prevent any twisting of the spine, it was necessary to keep Steven's spinal cord in line. It took eight people to keep his body in position when turning him over. "The tests themselves weren't difficult," he remembers, "but I was tired, so tired, so unbelievably, achingly tired. The neck brace was hot and sticky. I still had glass in my hair and cuts and scratches all over my face. My ear and parts of my face were pulled tight with stitches and they hurt with every movement of any of my facial muscles. I could reach to the back of my mouth with my tongue and feel where my teeth had split, but it all seemed so minor."

When they pricked his skin, he could feel the sharp sting of the steel tip on his neck and a little distance below it. He knew they were continuing to poke away at him with the little pins, but he couldn't tell them when or where they were touching him. When they asked him to move his toes, he thought he had moved them. It seemed odd to him that he couldn't feel his toes rubbing against the sheets, but he was certain that he had moved them all the same. He hadn't. His brain had sent the signal as it always had, but nothing moved.

"It was incredibly weird," he said, "I just assumed my toes, my arms and everything had moved on my command. But it seemed that my arms weighed a ton and just lay there, solid and still as a stone."

The neurosurgeon came in after the assessment to talk to Steven. Gently and clearly, he confirmed that Steven had indeed broken his neck. Steven asked him exactly what that meant. "Am I going to live?" he asked. The doctor replied that because Steven was young and in superb physical condition, he would live.

The doctor then explained the limited options immediately available to a victim of a high level spinal cord injury. He indicated that Steven could have a steel rod riveted to his neck to stabilize it, or he could have a "halo" installed to immobilize him. A halo is a metal ring attached to the patient's head with four equally spaced titanium pins. He also assured Steven that he could have a second opinion, and Steven said he wanted one.

"Just because the doctor said I was paralysed didn't mean that I was," he said. "I didn't want one person's statement to make it so." Aside from the fact that it was simply part of Steven's nature to double-check everything, he was hoping that someone had made a horrible mistake, and that his paralysis was temporary.

Racked with pain though he was, he still couldn't believe that he would never be well again. In searching for his second opinion, he checked with medical people he knew and trusted and was told that Dr. Ian Ross would be the best neurosurgeon for him. Steven wasted no time making his choice. "By the time Dr. Ross became my surgeon of choice," he says, "I would have done anything to get the pain to stop."

On January 13, two days after the accident, Steven had to be put on an assisted breathing device. Still able to speak, he spent much of the day trying to grasp the impact of his injury. After a lengthy discussion with the consulting nurse, he asked, "Will I ever be able to canoe again?"

"No," she replied.

"Will I be able to have children?"

"Probably not," she said.

He paused and said slowly, "I'm very sorry about that." It was his first acknowledgement that he understood his world would never be the same as it had been. Yet, deep down, he believed he could triumph over these adversities.

That day Claire visited him in the step-down unit on D2. She forced herself to move and talk quietly and calmly, concentrating on what she could do to comfort him. Yet she craved a hug, and wanted to steal him away from all the pain and confusion. She wasn't thinking about her own trauma at this stage; that would come crashing down later. For the moment, she was trying to surround Steven with positive energy and love, mentally willing him to be hopeful and unafraid.

For a while the room became still and quiet, and she began to sing a campfire song that the two of them had always enjoyed. Though Steven was wearing an oxygen mask, he had not yet been intubated and could still speak. The song, which they had sung around the campfire when they first met, was called *Glunk, Glunk Went the Little Green Frog*. It had facial actions that went with it. Claire always got the actions mixed up and Steven always laughed when she did. That day when Claire started to sing, he struggled to sing with her. It was a memorable moment, simply and sweetly uplifting.

That night, Steven's right lung collapsed and he was put on a respirator. Oxygen was pumped down his throat to his lungs. He had developed pneumonia and had a high temperature. He was rushed back to the ICU and intubated. A breathing tube was inserted through his nostril into his right lung, and a feeding tube through his other nostril into his stomach. No longer able to speak because of the tubes in his throat, Steven communicated by way of a letter board, blinking his eyes when the correct letter was indicated, laboriously spelling out a word or a sentence. A simple request for someone to scratch his head and give him relief from the unrelenting itching of his drying scalp wounds seemed to take forever to spell, increasing Steven's agony. Tears formed in David Fletcher's eyes as his son, now on life support, struggled to make himself understood.

After leaving Steven at the hospital, Claire couldn't stop worrying about him. Finally, she felt such a powerful urge to see him that she asked her mother to take her back. It was dark by the time they arrived on D2. When they learned that Steven had been sent back to the ICU because his lung had collapsed, Claire's immediate thought was she shouldn't have encouraged him to sing, that his struggle to accompany her had caused this new complication. She was wrong, of course, but the strain they were all under was beginning to take its toll.

Unable to see Steven, Claire returned home and called the Fletchers. Gordon began to give her the details about Steven's rushed return to the ICU, but became too upset to continue; his girlfriend, Jen Paterson, took the phone and explained further. This was Claire's awakening. Now, at last, it sank in just how traumatically Steven had been injured, and how serious was the threat he faced. Cold threads of panic began to grow within her. Her memories of the past and hopes for the future were weighed against the crushing reality of the present.

As friends and family heard of Steven's accident, those close to him began to receive phone calls expressing concern and offering sympathy. During one such conversation, Claire was asked, "How are you doing, Claire?" The question caught her off guard. *How am I doing?* she asked herself, and promptly burst into tears.

This sudden eruption of overwhelming grief was being experienced in one way or another by all those who loved Steven. Their anguish could only be contained for so long before it poured out, often unexpectedly, stunning them with its ferocity. It was as if in some metaphysical way the moose had damaged them too.

Once, Jen Paterson impulsively hugged Claire. "That hug came on a day when I really needed it," she says, "and it was so comforting. I was beginning to feel I would never be able to get back up." Like Claire, each family member had taken a hard fall; getting back up was difficult for everyone. Particularly at first, they didn't recognize that they, too, were victims in need of support.

For Claire, Steven had been her support and comfort. In times of stress it was him to whom she instinctively turned. What she really needed now was for him to comfort her. She wanted him to hold her and tell her that everything would be okay, but of course, that was impossible. Worse, she felt this need to be comforted was selfish; her personal needs had to be set aside in light of Steven's greater needs. To even think that he could be stronger than she was seemed absurd under the circumstances. He was the one for whom she was grieving. He was the one who needed to be strengthened by others, not the other way around. It was her turn to hold his hand as they stood at the edge of the cliff, and this role reversal demanded a difficult psychological adjustment that would take its toll as time went on.

As fluid built up in Steven's lungs, the hospital staff suctioned it out. This process had its own peculiar crackling, slurping sound, reminiscent, said one observer, "of a Grade B movie monster sucking on the flesh of its helpless victim ..." Steven described it less dramatically, as a sound "like wrapping paper being squished". Still, it wasn't a sound he particularly enjoyed, though it was caused by a life-saving measure.

There were often problems with the tubes through which fluid in his lungs was sucked out. The tubes were held in position with a cup-like apparatus; at times, the technicians would excavate for hours without being able to correctly position the tubes. Sometimes the tube was too short to reach its intended destination, and bodily material was sucked up from the wrong location.

Even inserting the tube, which was done through his nostrils, was difficult, bloody and painful. Steven could hear the cartilage cracking in his nose as the bulbous end of the tube was pushed through his nasal passage. The sound was amplified as it passed his middle ear. Struggling to ignore the pain and keep breathing was exhausting. When the staff failed to get the tube in properly and they had to put him through the whole horrible exercise all over again, he came perilously close to tears.

During one particularly dreadful hour-long period they had to do the suctioning four times because of accidents and mistakes. At one point the bulb or cup at the end of the tube actually burst while in his lung. He could hear the hated suctioning sounds, but worse, he could feel the tubes being moved from his nasal passages down his throat—a decidedly unpleasant feeling—and then ... nothing, nothing at all where his sense of feeling ended. It was disconcerting and terrifying. What was going on where he couldn't feel?

The suctioning was repeated over and over. Steven didn't know at the time that he would have to endure the process for hours on end, week after week, for months. But he had no choice; without the air that rushed in to replace the fluid being drained off, he would die.

Despite his inability to feel, Steven was aware in a deep, primal way that the suctioning procedure was painful. Something foreign and unnatural was happening and it hurt. Added to the agony of not being able to breath or sleep, he succumbed to an overwhelming and unaccustomed weariness as his body fought to survive.

For three agonizing days between the accident and his first surgery, with a broken neck and in mind-numbing pain, intubated and feverish, he had to be regularly turned. He couldn't tell if it was night or day. The ICU is the same all the time. "At night," he recalls, "they act like it is day and in the day they act like it is night." While this means there is no night-care slowdown, the downside is that the hustle and bustle of the day continues into the night. There is no whispering or tip-toeing. The activity and noise continues non-stop.

Steven became disoriented and was unable to sleep, a form of constant, unrelenting torture. There were times when he thought he'd lost his mind. Perhaps his belief that he was imprisoned in his own body was because he had become psychotic. It couldn't be an actual happening.

The ICU was highly staffed, but the critical care required by its patients meant the nurses were under great pressure. Numerically, there was one nurse for each patient on the unit, but each patient didn't have consistent one-on-one care. Constant emergencies, patient crises and even coffee breaks meant that patients were regularly left for short periods. Steven had serious problems breathing because of his pneumonia and tubes. Unable to speak or signal for assistance, he was never confident that help would be there when he needed it. It was frightening.

He said later that the first eight weeks after the accident could never be measured on any stress level chart anywhere on Earth. The pain, agony and fear were right off the scale.

Lying there, helpless and in pain, Steven was increasingly bothered by seemingly small irritants. "I remember a door that kept opening and closing, opening and closing, opening and closing until it nearly drove me mad," he recalled. "It was an endlessly repeating swishing sound and it was like torture to hear it going on and on. There was nothing I could do to shut the sound out. I couldn't get away from it. I don't know why it bothered me so much, but after a while I just couldn't stand it."

After extensive consultation and two medical opinions, Steven signalled that he wished to proceed with surgery to reattach his skull. His father, David, signed the forms. "There were a lot of bad memories from that year at the hospital," says David, "but one of the good memories was of Steven's neurosurgeon, Dr. Ian Ross. Neurosurgeons are pretty close to God at the hospital, right at the top of the totem pole. Steven's surgeon was skilled and also very informative. He clearly explained Steven's situation and what he was doing about it. We really appreciated that."

On Monday, January 15th, at 8:00 a.m., four days after the accident, Steven was wheeled into the operating room. There, Dr. Ross grafted bone from Steven's thigh to his neck. A forty-seven millimetre steel rod was put in place from the back of his head past his neck to between the fourth and seventh vertebrae and securely attached with screws. The accident had broken Steven's fifth and sixth vertebrae, but the neurological damage was at the C4 level, leaving him paralysed from the neck down. He finished the surgery in stable condition, but with the ability to turn his head now limited by the steel rod.

Once the surgery to attach his skull to his spine was completed,

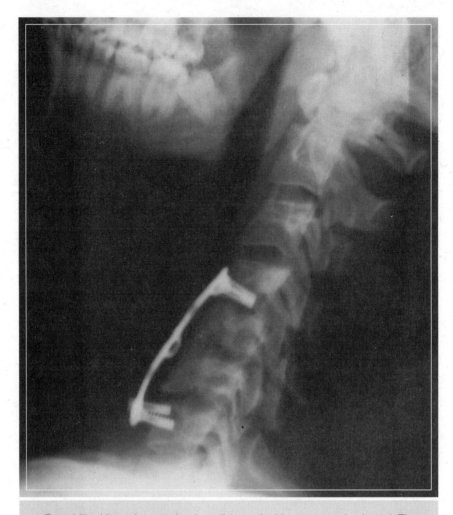

To stabilize his neck, a steel rod, easily seen in this x-ray, was implanted. The surgery was painful and permanently limited his ability to turn his head. But in typical fashion, today he quips, "People sometimes ask me whether I've got my head screwed on properly. I've had to admit it's tilted a little to the right."

physiotherapists came to "pummel" Steven. They spent hours pounding him, forcing him to cough in order to clear his lungs. Turning him over—no small feat—they pounded some more, cheering whenever he expelled damaging substances from his lungs.

THE day after the operation, Claire received a postcard in the mail. It was from Steven, who had written it while sitting in the doctor's office at Kirkland Lake, waiting to have his physical examination for the job at the Macassa Mine. He had mailed it from Kirkland Lake the week before, after he had been pronounced in superb physical condition. She stared at his handwriting, tracing his signature slowly with her finger, understanding that it would probably never be written again.

While Claire was reading her postcard, Stephen Davies, the chief engineer of the Kinross Gold Corporation at the Macassa Mine at Kirkland Lake, was writing a lengthy letter to David Fletcher.

> I am afraid words cannot express my sorrow ... our inter-
> view process is an intensive one ... the three-day process
> allowed us to evaluate Steven. Without exception, the deci-
> sion was to bring Steven on ... Steven met my conditions
> of a doer who would give 120% to a task ... His physical
> limitations are many but his mental limitations are none ...
> I want to place myself at whatever disposal I can to you
> and your family ... When Steven feels up to it he can call
> me at anytime as I wanted to be more than just an employer,
> but a friend to him ...

On January 28th, Steven was back in the operating room, where a tracheotomy was performed, creating an opening at the base of his throat through which air could pass. This opening (or "trach", as hospital personnel know it) had to be drained and suctioned at regular intervals. Inserting a catheter into the trach hole, nurses drained the phlegm that had accumulated, keeping the trach clear so that Steven could breathe. The trach was often clogged, and made a gurgling sound as moist air condensed in it. There was a constant worry that the airway would become blocked, preventing air from passing through it.

After a month in the ICU, Steven was moved back to the D2 ward, where he had been initially assessed. The ward had no direct twenty-four hour observation. While this was traumatic enough for Steven, the additional knowledge that the ward was horribly under-staffed made his situation almost unbearable. Medical personnel were often delayed on their rounds, and on many occasions didn't come to suction his trach on schedule. When this happened, he couldn't breathe, couldn't ring a bell, couldn't speak or make any identifiable sounds. It was torture. Listening to the gurgling in his trach, he knew that saliva, mucus and other fluids were accumulating. Gasping for air, struggling to breathe, he felt he was drowning.

Steven was unable to speak for more than three months. During that time, he developed a communication system by clicking his tongue against the roof of his mouth. One click signalled "yes", two meant "no" and repeated clicks indicated distress. This communication improved his situation, but still there were far too many times when he lay clicking desperately for attention, but without avail, for the clicks were too faint to be heard in the hallway. Even today, many years later, when he is in trouble his first inclination is to click his tongue against the roof of his mouth.

At one point, he was given a speaking trach. Julia had the day off school, and she stayed with him for fourteen hours. During this time, she and her brother tried to converse, but his speech was not clear. "Steven," she noted in the journal, "was talking like Darth Vadar."

The trach was finally removed in April, three months after the accident, and as soon as the hole in his throat healed, he regained the ability to speak. To finally be able to talk with his family and the hospital staff was an immense relief.

Steven was used to facing and overcoming obstacles. Nothing in the past had stopped him from accomplishing his goals. His expectation that he would recuperate fully from his meeting with the moose, and be well again in a relatively short time, was completely in keeping with his character. Even when told that his broken body could not be mended, he believed he would be the exception to the rule. He would overcome. He would prevail. He would work hard and be whole again. His medical charts during this period include this entry: "patient has unrealistic expectations ..."

Awareness of the bitter truth came slowly, in stages, a gradual, persistent dawning of a reality too horrifying to contemplate. From this dark and dreadful pit of knowledge, he would eventually surface, struggling through levels of understanding each more terrifying than the one before.

VII

A Time of Crisis

In the immediate aftermath of the accident, Steven's younger brother Gordon stayed at the hospital, intent on being by his brother's side. As it became clear that Steven would live, but would be hospitalized for many months, Gordon was advised to go back to school. Initially, he says, it was "a colossal waste of time. I was a total mess." Unable to focus or function, he broke down during the first class on his return. "You think you understand, until it gets worse and it really sinks in. You think it can't get any worse and it does."

The family was encouraged to return home to sleep and to try to resume some semblance of normalcy. The neighbours were generous and brought food to the house. Joanne asked Gordon to be there to receive these gifts and keep the neighbours up to date on Steven's condition. It didn't take Gordon long to realize that most people didn't know what to say to him, but it didn't seem to matter. He felt the depth of their distress and sympathy merely by their presence at the door. He realized how much it meant just to have someone show up.

Nothing drove this point home more sharply than the day that a neighbour came to the door. Her son had been killed in an accident just two months earlier, and now she herself was ill. Gordon didn't know what to say to her. There she stood, with homemade pea soup, and all Gordon could think of was that he had done nothing for her when her son died because he hadn't known what to do.

"I was completely stunned to see her," he said. "Most of the people who had come by were close friends, but this neighbour wasn't someone we saw often. Here she was offering comfort to us with all her own sorrow to handle. I felt terrible and wished that I had gone to see her when her son died, even if I hadn't known what to say or do. She showed me what compassion is all about by offering it to us when things went wrong for us. She knew from her own experience what was needed, and she gave it generously.

"I got a lot of eye openers that year. Steven was in hospital for 333 days, and I learned a lot about people by their hospital visits. Jennifer Paterson, my girlfriend when Steven's accident occurred, visited Steven as often as the family did. When we broke up, she continued to visit Steven on a regular basis, and her visits were good for him. Steven says that Jen was wonderful—really wonderful—in the companionship and comfort she provided. Such caring people, he says, gave him strength and helped him in his painful struggle to get through each day."

Neighbours David and Marilyn Jones, who had been contacted by Jean Burton from the hospital the night of the accident, headed over to the Fletcher house in the early morning of January 12th. Julia had already arrived home and was shovelling snow off the driveway. When she saw Marilyn, she dropped the shovel and held out her hands. The two of them stood, holding hands and weeping, unable to speak. Marilyn echoed the thoughts that so many others were thinking: "It's a nightmare."

Later that day, Marilyn went to Health Sciences Centre to sit outside the ICU, to be with Joanne. Over the difficult days to come, it became a routine.

"Joanne needed someone just to be there, someone to be able to talk to," Marilyn recalls, "Nothing more could be done than what was already being done for Steven, and Joanne felt powerless and helpless, unable to do anything that would make things right again. I thought of all the times that Joanne had been there for me, how she took such good care of Bill when I had a tubal pregnancy and lost the baby, how she taught Bill to ride a bike during that period when I was so sick. I could always count on her and now she needed me. I hoped that my presence in the hospital would help soothe Joanne in some small way. Sometimes you just need a friend to lean on."

Since admittance to the intensive care unit was restricted, non-family visitors were usually not allowed in. Despite that, Marilyn Jones would regularly come to the hospital and sit in the waiting room, to be present when Joanne came out for a break. For what seemed like endless days, she sat waiting, just to be there for those few moments when her friend needed her.

One day, Joanne was able to get permission for Marilyn to come into the ICU with her. Standing by Steven's bed, Marilyn had a hard time believing what she was seeing. The energy that had always seemed to emanate from Steven was gone. He lay impossibly still, almost comatose, with wires and tubes going in and coming out of him, all connected to equipment and machines that made noises foreign to Marilyn's ears. Steven didn't know they were there and Marilyn later observed that, "it was hell on Earth for Joanne to see him like that." After they left his bedside, Joanne turned to Marilyn and told her that she wished she could climb into Steven's bed and take his place so that he wouldn't have to suffer so.

After Joanne eventually returned to work, Marilyn sometimes picked her up and took her out for lunch. They talked about Steven and cried until Marilyn said, "We have to stop crying now," and changed the subject. "It was cathartic, I guess," she recalls, "and the crying provided a temporary release, but it was so hard to cope."

As the weeks passed, the family members gradually fell into a routine of sorts. Joanne and David returned to work and Julia and Gordon to their studies. Joanne went straight from work to the hospital, while the rest of family would join her at Steven's bedside as soon as they had completed necessary errands, household chores and daily duties. They were going through the motions, doing everyday things, but it was like walking in water; everything took extra effort to accomplish.

Once Steven was out of intensive care and able to have regular visitors, a multitude of people started coming to see him. These visitors recalled good times from the past and exuded confidence that there would still be good times to come. While Steven was not wholly optimistic that good times lay ahead for him, these visits were uplifting and afforded him fleeting moments of hope.

Also offering hope was a cheery banner, created by his artist friends Jim and Leslie Kirby, which hung by his bed. "Get well Steven", it read, a consistent reminder there were others hanging in there with him.

Along with the banner, a newspaper article that had appeared on the front page of the *Winnipeg Free Press* ten days after the accident was also displayed. Entitled "Moose collision shocks naturalists" and written by Bill Redekop, it spoke to the irony of how an individual who so loved the wilderness could be harmed by it. It also served as a notice to those who had not yet learned of the accident, sparing the family the need to repeat painful details to the many people who cared about Steven. Lying there, unable to move or speak, staring at the ceiling, Steven was immensely grateful for that article. It helped to remind the hospital staff that Steven was a person and not just a body.

As the disquieting nature of Steven's injuries became more apparent to Claire, she found herself wandering about the University of Manitoba, haunting the places she and Steven once frequented. She often stopped and contemplated his graduation photo, which hung in one of the engineering buildings. It was there, as she stood in front of the photo, that she recognized and accepted that she would forever mourn the future that could now never be, and yet at the same time she would rejoice in the good things that, despite everything, were sure to come.

This would become her mantra. Steven would never return to the life he had known, nor would she, but hope and opportunity could

Steven's engineering graduation photo, 1995.

be actively sought for a prosperous future. They could choose how they would face these horrific circumstances, either be beaten by them or beat them back. Claire would support Steven through the terrifying challenges ahead of him and try to set aside her own fears and needs.

She was a constant visitor to the hospital, often bringing Steven small items she thought might cheer him or encourage him in some way. One was a toy fish that Steven had given her the previous Christmas. It made a loud kissing sound when it was squeezed and it made Steven laugh. They nicknamed it "Mr. Blowfish", because it blew kisses. "I guess it sounds kind of silly in retrospect," says Claire, "but it was a bit of fun at the time, and helped brighten the dark days."

Once she brought the packet of letters he had sent her from Bissett and they went through them together, taking a figurative walk down memory lane. They found it a cathartic exercise, and Steven told her that he, too, had saved all her letters.

On occasion, Claire brought classroom assignments with her. She remembers studying for her computer science exam by the light of Steven's bedside lamp. "They weren't ideal conditions for studying," she admits, "but there was an engineer in the room in case I needed help, and I did pass, just as Steven had promised me I would."

Family members took turns staying by Steven's bedside during the night. Though they were exhausted, night time was a special time of intimacy and closeness for all of them, for it was then that they were genuinely protecting and watching over him and he was comforted by their presence.

"I stayed overnight only once," says Claire, "and it meant a great deal to me to be there. Just watching him breathe, watching his heart beat, watching him being able to catch a few moments of precious sleep, this was something for which I was extremely grateful."

Steven's boyhood friend, Bill Jones, became a regular Sunday visitor. In elementary school, at that magic age when they were old enough to play outside by themselves, but not old enough to go too far from home, still too young to notice girls or to think of having to get a summer job, Steven and Bill spent several summers building forts in the woods behind their street. Gordon Fletcher often tagged along with them, and many years later, these summers were remembered as wonderful, adventurous times by all three young men.

Daily they trudged off into the trees, with bag lunches provided by their mothers. "It was great," one mother recalled, "they would drag discarded pieces of wood from construction sites around the neighborhood into the forest. Then they would climb and hammer and saw all day long and come home ready to sleep like logs."

Their fathers regularly inspected the structures the boys were creating, to make sure they were safe. It was with pride that the boys would be told that their forts were "well-engineered". They were, after all, their fathers' sons.

They were healthy, happy, memorable summers, carefree and unburdened, as summers should be, and though they didn't realize it at the time, building the forts was a significant factor in their formative years.

The cards, letters and hospital visits were a significant part of the good medicine that Steven received. They linked him to the real world and to his various communities of friends. They kept his mind from dwelling endlessly on his circumstances and gave him ongoing interests outside the hospital. It was pleasant to have people come, even when he was too tired to talk much.

"They taught me a lot about the true meaning of compassion," Steven has often said. Many who came had been touched in their own lives by some tragedy, and they seemed to realize how much their presence was needed. These good visitors stand out in Steven's memory and they were an important factor in his mental and spiritual healing.

Despite all this, Steven's two months in the transition ward were deeply depressing. Still unable to speak, communicating only by clicking his tongue or blinking his eyes, he worried constantly about choking. By the end of January, he was experiencing problems with the respirator. A series of unfortunate mistakes had frightened him and his family.

One night, while lying in D2, in a cold room with one other patient, neither of them under twenty-four-hour supervision, Steven began to choke. His trach and tubing had become clogged and he couldn't breathe, call or buzz for help. As he struggled to get some air into his lungs, coming close to passing out and drowning, the elderly man in the other bed woke up. Seeing Steven in distress, he called for the nurse, who came running to suction the trach and tubing. The next morning the old man lay unmoving in his bed; he had died during the night. He had been lying next to Steven for less than twenty-four hours, but without his presence, Steven would surely have died. Family members could only thank God for placing him beside Steven that night.

The same choking ordeal happened more than once while Steven was untended by medical staff. When these terrifying episodes occurred, he would lie there desperately clicking his tongue trying to get attention before he suffocated. On more than one occasion, other patients rescued him, though they were not always as purely motivated to help as was the old man who saved him that memorable night. One roommate was so annoyed at Steven's rapid clicking that he called the nurse to complain, drawing Steven's situation to her attention. She immediately rushed to his aid. As Steven says, "The guy got his peace and quiet back and I got to live another day."

Increasingly concerned about the periods at night when he was unattended, his mother and other family members took turns staying by his bedside at night. Then the hospital decided not to allow overnight visitors. While barring overnight visitors may have been a sensible rule in most ordinary circumstances, Steven's circumstances were exceptional. How could he get attention when he couldn't talk or move? What was he to do when he thought he was suffocating and couldn't call or ring for help?

With Rob Burton's assistance, David Fletcher approached the Manitoba Public Insurance Corporation, the holder of Steven's vehicle insurance policy, to seek help. After negotiating with Steven's family, the insurance company indicated that it was willing to pay for a private night nurse to be with Steven.

To the family's distress, the hospital refused permission for the private nurse to attend Steven, claiming it was unnecessary. Did the Fletchers think that Steven was more special than other patients? Did they doubt the hospital's quality of care? In fact, Steven's condition was far worse than any other patient in the unit. If he faced a sudden crisis and the nurses were occupied elsewhere, even for a few minutes, he could die. The Fletchers stressed that they didn't feel the nurses were incompetent, but rather that there weren't enough nurses to give Steven the monitoring that would guarantee his safety. They strongly suspected that the hospital's accepting a private night nurse would be an acknowledgment that it wasn't adequately staffed.

The incident was but a small but significant forewarning for the Fletchers. Over the years to come, the politics of health care delivery in an autonomous public system would become a serious challenge.

Despite the hospital's explanations, the family had difficulty understanding why they could not have a private night nurse for Steven. They argued that an extra nurse, charged only with his care, would have helped everyone, providing assistance that would not even have to come out of the hospital's budget.

The family searched for something else to ease Steven's nighttime anxiety and to attract attention when he began to choke. A nurse, newly arrived from another Winnipeg hospital, told them about an alarm device that might help. It had a tube into which a patient could blow to set off an alarm. The hospital ordered the system, and it gave Steven some degree of comfort, provided the tube stayed positioned within reach of his mouth and didn't slip out of range when he needed it.

In addition to improving his ability to communicate, the presence of the alarm indicated that the hospital staff understood that he wasn't trying to make trouble. He was just trying to stay alive.

When he was first injured, Steven's physical agony was so intense that he couldn't think about anything but release from his torment. The overwhelming, unimaginable and indescribable pain in his neck and head rendered everything else about his body insignificant. He couldn't feel anything below his neck, but that disturbing fact hardly registered as he struggled to endure the pain. He didn't know what a catheter was or where it went or what it did, and didn't care. In any event, he couldn't feel its presence or the discomfort it routinely causes because he had no sensation from the neck down. Even the indignities inflicted on him during that first devastating period of time went unnoticed.

As the weeks and months went by, however, he became aware of the myriad ways that dignity and privacy are stripped from long-term hospital patients. Used to respecting and expecting privacy, he was sensitive about the elimination of bodily fluids, to his bladder functions and bowel routines. As much as possible, he wanted such things to remain private, as they are for "normal" people. Yet, unable to sense when his bladder was full and lacking the muscle power to empty it, Steven had to be catheterized in the hospital. This meant draining his urine into a plastic bag using a tube, or catheter, inserted into his bladder. To medical staff, leaving a patient's bladder bag hanging in full view off the side of the bed might seem a relatively minor thing, but to Steven it was embarrassing. He wanted the bag placed under the bed covers, out of the sight of visitors and passers-by. It would have taken only a moment to hook the bag up out of sight after tending to it, but this was seldom done, and Steven, of course, could not move it himself.

Most patients are in hospital for relatively short stays. A few days or a couple of weeks of having one's body waste on display is a temporary matter, which ends when the patient's everyday life resumes. When someone is in hospital for a year, however, the hospital becomes that person's dwelling place, where everyday life is lived. It's likely anyone in Steven's circumstances would have been as uncomfortable as Steven was about the lack of privacy.

The bowel routine for quadriplegics is even more challenging and upsetting than bladder catheterization. To remove solid body waste, a catheter is inserted into the patient's colon to drain fecal matter. If this sounds rather straightforward, it isn't quite as simple as it sounds. The many facets of this unpleasant procedure go right to the core of a quadriplegic's vulnerability and utter dependence on skilled and competent health care professionals.

Waste cannot be allowed to accumulate within a patient's body, as it can result in serious damage to the bladder or bowel. A full bladder can cause urine to back up and damage the kidneys. Urine and fecal matter remaining in the body for too long can cause infections. And stretching of the bladder or bowel walls can cause them to lose elasticity or become dangerously thin. As a result, the procedures for clearing bodily waste are vital to sustaining life.

Emptying the colon begins at night. The patient is placed on his or her side on a plastic sheet, a suppository is inserted to soften the stool and over the course of the night the waste is drained out. If the bowel is not completely emptied by morning, external abdominal pressure is sometimes applied, and occasionally digital anal stimulation is required.

In the hospital, this "undignified process" was rarely conducted in privacy. There were patients and other people in the room. The bed curtains were not always well closed. Sounds, odours and sometimes sights were often noticed by total strangers. Steven would try to concentrate his thinking on something else, focusing on anything other than his vulnerability, his exposure, his embarrassment and shame. "I felt like a helpless baby," he told me, "and like a baby I would invariably cry myself to sleep after the staff had finished with me. Sometimes I would weep while the procedure was going on. It was humiliating. I know one shouldn't be ashamed of natural body functions, but I was twenty-three-years old, and of a private nature. I have to accept what is necessary—I have no choice—but I still dislike the process."

On the mornings after his bowel routine, Steven would be given a shower. The shower room was down the hallway and Steven was taken there on a stretcher. While waiting to be taken to the shower room, Steven would often find himself lying naked, or inappropriately covered, on his bed or on the stretcher without his bedside curtains closed. On the return trip, from the shower room to his bed, more than once he was exposed to public view in what he felt was an indecent manner. These humiliations were all part of his living nightmare.

Steven had many personal experiences when nurses were callous, or worse. His needs were too often seen as secondary to the needs of those working in the system. One example sticks in Steven's mind. Medical staff members are supposed to use a fresh catheter every time they do a new intubation, to prevent infection. On ward D2 they sometimes "double dipped", using the same tube over again after a failed intubation attempt. After one such incident, Steven asked his father, via his letter board, to speak to the nurse in question about the danger of infection. David spoke to the nurse and to his surprise and shock, the nurse replied that it was okay because she, the nurse, had been wearing gloves, which would protect her from any germs Steven might have. While recognizing the very real need to protect medical personnel from germs, Steven also knew that the nurse's rubber gloves were supposed to protect the patient from the nurse's germs, which the nurse had not thought to mention. The nurse's stated concern for herself and not for Steven was revealing.

This incident with the gloves made such a lasting impression that more than a decade later, when, as a Member of Parliament, Steven was asked about the various causes of hospital infections such as *C. difficile*, his first thought was the necessity for an increased emphasis on hospital hygiene to protect both staff and patients.

On D2, he would experience this "me first, patient second" attitude all too often and it worried him that it permeated the entire hospital in many subtle but significant ways. The directive, "patient first", was not necessarily deliberately ignored, but it was not necessarily deliberately followed either. Florence Nightingale no longer roamed the corridors with her lamp.

Steven's depression deepened. The recognition that he wasn't in the throes of some unspeakable nightmare or fear-filled, insane psychotic episode, that he was living in a hell from which there would be no escape, stirred in his soul a deep and passionate yearning for death.

Death would not come however. The strength of his body, his years of strenuous activity and his highly conditioned muscles, held it at bay. His horror rose as the total hopelessness of his circumstances engulfed him. There would be no escape. He was trapped. How bizarre, how macabre, how ironic that the body he inhabited, the body that was too strong to die, would at the same time have no strength to help death come for him.

He was pinned down, kept in place by the weight of his flesh, flesh that he could not feel, flesh that would not move, flesh that refused to serve him, but would not let go of him. He was acutely aware that his head and neck were sources of great, sometimes almost unbearable pain, yet pain that he had no choice but to bear.

What he knew of the rest of his body was less certain, except now, finally, this full realization: that his body was gone from his control and it wasn't coming back. This was no temporary paralysis, no hallucination. He was never going to feel or touch or move again. He was trapped inside a heavy mass he could not fathom, doomed to live a half-life from which he was powerless to flee.

This awareness sent him into depths of depression that observers indicated was "quite understandable under the circumstances." But only he knew how deep was the descent and how black the hole through which he fell.

The "understandable" depression flowed from the details he was given about his condition. The initial information was direct and clear. "Your spinal cord has been severed at the fourth cervical. You are, and will remain, completely paralysed from the neck down for the rest of your life."

The implications and consequences of this clear fact revealed themselves over time. They were far-reaching, complicated and staggering in their impact. He could not imagine that his life would ever again be worth living.

Steven knew that his desire for death could not be realized. How can a completely paralysed man commit suicide? He could not expect help from others. Medical staff members were sworn to uphold life. Asking his parents to assist him would destroy them forever. They were so full of hope, so grateful for every breath he took, that he could not impose even the knowledge of his desire upon them. His love for them was greater than his wish to end it all, and it was that love that saved him.

The episodes of depression were ghastly. What reason did he have to live? He was more than half dead already. His body had ceased to function. He began to meet with the hospital psychiatrist, Dr. Pat Wightman, and unburdened himself to her. "She understood," Steven said, "and she never condemned my anger, my wanting to end it all. She helped me, but I still couldn't believe I would ever again be glad to be alive."

VIII

More than He Wanted to Know

It was clear from the start that Steven Fletcher would not be the stereotypical helpless patient. He was not the type of person the hospital was used to having in the ICU and he posed a real challenge for the tired, overworked staff. For starters, he was far too inquisitive, always wanting to know what they were doing to him and why they were doing it, questioning procedures, objecting to certain medications, and generally wanting to take charge of his own life.

Many observers would find Steven's intense interest in his medical treatment quite natural under the circumstances, but in a busy ICU, where most patients are either unable or too passive to bother staff with questions, young Mr. Fletcher's "this-is-my-body-and-I-want-to-be-involved-in-what's-happening-to-it" attitude had the potential to interrupt established hospital routines.

When faced with a problem, Steven's automatic inclination was to begin trying to solve it, something he learned as a child. "In our family," David Fletcher says, "we were expected to do well at whatever we did. There was an expectation that was ingrained. We reached for excellence in conduct, in fulfilling our potential and in serving others. If we didn't do well, it was considered that we had let our side down."

Steven's intellect, educational background and life experience added strength to this natural bent. His transfer to the D2 ward only added to his determination not to be left out of the decision-making surrounding his tenuous hold on life.

However, the medical staff grew impatient with Steven's

persistent interest in his health care. It was as if, by questioning
what was being done to him, Steven was somehow overstepping his
bounds and not behaving as he should. Examples of small but stinging slights by staff began to accumulate, adding to Steven's feelings
of frustration and his family's distress.

On the whole, the Fletchers were secure, confident people. While
unfailingly respectful, they were not easily intimidated. They appreciated
medical expertise, but did not stand in awe of medical professionals.
They recognized that Canada's health care system had identifiable flaws
and that the people working in it were not infallible. Most important,
they would do everything in their power to help and protect Steven
and he, in turn, would do everything in his power to assist them.

For Steven, the stay on ward D2 seemed interminable. He was
anxious to be moved into the rehabilitation unit, commonly called
"rehab". There he hoped to strengthen what parts of his body he
could and to maximize his ability to function as independently
as possible.

He also wanted to get off the ward, for his experiences connected to staffing shortages in the ICU paled next to his experiences
in the D2 ward. While there were still a few altruistically motivated
nurses on the ward who went the extra distance to alleviate patient
suffering, for the most part the nurses on the ward had become jaded,
bitter and had abandoned their passion for their work. Many refused
to do anything not specifically mentioned in their job descriptions.
Strongly affected by a militant union atmosphere, the work environment was dismal and it seemed that very few were willing to accept
personal responsibility for their performances.

There were a few absolutely outstanding nurses who tried to
make things better for everyone. "These exceptional professionals
excelled in their work and really cared about the patients. They saw
their work as more than just a job," Steven says, "and yet they were
drummed down by their colleagues shift after shift, day after day,
week after week for setting too high a standard. If they skipped their
coffee break, or stayed a bit overtime, or stopped to give some comfort to a depressed patient, they were criticized for making the others
look bad. There was a fear that if the administration saw that one nurse
could do more than expected, everyone else would have to do more
also. I can't imagine being in a work environment where enthusiasm
and empathy are criticized. No wonder morale is so poor."

Steven believes that people who go into nursing don't start out
with the negative attitude many of them eventually adopt. "I can't help

but feel that when they wrap themselves in that mantle of negativity, they are going against their natural grain. It must create a lot of inner conflict. Perhaps they need management principles where excellence is rewarded and mediocrity is not. But that is not likely to come anytime soon, because it would require a major cultural shift."

He always tried to make a point of thanking the exceptional nurses, to encourage them and let them know their efforts were worthwhile. He knew his day would be all right if certain nurses were on duty. Unfortunately, he also knew that he could expect "eight hours of hell" if certain others were having their shift.

There are both blatant and subtle ways of creating hell in a hospital setting, and most patients won't complain about either for fear of reprisals. The subtle things—not hearing you on purpose, leaving your bed curtains open when they know you want them closed, leaving you waiting for a much needed cleaning while they laugh and socialize at the nursing station—are intensely frustrating. The blatant ones are more easily recognized and can include sharp, hurtful comments and obvious passive-aggressive behaviour. Serious adherents of the "I can make your day hell" philosophy are careful to do the minimum work requirements that might be demanded in a work-to-rule situation.

The passive-aggressive "it's not my responsibility" attitude sometimes robbed patients of their sense of worth and dignity. Julia has never forgotten how sick at heart she felt when one of Steven's ward nurses was very reluctant to hold the hospital cafeteria door for her as she tried to take her brother downstairs in his wheelchair. "This is cutting into my lunch hour," the nurse responded when Julia asked for help with the door. Recognizing that any time is an appropriate time to show common courtesy, Julia says the incident callously diminished Steven at a time when he was struggling to re-enter the everyday world.

"It was a small cruelty," Steven said later, "but it made me feel terrible, especially when it emphasized to me that some of those who provided my medical care resented me to that degree. I felt the burden of being a high-maintenance patient, as I never had before, and hated my helplessness. Small cruelties can eat away at you. Julia was really upset, because she had wanted to get me out of the wardroom for a positive 'normal' kind of experience. I don't know who felt worse, me or Julia."

At times it seemed impossible for Steven to preserve even a modicum of dignity and self-respect. Marilyn Jones recalls one remarkably insensitive incident when Steven's request for adequate covering was sarcastically treated by staff as an annoying inconvenience. There is something terribly dehumanizing in being treated like an object, with needs that are reluctantly serviced.

Most of the patients in D2 were either amputees or paraplegic patients who had functional movement of the arms and hands, allowing them to live with less nursing care than Steven required. Despite this, the nurses allotted him the same amount of time to tend to daily routine care as they gave to other patients. It didn't seem to matter that the others could brush their teeth and hair and he couldn't. Everyone got the same time. And to make matters worse, some nurses felt they were above performing bedside tasks and left them undone.

Not long after the accident, Joanne had an altercation with one of the nurses. She had approached the night nurse, who was writing up her report, and asked if someone could loosen Steven's neck brace, because it was very tight and causing him pain. Ignoring her, the nurse went on working on her report. Joanne asked again, and the nurse responded brusquely, clearly annoyed at the interruption. "She was rude and abrasive and didn't care that her patient was in pain."

"This was my son," Joanne recalls, "seriously injured and suffering. Nothing was more important. A few minutes to adjust his brace—was that so much to ask?" Impatient with the nurse, Steven's mother raised her voice. "She didn't like that."

Recognizing that she was still in a stage of shock, she wondered aloud if her emotions were running wild and she had overreacted. Steven indicated that he wanted the alphabet board, and began spelling out a message, which Joanne carefully recorded letter by letter. When he was finished, she read the note aloud. He had spelled out, "the nurse was horrible you were right mom." The note was tucked away in the journal that was kept of Steven's time in the hospital.

With the help of Dr. Conrad Hoy, the physiatrist (a doctor specializing in physical medicine and rehabilitation) assigned to him, Steven was finally able to get off ward D2 and into rehab. Since rehab doesn't usually take patients who have trachs, Steven was grateful to Dr. Hoy for his advocacy. Being on rehab was infinitely better than being on the ward, but even there, a shortage of staff and negative attitudes impacted his treatment. The doctors had told him that without physiotherapy his fingers would tighten and curl, his muscles would atrophy and his bones would lose density.

One of the physiotherapists was a good-natured woman from Scotland named Denny Elliott. With her heavy Scottish accent, cheery manner, and her determination to make each therapy session count,

Denny endeared herself to Steven, despite the discomfort of the regular assault she waged on his body. She often came into his room on the night shift and made the end of his day seem better. She took care of Steven on the surgical ward, in the ICU, on the D2 ward and in rehab.

"Denny had, without a doubt," Steven recalls, "the best, most effective pummelling technique of anyone I know. She was brutal."

Pummelling him ferociously on his back, on his chest and on both sides on his rib cage, Denny forced him to cough continuously throughout the session. Her pummelling loosened the phlegm, mucous and other fluids filling his lungs. He would start to cough and she helped him cough more by performing an assisted cough procedure on him. After that, a tube was inserted down his throat and, gurgling and bubbling sound, it sucked up additional liquid from his lungs. He couldn't believe how much fluid his body held. The sound of it in his trach and in the tubes was offensive to his ears, but the process was essential to his survival. It had to be done. Without Denny's strong hands pummelling him night after endless night, Steven would have drowned. Every evening, she literally saved his life. She was thoroughly professional, and a lot of fun to be with. Steven found that he could talk to Denny, really talk, sharing with her his innermost thoughts. Using the alphabet board, Steven told Denny that he "felt like a thinking plant". This was not something he said to others, but Denny seemed to understand exactly what he meant and never seemed upset or shocked by anything he said. "She was joyful in the true sense of the word," says Steven, "in that she was filled with joy, always happy and perky."

The night sessions were long and exhausting for both Denny and Steven, but despite this, at the end of every one, she took extra time to help alleviate the severe pain that he experienced constantly in his neck. The thick neck brace he had to wear made his neck hot; soaked with perspiration, it caused his skin to feel itchy and raw. The neck itself was incredibly stiff and the muscles were so tense and tight that they felt like they were made of steel. Having been held immobile for the long period of post-surgical healing, his neck muscles had begun to atrophy. Removing the brace and massaging his neck muscles with a firm, deep pressure, Denny's therapy was excrutiatingly painful, but gave great relief at its conclusion, as the muscles relaxed and became more flexible.

Before his accident, Steven had built up thick calluses on his hands and feet from extensive canoe and kayak paddling. In the weeks following the accident, with no hand or foot movement at all, these calluses began to grow out and fall off, rather like a snake shedding its skin. Denny massaged his hands and feet, rubbing off the peeling dead skin and softening the tissues underneath. Though he couldn't feel it, the treatment was somehow soothing. But the truth was stinging. The evidence of years of activity and joy were literally being peeled away from him.

Steven was deeply grateful for wonderful people, such as Denny, that he discovered in the health care system. Proficient and caring, they held themselves to high standards, and took pride in their competence and professionalism. He was less than delighted, however, to find that his ability to participate in therapy sessions depended entirely on members of the ward staff who were not always able to get him to the physiotherapists in time for his appointments.

The clock above the elevator in the hospital hallway outside his room was right in the center of his line of vision. He often watched it with frustrated fascination as he waited to be taken to his physiotherapy appointments. He recorded some of these waits for posterity and for discussion with his caregivers.

He noted, for example that the morning shift change took place at 8:00 a.m., while patients were being presented with their breakfasts. At 8:30, the first set of nurses went for their coffee break. The fifteen-minute coffee break usually lasted almost half an hour, and then the next crew took their break. Steven's physiotherapy appointments were at 10 o'clock. While other patients were whisked over for their therapies fairly quickly, it took a long time to ready him for his sessions. He was frequently late for, or entirely absent from, his physiotherapy sessions, because many of the staff had been away on coffee breaks and those left on the floor couldn't ready him in time. When they did manage to get him ready, the nurses couldn't always deliver him to rehab on schedule because by then they were busy with other tasks.

In discussing these timing problems, Steven asked the nurses why they couldn't work until 9:30 or 10 a.m. and then take their coffee breaks, while the patients having physiotherapy were gone from their beds for a couple of hours. He also asked why they needed to take their breaks in groups, suggesting that if they left the floor one at a time, more staff would be left to tend to patients. Steven thought these were immensely sensible suggestions, but they were rejected out of hand, because "that's not the way things are done". Advice from a pushy patient about scheduling, with its implied criticism, was not welcomed.

Those who agreed with Steven, who saw merit in his suggestions, were quickly silenced. "Basically," said Steven, "those with a solid

work ethic were beaten down for considering accommodating identified patient needs." Steven was more sensitive to these issues than
other patients because he was so totally reliant on the staff. The other
patients, while severely damaged, had more physical flexibility and
mobility than he did and were not so completely dependent.

Missing his medically prescribed physiotherapy sessions entirely
or in part worried Steven greatly. Half-hour sessions were not what
the doctor had ordered and to lose any portion of the limited number
of physiotherapy options available was more than frustrating. It was
frightening. Realizing that he would never be restored to his former
strength and agility, Steven recognized the need to strengthen his
body as much as he could in any way possible. Interference with
opportunities for therapy was therefore traumatic.

"We became disillusioned as time went on," David Fletcher
recalls. "The staff seemed to work very hard, but not always in a
useful way. When Steven first went into the rehab unit there were
posters all around saying that this was a place for teamwork, that the
patient, doctor, nurse and therapist were a team. The posters had little
connection to what was actually happening. The nurses made arbitrary decisions about his care, but seldom, if ever, consulted Steven."

Gordon Fletcher, who at the time still believed his brother would
get better, couldn't understand why breaks in Steven's therapy were
allowed. Years later, Gordon admitted that it was months before he
realized that Steven's condition was permanent. When the doctors
had originally told the family that Steven would never be able to move
again, Gordon believed they had said that to lower the family's expectations in case Steven was unable to move. Gordon kept anticipating
the end of the medical treatment, when Steven would be told that he
would always walk with crutches or a cane, or get himself about in
a wheelchair. When the truth finally sank in, that there was going to
be no recovery, it was heartbreaking.

However, the acceptance of truth frees a person to deal effectively
with reality. In the close-knit Fletcher family, it was crucial that each
of them faced reality. When they did, Steven began to set goals, which
became family goals. Together they prepared for Steven's reintegration
into society. Steven has repeatedly said that without the devotion and
dedication of his family, he couldn't have made it through the tough
times. In the family and with close friends, the terms "pre-accident"
and "post accident" became as relevant as BC and AD in marking
an event so significant that all time is seen in relation to it.

The first goal, after the obvious one of survival, was to get

Steven out of the hospital and living as independently as possible. Physiotherapy was a necessary step toward achieving this goal.

At the end of July, he was unexpectedly told that he wouldn't be going for physiotherapy sessions during August. Knowing that physiotherapy was the only chance he had of getting back any possible movement and realizing that any break in that treatment would be a major, perhaps irreversible, setback, he was upset. He asked why were his sessions being cancelled and was told that no physiotherapists were available because they would all be on vacation.

"Why," asked Steven in openmouthed disbelief, "are they all taking their holidays at the same time?" The department head explained that staff had all booked their vacation time in August. Steven replied that it seemed odd that the staff members would all be granted the same period of time off when it would be so obviously to their patients' detriment. "That's just the way it is," he was told.

David immediately checked with other hospitals and found that elsewhere holiday time was staggered to meet patients' needs. His fury and frustration were somewhat mollified when he was told that there would, in fact, be at least one physiotherapist on duty at the Health Sciences Centre in August.

The relief was short-lived, however, as it became clear that the therapy available would be mostly provided to patients less seriously injured than Steven. Why? Because those patients could be more easily restored. In 1996 and before, accident victims with high-level spinal cord breaks usually died, if not immediately at the accident site, then later due to complications. Perhaps that knowledge, plus the fact that Steven would always remain a quadriplegic, caused medical people to give up trying to do much for him other than to keep him breathing and conscious. Other patients, those more easily "fixed", were the priority for intensive rehabilitation. Since severely injured patients require more time and effort to accomplish even minimal improvements from physical therapy, when resources are lacking the severely injured are often left to wait.

While it is true that patients with "fixable" injuries can make fast and almost full comebacks in a relatively short time, and severely damaged patients require tremendous resources and months upon months to achieve almost unnoticeable results, it is also true that even the tiniest improvement can make an enormous difference in the lives of the severely disabled. Left to atrophy, the limited abilities of a quadriplegic are rendered even more limited.

After much resistance and denial, Steven had eventually accepted that he would never be fully restored physically. But he longed to accomplish some small task to improve the quality of his life, even if it were simply swatting a mosquito.

Once, in the early days while in ICU, as Marilyñ Jones was sitting alone with Steven, he asked her if she would scratch his head because it was horribly itchy. Marilyn had often seen Joanne do this for her son, and so she gave Steven's skull a vigorous scratching. She found that she scraped off dozens of dried scabs that had formed over the cuts he had sustained in the accident. The nurses didn't tend to this type of annoyance and it was driving Steven to distraction. Marilyn imagined an itch that you couldn't scratch and knew you would never be able to scratch. Feeling Steven's helplessness in being unable to meet even his smallest needs, she was moved to tears.

✦ ◼ ✦ ◼ ✦

THE room in which Steven was housed in the rehab ward had four beds, all full. With four patients and concerned friends and relatives in attendance, the room was always crowded.

There were not enough chairs if all four patients had visitors at once, which they always did, since the four patients in the room were all seriously damaged. Family members tried to accommodate one another, and medical staff made their way through the crowd to tend to their patients. But no matter how considerate everyone was, everything was on display all the time.

Joanne found this particularly difficult, and the constant presence of strangers bothered her immensely. Bed curtains provided a temporary shelter from curious eyes, but there was no noise barrier and every sound made at every bedside could be heard through the whole room.

Though there was a constant turnover of patients in the other three beds, the four patients were often of different backgrounds and cultures, each with his or her way of responding to crisis. Two of the other patients had large families who came faithfully to visit, adding to the stress and confusion. There was no sense of consistency and any semblance of dignity was impossible.

Steven was conscious of his roommates' circumstances, as they were of his. It was impossible not to be aware of everything happening to each of them. At one point, a young father from a First Nations reserve occupied the adjacent bed. He had been in an accident that had left him paralysed. Though he couldn't hold his baby when it was held up to him, he was calm and accepting of his fate, as were many of his relatives who visited him daily. There was no calm acceptance from a patient whose legs had been severed in a fall from a train, however; he fought his tragic circumstances with steely determination.

The drama and stress were heightened by the many irritations of hospital existence. Joanne preferred to sit with the curtains pulled around Steven's bed, so he could have some privacy. When the nurses told her to open the curtains, she replied, "I didn't come here to socialize with other people, I came to be with my critically ill son."

In retrospect, Joanne says she must have seemed rude at times. "It wasn't that I didn't care about the other people in the room. It was just that I didn't have the strength to cope with any other burdens. It always seemed so crowded and noisy. Like being in the middle of a crowded shopping mall and having to handle nightmare problems when you were being crushed by all those busy, noisy people.

"I realize now that I walked around like a zombie for a year. The whole world seemed so clouded and scary."

Sunday, when she spent twelve hours at the hospital, was an unusually hard day for her. Regular visitors lightened the day, and she welcomed the time spent with Steven, but Sundays made her conscious of her far-away family. Their relatives and extended family lived in New Zealand, Eastern Canada or on the West Coast. David's work took him all over the world and he and Joanne felt it was important for Gordon and Julia to get back to their studies.

"I don't know how they ever managed to get through their academic years because they spent so much time at Steven's side," Joanne recalls. "They were so good to him and so good for him—as he would have been for them if the circumstances were reversed. But sometimes I felt so alone and so afraid, though of course I didn't want anyone to know that because it was important that I be strong."

From about mid-March to December, Steven lived in this hectic four-bed room, though both family and visitors noticed there were unused hospital beds close by in empty rooms on the ward. No effort was made to relieve the crowding by moving two of the four patients into these available spaces, however. One can speculate on the justification for the crowded condition—as many beds as possible in one room might be more cost-effective or more efficient—but that doesn't change the reality; four suffering patients and their anxious families simply had to endure the close quarters and try to stay out of one another's way.

Steven vowed to never go back to the hospital. But, ironically, when he became a Member of Parliament, his first position was that of health critic for the Official Opposition. In that role he toured dozens of hospitals around the country. On these tours he always looked for appropriate and workable architectural design and found some ICU units that are designed to function in a masterful way.

"There is one ICU design in particular that works extremely well," he says, "and that seems to provide solutions to the many problems that frustrated me so much during my year in hospital. All the beds in this unit are visible from the nursing station. They are individually enclosed with sliding glass doors, which have curtains that can be pulled for visual privacy. There is privacy for visitors. Smells and sounds are contained and yet nurses can see the people. Air temperature can be better controlled to suit individual patients." Such designs exist, but not in many parts of the country.

Steven observes that the quality of medical treatment for accident victims depends on where an accident occurs. Depending on which province, which city, town or rural community delivers emergency care, a patient can expect widely varying results in medical treatment. "There is a myth that there is equal delivery of health care across the country," says Steven. "This is not true by a long shot. Is there anyone who truly expects such equality? Think about it. How could a small rural community of 300 people replicate the health care delivery offered by a large city hospital that has thousands of people on staff and state-of-the-art medical equipment?

"Equality, as some envision it, has a strong potential to lead to overall systemic mediocrity. I wouldn't want equal care if that care has to be mediocre or inferior. Equality at the lowest common denominator has little appeal for me. Better and more timely access to high quality care for everyone is the answer. With sophisticated technologies and highly trained paraprofessionals steadily improving the care in small and remote communities, such timely access is beginning to happen."

IX

Fighting Back

Steven had never cared for medications, but recognized that under his circumstances pharmaceutical intervention was probably necessary. He routinely asked the medical staff what he was being given and why. At one point his doctor told him "Steven, I have just returned from a medical conference where I learned of a pill that can help you sleep better at nights. Would you like to try it?"

Steven agreed to try this new medication since he had been having trouble sleeping. When the nurse brought this medication, she said merrily, "Here's your Trazadone!"

"What is that?" Steven asked, and the nurse replied that it was an anti-depressant. "And why am I being given that?" After he asked to see information on the medicine, the nurse went and got it for him. This pill, which would help him sleep better at night, was indeed an anti-depressant, a mood-altering drug that had as an incidental side effect "drowsiness". Steven was furious. He felt he was being given medication under false pretenses. Told he was being given a simple sleeping pill, which was subsequently discovered to be a heavy tranquillizer, Steven could only assume that it was being given to quiet him, to stop him from asking so many questions.

Angry at the deception, he refused to take the pills. He told the nurse he didn't want to "be drugged up like a zombie" and said he wanted everyone to know that he didn't appreciate being deceived or misled. He pointed out that his mind was all that he had left, and he was going to remain mentally alert, aware and capable, no matter how inconvenient it might be for others, or for that matter, himself.

In another frightening incident while on the D2 ward, a nurse tripped on his intravenous stand and ripped the IV right out of his arm. Though he couldn't feel the pain that would have ordinarily accompanied such an accident, he could see what had happened and felt a natural sense of panic. Once again, he was deeply aware of his inability to move as he waited helplessly for rescue.

Because Steven had been told he would not be able to move any part of his body unless he had sensation in it, his parents and siblings took turns running objects up and down his chest to see how far his sense of being touched extended. Initially, it had seemed he had some sensation on his chest and upper shoulders. The family marked his body on the spots where Steven indicated he felt sensation. The family noted these marks as credible because, while Steven couldn't see where they were touching, he nevertheless correctly identified the location of each touch.

Later, the areas of sensation lowest on his chest began to diminish and disappear. Steven asked to see his medical records, to compare his current sensation level against the tests taken when he had first entered the hospital. He was told that there were no written records of these initial sensation tests and that it was hospital policy not to take these levels on seriously injured patients.

Steven assumes this policy existed because the hospital had no expectation of improvement for the catastrophically injured beyond keeping them comfortable and at peace. Still, he understood that when the spine is dealing with shock it swells, that swelling can take up to a year to subside, and that there is always a chance that some feeling could recur during that time. Therefore he couldn't understand why no records were kept of his initial sensations.

Concerned that he was losing feeling, at the end of March, after two-and-a-half months in hospital, Steven asked Dr. Hoy for a magnetic resonance image (MRI) of his chest and upper body. The doctor refused, telling Steven he had no need for an MRI, because there was no proof that there had been any sensation in his upper body in the first instance. Steven made repeated requests for an MRI throughout that spring and summer and the consistently negative responses he received to those requests both angered and disappointed him. Having not had an MRI at any point since his accident, he felt that he was missing out on the use of a modern diagnostic tool that could effectively assess injury severity and treatment. The imagery revealed by an MRI would definitely provide further insight into his condition.

Feeling that their findings of a loss of sensation on Steven's chest were accurate, his parents asked again for an MRI and were again refused. They knew that MRIs were expensive, that there weren't enough operators, and that doctors were not able to order the test simply because patients asked for it. However, they felt that Steven was being written off, treated as if there was no point in doing anything further for him. In July, David wrote in the journal, "Dr. Hoy's interest seems to be to get Steven well enough to get him out of the hospital, while Steven's aim is to get back as much [ability from therapy] as possible before leaving the hospital." Doctor and patient appeared to be heading down different paths.

Steven asked for a second opinion. The Manitoba Public Insurance Corporation agreed to pay for a second opinion and suggested Steven visit a Winnipeg specialist who worked with Dr. Hoy. Steven felt the ties between the two doctors were too close to provide objectivity and considered instead a doctor recommended by the Canadian Paraplegic Association. The specialist was familiar with this kind of trauma and had worked at the Health Sciences Center, but was no longer in Winnipeg. To see her, Steven would have to travel to London, Ontario.

Because there were very few spinal cord experts in Manitoba, MPI said it would pay for the second opinion in another province, but not for the travel expenses to obtain it. David Fletcher unhesitatingly agreed to pay for two people to go to London.

When Dr. Hoy realized that Steven was actually going to London, he suddenly authorized the long-denied MRI, to be done before Steven left Winnipeg. All his earlier excuses and reasons for denying the test vanished like fog in the sunshine.

Though the incident had created tensions with Dr. Hoy, Steven knew he had to focus on his own health. He'd had the test he believed he needed, and when the doctors in London asked for his Manitoba MRI results, he would be able to produce them.

It was now October, eight months since the accident and six months since Steven's first request for an MRI. With considerable difficulty, David and Joanne made the arrangements to get Steven to Ontario. He and a health care attendant would travel together, without any other assistance. To prepare for the experience outside the protective confines of the hospital, they did a dry run at a Winnipeg hotel. The patient and his attendant checked into the hotel, made their way to the hotel room and went through all the medical procedures Steven required on a daily basis. Then, working with Air Canada, on a bitterly cold day, they took a 737 to Toronto. This first leg of the journey was relatively easy since covered gateways accommodated Steven's wheelchair and eliminated the need for stairs.

Travelling from Toronto to London was a different story. The regional plane was much smaller, and had to be accessed by stairs rather than an enclosed gateway. To get Steven into the plane, the baggage handlers loaded him in his wheelchair on to the plane's food trolley and hoisted him up, lifting him from his specially equipped wheelchair to a narrower one, and from that into an airplane seat. When they arrived in London, two baggage handlers carried him down the steep airplane steps in a narrow chair. It was, Steven says, absolutely terrifying, but the baggage handlers performed superbly and Steven was successfully transferred to an accessible ground vehicle.

The trip was risky, but Steven was determined to have his condition correctly assessed. By the time he arrived at London's Parkwood Hospital, he was choking and coughing so severely that he had to be intubated immediately. Once he was stabilized, Dr. Gail Delaney, the physiatrist to whom he had been referred, examined him and the MRI done in Winnipeg.

Dr. Delaney spent more than four hours with Steven and discovered he was suffering from post-traumatic syringomyelia. Following a traumatic spinal cord injury, a cyst, known as a syrinx, can develop within the injured spinal cord. The term syringomyelia is reserved for large cysts that are associated with loss of neurological function. Dr. Delaney found the cyst at the top of Steven's spine. "In my opinion," she wrote in her report, "There is a true post-traumatic syringomyelia here.

"I took the liberty," she went on, "of reviewing these scans with a neurosurgical colleague, Dr. Parrent, with whom I have worked on previous cases of post-traumatic syringomyelia. He has concurred with me that this is a significant-size syrinx worthy of consideration for surgical shunting."

Dr. Delaney indicated that Steven should have surgery immediately to remove or mitigate the cyst because it could indeed block sensation and it was getting bigger. The consulting neurosurgeon agreed.

On returning to Winnipeg and providing the results of the second opinion to Dr. Hoy, the Fletchers were stunned to hear him say that he had a difference of opinion with the doctors in London. He would not authorize the surgery, saying it would unnecessarily expose Steven to danger.

Undaunted, Steven appealed to Dr. Ian Ross, the neurosurgeon who had done his earlier surgery. Dr. Ross scheduled Steven's surgery for noon the next day. It was risky surgery, and with David in China, Joanne signed the consent form, though she was terrified. Then, with Gordon, Julia and Claire, she followed Steven's stretcher to the operating room. Still stunned at the speed with which the surgery had been arranged, they waited. Later she realized that Dr. Ross had foregone his midday lunch break to make time for Steven's surgery.

When David returned from China, he could immediately see the improvement in Steven. His cheeks were rosy, he seemed brighter, his voice was stronger and his breathing less laboured. Dr. Ross, who took over Steven's care for the rest of his time in hospital, had done much more than eliminate the damaging effects of a spinal cyst; he had given Steven confidence and hope, along with the peace of mind that comes from knowing that everything that can be done is being done. Joanne adds, "We had prayed for help and God sent us Dr. Ian Ross. Everyone was amazed that the surgery had been done so quickly and that everything had gone so well. It was a tremendous relief for us all."

X

Standing By

Julia Fletcher faithfully visited Steven every day after school. She was terribly sad, and cried for her brother. Because she spent every evening at the hospital, her homework suffered that second semester. Her presence and her devotion paid dividends for Steven, however, since Julia had an ability to communicate with Steven that she herself describes as "almost spooky".

In intensive care, unable to speak, unable to move, Steven relied on the alphabet board, which enabled others to laboriously spell out words and sentences for him. The person with whom he was "speaking" pointed to letters in the alphabet printed on the board, and Steven blinked when the correct letter was touched. In this slow and ponderous manner, he could send messages.

Steven's mind, however, was not slow or ponderous and his frustration was obvious. Julia's relationship with him was unique. She almost felt she could read her brother's mind, anticipating what he was trying to say, and eventually becoming proficient at lip reading as he mouthed silent words for her to "hear".

Steven and Julia were connected. As his external wounds healed, his dry skin itched terribly and made him miserable, since he could not scratch. But a mere glance or a movement of his lips and Julia knew that Steven needed his eyebrows or his head scratched. She knew what he wanted, what he needed and what the nurses could not provide. One day he spelled out, "shave my head hair itchy". So she rid him of his hair and felt the relief along with him.

Before they were told they could no longer stay all night at his bedside, family members watched over him at night. David spent so much time standing by his son's bed that his legs required medical treatment. Once or twice, Julia climbed up on the bed beside Steven and dozed off with her arms around him. "I guess," she recalls, "as far as the staff was concerned, we were probably in the way, but we weren't thinking about the needs of the staff. Our focus was where it was supposed to be. We needed to bring Steven back to us in every way."

In the early months after the accident, Claire also came almost every day, but over time, she fell into a deep sadness. She tried to ignore these feelings, believing they were secondary to Steven's needs, and not wanting to upset him. In stifling her conflicts and sorrows, however, her own legitimate needs went unmet, which wasn't healthy for either of them. It created a strained and unnatural distance between them, since they had always shared their feelings fully and openly. Claire also became independent in a way that had never been part of their relationship. Still, they had great trust in each other, because in addition to everything else, they were best friends.

Over the months, however, communication became increasingly difficult. In addition to the lack of privacy and Claire's nervousness about sharing her negative feelings, the physical impediments were overwhelming. Steven's intubation, the alphabet board and the tongue clicking made it hard for him to share his thoughts. Though she tried to anticipate what he wanted to tell her, to save him from having to go through such labours to get his message out, it was a dramatic change from the long, private talks they'd once had. Even when Steven could at last communicate, there was no privacy to discuss deeply personal things. Her sadness deepened. She didn't feel able to be open with him or to ask what he was feeling. And sometimes he was deeply depressed and didn't want to converse at all.

"He sometimes had such a heart-wrenching look, one of despair so deep," she said, "that it frightened me." She worried so much about him that there were days when she just got up and walked out of a university class halfway through and went straight to the hospital. As she drove she thought, *Steven, give me a sign that you're going to come out of this all right.*

Eventually, Claire knew she had to get help for herself or she would become dysfunctional. Before Steven's accident she had done volunteer work—ironically, for the Society for Manitobans with Disabilities. She turned there for guidance, and then went to the hospital staff for professional help.

Though she was more than a friend, she was not next-of-kin,

and therefore not officially a person to whom the hospital provided reports on Steven's condition and prognosis. She knew what was happening, however, because his parents were kept informed and they gave her updates as they received them.

"I could see what they were going through," Claire said, "and I knew how hard talking about these things was for them. I was conscious of my role and place and didn't want to upset the family by asking them about medical details that confused me, so sometimes when I had additional questions to ask, I had my own conversations with medical staff. I felt my role in Steven's life would develop naturally over time, but sometimes it was a bit awkward not being clearly defined. There were so many of us who were deeply concerned.

"It's ironic. When your senses are being bombarded from all sides, you become more conscious of things. It was bitterly cold the whole time Steven was in the ICU, about 25°C below for the whole time. That isn't so terribly unusual for Winnipeg in the winter, but the emotional pain I felt inside seemed to magnify the physical pain outside to the point where the cold actually felt much colder than it really was. Everything seemed more intense."

When Steven was moved to rehab, Claire initially gained some hope. The place had a good reputation and held some positive memories for her, since her mother had worked there when Claire was young and she had occasionally accompanied her mother to the cafeteria for lunch. Enthusiastic about the move to rehab, Claire talked it up with optimism and humour, encouraging Steven to get excited about his physiotherapy program and what it might achieve. "We had never said that we didn't expect some sort of progress, even small finger movements," she recalls, "but maybe encouraging him to hope for so much wasn't beneficial, because he was so continually let down."

As the months progressed, Steven and Claire occasionally stole away for brief periods to a small hospital room that had been transformed into a chapel. There, free from intrusion, they were able to be boyfriend and girlfriend, if only for a short time.

After personal counselling and much introspection, Claire allowed herself to look ahead. She knew she had to start thinking long term. A job opportunity in a career-related field became available in Ontario for the summer of 1996 and she was encouraged to apply. She wanted to take the job, if she could get it. It was appealing and would benefit her both in the short and long term. She spoke to Steven and told him she wanted to take advantage of the opportunity. Though he was aware the separation could well become permanent, and he knew how he would feel with her not being near him, he didn't discourage her. But Claire was torn with indecision. She hesitated until the last minute before sending in her application. She got the job.

When she left, Steven gave her his childhood teddy bear. He dictated a personal and private note to her, which his father carefully wrote out for him. The great love that David had for his son, and his son's absolute trust in him, enabled them to complete this intimate task with Steven's privacy and dignity intact.

Then Steven disappeared.

He had been learning to operate the controls of a specialized wheelchair that was manipulated with head movements. To allow his body to become used to being in a sitting position, he was placed in the chair each day. This was not as easy as it might seem to able-bodied people and Steven sometimes passed out while being moved from a horizontal position to a sitting one. The stress on his paralysed body from being kept upright for a prolonged period was intense. He wasn't yet ready to be left alone in his chair, but after Claire had gone, finding himself unattended in his power chair, Steven left the hospital ward without telling anyone and found a place where he could be alone. He wasn't trying to create a panic on the ward, though one ensued when no one could find him. He simply had to be by himself, without being monitored, while he gave himself up to his grief.

He knew he was going to lose Claire, lose the hope of a wife and children. He had already lost his dreamed-for mining career, his beloved canoeing and kayaking trips, his ability to take a walk in the forest by himself. He had even lost the ability to be alone for a couple of hours without having to account for his whereabouts, to deal privately with the overwhelming sorrow of being locked in a body that didn't work.

The nursing record reveals how his emotional turmoil and sense of impending loss affected Steven. The care nurse reported Steven wept and told her, "We had so many plans for the future ... Why didn't the moose damage me 100 per cent? ... Look at me. I have to get someone to feed me ... I don't think Claire understands how serious this whole thing is ... I can't be a husband to her, not a real husband ... I can't ..."

Later, in August, the nurse recorded in the chart, "Patient crying. With a lot of encouragement patient stated 'My girlfriend is dump-ing me, but it's not her fault' ... Patient says he just wants to sleep ..."

Still later, in September, the medical chart states, "Patient refusing to eat or drink, when confronted with potential risks to his condition, patient became upset and stated, 'I want to die' ... Patient regained composure ... and requested that he be left alone."

Shortly after, a psychiatric nursing note states, "follow-up visit, major issue is the potential break-up with girlfriend Claire, a loss he is not able to comprehend." And "Patient says, 'I can't take this anymore.'"

Claire found out later that Steven had left the hospital ward alone without notifying anyone and that he had been gone for hours. "I created that grief, that lowest point for him. I was heartsick to have hurt him so. Here I am always trying to find something positive in everything that happens, to find the hidden benefits, but all I could think of was how much he was suffering and it was hard to find the positive in that. Still, I knew I had to go to Ontario, and that ultimately it would prove to have been the right thing for both of us. I think that that summer, Steven started to move on, not necessarily accepting his fate, but forced to take his fate into his own hands."

The canoeing community was faithful in its hospital visits to Steven. The members of the Manitoba Naturalists Society (of which Steven was a board member) and the Manitoba Recreational Canoeing Association, as it was then called, (of which Steven was president) came frequently. The members of these organizations actually had to coordinate a visitors' schedule to accommodate the number of people who wanted to see Steven. It brightened his days to have them come.

These lovers of the wilderness perhaps understood better than most people that Steven was losing more than just an ability to move. He was losing the central part of his life. The MRCA held monthly meetings, which the president chaired. Since Steven was the president, the association simply moved the meetings to Steven's hospital room, which, lying motionless in bed and scanning notes over his head, he continued to chair.

"It was," his father said, "actually rather amazing to witness, and quite far-sighted of the board." In testament to Steven's commitment and the members' confidence in him, Steven ran and was elected for a second term as MRCA president.

Most of his University of Manitoba engineering buddies came too, and their straightforward commonsense approach to problem solving and their basic good fellowship were uplifting. Don Shields, dean of the Faculty of Engineering, and the senior stick of engineering dropped in to the hospital with a huge banner made by the students, covered completely with signatures and good wishes. It was a welcome and thoughtful gesture and, as the journal notes, "Steven was pleased."

In February, paraplegic Rick Hansen, well known across Canada and internationally for his prowess as a wheelchair marathoner, and the inspiration for the Man in Motion Foundation came to visit Steven. Hansen shared his experiences and indicated the approach

In 2004, Steven, right, joined disabled activist Rick Hansen, centre, and Vancouver Mayor Sam Sullivan at the University of British Columbia as they launched the latest line of Trail Riders.

that Steven would have to take to face his new world. Hansen's visit was positive and uplifting for Steven and the two have maintained contact. In 2007, Steven and Prime Minister Stephen Harper announced a $20 million investment in the Rick Hansen Foundation.

As time went on, however, visits dwindled in number, as was to be expected. After all, people get busy. They have their own lives to lead, and things they need to do. They get new jobs. They get married. They move away. They have problems and worries of their own. They didn't forget Steven and continued to care about him. They just couldn't keep up the routine of visiting with the same diligence they did in the beginning. But they were there for him during those first dark, terrifying months, and for the time and encouragement they gave him when he most needed it, he and his family are deeply grateful.

XI

Spell It Out for Me

Claire and Steven were beginning to redefine their relationship. They had not officially broken up, but they began to relate to each other more like old friends than people who were romantically involved. Without actually discussing it, they both knew what was happening. They talked a lot on the phone that summer she was away, and sent little things back and forth. She told him about her job. He let her know about his progress.

Claire's absence from the hospital during her summer in Ontairo provided a complete shift in her environment. Though she was only twenty, she felt rejuvenated. She realized she had begun to feel old—not mature—just old and worn. Now she felt young again—not carefree, she would never be young and carefree again—but young. She awakened to the thought of new adventures and dreams of the future. One day, she actually felt happy and recognized that she hadn't felt happy in a long time. Adding to that happiness was the knowledge that she was still capable of experiencing joy. She thought that capacity might have gone from her forever. Yet guilt often permeated her thoughts. *Why can I run and play and Steven not?*

She returned to Winnipeg for a short time during the summer. It was late when she arrived in the city and the night was very hot. She went straight to the hospital, straight to his room and just stood by his bed watching him sleep. Sensing a presence, he opened his eyes. Years later, they both remembered the moment and what she was wearing. It was a black dress with red flowers on it.

When she came home for good at the end of the summer, she

had a fresh perspective. There was Steven, and there was Claire. Was there still a Steven-and-Claire? The cruel reality was that their relationship had been drastically altered by their circumstances.

They never actually said, "It's over," which in retrospect Claire feels was a mistake. "We were so young and vulnerable and we didn't understand that we needed to talk it out at the time. We were so sensitive to his quadriplegia that we avoided saying all that needed to be said. That was strange when I look back, since we had always talked everything out in detail before. But everything was altered, and became ambiguous and we were having trouble handling things. We, who had prided ourselves on our ability to communicate so well, had flawed communications so much of his time in the hospital. If we had talked as we should have, we could have helped each other so much more effectively."

Claire saw Steven every couple of days that fall. They had good visits, but avoided romantic overtones in their conversations. About a year and a half after the accident, Claire decided to transfer to the University of Toronto to complete her engineering degree. There were logical reasons for this decision. Enrollment was low in the University of Manitoba's geological engineering program and the university wanted to transfer budget dollars from geological engineering to other branches of engineering. Claire realized it was not the best strategy to indicate on your resume that your degree is from a faculty that closed its doors the year you graduated. The U of T is a prestigious institution with a good reputation; a degree from it would enhance her career opportunities.

As well, she wanted to use her talents and interests. She talked to Steven about her desire to explore and grow and achieve, to seek adventure. In short, without realizing it, she described her desires to do many of the things that Steven had wanted to do. He recognized her need to soak up life. She told him she would always be a part of his life, but not in the way they had originally planned. The conversation was about as painful as it could be, for Steven knew her departure was inevitable. "She was young and had her whole life to live," he says. "We remain friends and will always care about each other."

Looking back, Claire says, "We were in a holding zone for a long time. We never decided it consciously, but there were some places we just didn't go. We didn't talk about personal relationships like him dating others or me dating others, for example. We didn't talk about his battles with MPI or his personal care complications, or about things that were impeding his future. Now we do.

"I believe that fate played a big part in what happened to us. That drives Steven wild because he doesn't believe in fate or predestination. I tell him that he is his own fate. He has allowed himself to become the role model he never set out to be. Ironically he is doing those things that an apparent fate has positioned him to do.

"Steven still seeks true inner peace," Claire continues. "He has conquered so much. He keeps himself so busy that he doesn't have time to think about his pain. I go over a bridge regularly and I always toss in a penny and make a wish. My deepest wish for Steven is that he can find peace.

"It is hard for me and for Steven to talk publicly about our relationship, either as it was in the past, or as it is now in the present, but I think it is important for people to understand that high level spinal cord injuries affect more than the body. They affect the mind and the soul and alter human relationships in myriad ways."

Claire attended Steven's convocation ceremony when he received his MBA. She sat in the back, apart from his family and when he rolled up to get his degree she cheered loudly. The person beside her smiled and said, "You must know him." Claire returned the smile and replied, "Yes, I do. I really do."

Eventually Claire began to date one person exclusively and she wanted Steven to know. Telling him about this was emotionally difficult for Claire, and hearing about it was hard for Steven. As if to underscore the way in which their lives had changed, Claire realized that she had left the intercom to his health care attendant on during their entire "private" conversation. They never knew if they had been overheard, but no one has ever made reference to the conversation.

Claire's relationship became serious and during Christmas of 2004, while visiting her mother in Winnipeg, she became engaged. The next day she went to tell Steven. He wasn't surprised. He was, Claire said, "cool as a cucumber, steady and gracious, as if he had expected this news and was demonstrating that he could handle it."

It was not the way Steven had hoped things to be, but then what in his new life was? Losing the precious things that had meant so much to him before he met the moose was part of his new reality, and he had the courage and strength to survive and prevail.

Claire thought carefully about what her wedding might mean to Steven, and after long and painful consideration she decided not to send him an invitation to the ceremony or to tell him of the exact date chosen for the event. She didn't want him conscious of the ceremony as it was occurring. It had been almost ten years since his accident and Steven was by now the Member of Parliament for Charleswood-St. James-Assiniboia. Claire's wedding took place a week before Steven was to attend meetings in Toronto. The two met for dinner and she told him that she was now married. He was, again, gracious. Claire and Steven's relationship continues to evolve and be continually redefined as they grow more comfortable with their changed lives.

XII

Don't Fence Me In

Having become aware he would never recover from his injuries, Steven Fletcher made a decision. If he was doomed to live, then live he would—but not as a cold lump in a bed taking up space in a medical institution. He would live as fully and productively as he could. And he resolved to live in the world, not removed from it.

Gradually, he began to identify what he would need to become part of the world again. The first, because of his many physical vulnerabilities, was twenty-four-hour medical care, whether he was institutionalized or not. Health care aides selected to look after him would have to be able and willing to see themselves as facilitators, whose purpose would be to help him live as full a life as possible. How could he get such medical care outside of an institutional setting?

He needed to be able to communicate effectively. He could see and hear and had regained his ability to speak. But he couldn't use any part of his body below the neck and, because of the stabilizing rod, could turn his head only slightly. What new technologies would allow him to telephone or use a computer?

He needed an effective means of mobility, a specialized chair with a mechanical system he could direct using limited head movements. Only in that way could he attain a measure of independent mobility.

He needed reliable transportation in which, because his body took on the ambient temperature of his surrounding environment, a certain temperature range could be maintained. It would have to be a van equipped with an emergency generator, modified to contain his specialized chair. He felt his health care aid could double as his vehicle driver, since he or she would accompany him everywhere he went.

He needed wheelchair-accessible living quarters that would allow him a degree of freedom and privacy, as well as space for his health care aide and all his medical equipment.

Returning to university for further education would help him become productive again. Having noted that there were no wheelchair-accessible gold mines around, Steven decided to begin studies for his MBA. This was in keeping with his pre-accident goals, but he wondered how accessible the university campus was. Even if the physical layout was accessible, he would need a specially adapted computer to do assignments. And what other obstacles would he need to overcome?

He had begun his restoration subconsciously within days of his accident, at the sound of his father's voice. "Blink your eyes. Blink your eyes, Steven," his father had commanded. Steven had blinked.

They know I'm still in here, he thought, emphasizing the point to himself. Knowing that his intellect and ability to reason were unimpaired gave him incentive to carry on, to become of value to society.

One must not underestimate the powerful influence of Steven's family in giving him that incentive. Steven's parents had raised him to be strong and self-reliant. One might say that because of them, he had acquired the backbone he needed to stubbornly push ahead, no matter what the obstacles. Now, as he recognized that his life was irrevocably changed, he began to focus his energy on new goals, new dreams and new ways of doing things. It was time to start over, to be braver and more fearless than ever before.

That fearlessness was something with which he may have been born. Joanne was six months pregnant with Steven, their first child, when the Fletchers moved to Brazil, where David was working on a large engineering project. Joanne gave birth in a hospital run by nuns who spoke no English, where everything was unfamiliar. It may be that when Steven took his first breath, he drew in with it his young mother's courage and ability to adapt to her circumstances.

Those qualities of character displayed themselves early and frequently. Steven learned Portuguese and attended a Portuguese kindergarten, and then the British school in Rio de Janeiro. As a young boy, he was thoroughly and comfortably at home in Brazilian culture. He corrected his parents' Portuguese when they were out shopping, as a new Canadian child might correct his immigrant parents' English. Indeed, for Steven, moving to Canada when he was five was an experience not unlike that of an immigrant child. He was not nervous or timid, but excited by the move, and fascinated that, in Canada, it was not just his parents who spoke English. His sense of adventure and his eagerness to explore new territories—both physical and cultural—gave him an ability to adapt that would later prove essential.

In 2006, in his role as parliamentary secretary for health, Steven travelled to Rio for an international public health conference. He was able to visit his old alma mater as Canada's first Brazilian-born Member of Parliament, delighting the students—and himself—with the event. Later the school sent him a newsletter telling of his visit, and featuring a photo of his primary class, with a caption identifying Steven in the last row, where the tall kids were.

Steven spent almost a year in hospital. Some of that time he cannot recall, but most of it he can. Because of his experiences, and through further study and research, he has become an expert on spinal cord injuries. More than that, though he didn't set out to become a spokesperson or advocate for the severely disabled, he has become just that.

Blessed with a natural ability to explain things, Steven has been able to help others understand the various problems paralysed people face and to educate them about spinal cord injuries. Though he didn't talk publicly about his accident until 1999, when he was asked by a friend's mother to speak about it at a local junior high school, he has since become a popular and articulate guest speaker. His mere presence at a podium helps audiences to see ability rather than disability.

Asked the difference between a quadriplegic and a paraplegic, Steven carefully explained that a quadriplegic had all four (quad) limbs paralysed and a paraplegic paralysis in just the lower two (para) limbs. He went on to say that, depending on where the spinal cord was broken, some people would experience more severe paralysis than others in the same category.

"The closer the spinal break is to the head, the greater the paralysis the patient experiences. It's all a matter of perspective. High-level quads, like me or the late Christopher Reeve, who are paralysed from the neck down, wish we could be lower-level quads like Vancouver mayor Sam Sullivan, who has partial use of his upper arms. Lower-level quads want to be paraplegics like Rick Hansen, who can use his arms and his body above the waist. Paraplegics wish they could be below-the-knee amputees who can use prosthetics and walk; below-the-knee amputees wish they were Tom Cruise—that is, if they are men." Because he uses humour and real people as examples, listeners remember his explanations.

For most of Steven's wide circle of friends, just knowing him has increased their awareness of physical challenges. It has also given them a more in-depth understanding of the details of his particular disability, though most of the time those who know him well are too busy trying to keep up with him to notice.

The British School kindergarten class in Rio de Janeiro, 1976.
Steven, circled in this photo, stands in the back row.

XIII

Returning to the World

J ean Burton was a godsend for her friends in more ways than one. A registered nurse at the time of Steven's accident, she was providing home care to patients whose medical conditions required regular professional intervention. Her in-depth knowledge of how home care and independent living worked would prove invaluable to the Fletcher family. As the time for Steven's release from hospital drew near and it became clear that the medical authorities were looking to house him in a personal care home, she expanded her support and got involved in Steven's health care as well. She knew Linda Greenhalgh, the discharge nurse at the Health Sciences Centre, who usually dealt with "challenging discharges". Jean called her and asked her to talk to Steven. Familiar with community living, Linda understood what could be done, even with a case as severe as Steven's, and became his advocate.

As he prepared to leave hospital, Steven was asked to attend a meeting of all the health care professionals who had been involved with his care. It was a large group. Sitting in a circle, they discussed what should be done with Steven. The first speaker suggested that the best situation for him would be to a personal care institution or group living centre; others quickly picked up on the idea. Moving around the circle, each in turn agreed with the recommendation.

"Yes, indeed," they all said, "that will be the ideal place for Steven. He would be well-cared for and looked after there." It was clear they had made this decision prior to meeting with Steven.

A wave of despair washed over him. Being confined to such an institution would be, in his words, "like putting a sane person into an insane setting." Once placed there, he believed he would never get out and would end up being heavily drugged to keep him calm and not upset the institutional routines. He would lose his mind, the only thing that he had left. And his life, at age twenty-four, would essentially be over.

The last person in the circle to speak was Linda Greenhalgh, who had a very different take on things. She not only disagreed with the consensus, she disagreed vehemently. A personal care institution would be horribly inappropriate for a person like Steven, she said. He would not fit into such an environment and would not do well there. She told the group that institutionalizing Steven would be destructive to his sense of self-worth and would be counter-productive to his overall wellbeing. Instead, she advocated independent living.

Finally, Steven was asked for his opinion. He told them that he wanted to go into self-managed care. Genuinely worried that this would be unworkable, the group members asked him how he would manage all the people who would work for him under such a program. Steven indicated that he was up to the challenge of managing his medical staff.

Eventually, the hospital staff members were persuaded to try this innovative alternative, and to their credit, worked very hard to make it succeed for him. He was the first profoundly injured person in Manitoba to go straight from hospital into self-managed care.

However, creating an effective, smoothly functioning, self-managed care program for Steven was a process filled with seemingly insurmountable obstacles, particularly during the first year. With the help of his caseworker, he rented an apartment in a residential district in Winnipeg, close to his father's office. While the apartment was in a regular building, it had a street-level doorway, an elevator, doorways wide enough to accommodate his specialized chair and a room for his attendant. It would serve as a temporary dwelling until he could find accessible housing. And he had achieved his goal of leaving hospital before Christmas, just a few weeks before the first anniversary of his accident.

Finding qualified health care attendants, however, was more challenging. At the time, self-managed home care was a relatively new alternative in Manitoba. In 1991, the provincial government had initiated a two-year pilot program that allowed disabled individuals to hire, train and manage their care requirements independently. Reports were optimistic about the potential of such a program and the pilot project was successful enough that, in 1995, it was expanded into a care option for adults with disabilities.

Despite this, the program was still in its infancy and had not yet been tested by patients as catastrophically disabled as Steven Fletcher. For his purposes, the self-managed care program was vastly underfunded; yet he was determined to make it work.

He found a company, Gentle Touch, which was willing to take a chance on him, even though funding was only provided for twenty-one hours a day. But Sharon Marks of Gentle Touch was imaginative about how the care was arranged, and stretched the available dollars over twenty-four hours, to give Steven round-the-clock supervision. Nevertheless, working with such limited funding, finding attendants with the specialized qualifications needed to assist Steven was difficult. The wage scale for home care attendants was relatively low, since for the most part their tasks were fairly simple and straightforward. However, Steven needed aides who were aware of the many complications associated with high-level quadriplegia and who were capable of performing complicated medical procedures such as catheterization. Such individuals were in short supply. To compensate, Sharon jockeyed schedules to give Steven a person capable of doing a bowel routine when he needed one, and placed a less qualified person on duty when such tasks were not scheduled. Despite her best efforts, there were times when Steven thought he'd never be able to make self-managed home care work for him. It became critical to hire more qualified aides, but how could he do this with such a shortage of money?

Fortunately, one or two attendants that Sharon found turned out to be exceptionally good, and one of these, Susannah Mah, was a life saver—perhaps literally—for Steven. Susannah came to work for Steven in 1997, during one of the lowest periods in his life. A well-spoken, intelligent woman of Chinese and Filipino descent, Susannah had moved to Winnipeg from Prince George, British Columbia, shortly after Steven was released from hospital. She was studying nursing at the University of Manitoba when she began to work as one of his health care attendants. Close to Steven in age, she had great empathy for his situation. Right from the start she proved to be unusually competent and, as a result, Steven relied upon her to do the less pleasant procedures others couldn't perform well.

Susannah recognized that the young man she was tending was deeply depressed. And why shouldn't he be depressed? she asked herself. He had lost so very much, and everything that meant something to him—his kayaking, his career, his girlfriend—everything was snatched away in the blink of an eye.

At times, Steven seemed to have no motivation to continue living. He was grieving the loss of his romantic relationship with Claire; he had money worries and he was in a battle with the insurance company over expenses. He had no vehicle to transport him to the places he needed to go, and he had huge staffing problems that were literally a matter of life and death. There were days when Steven wouldn't get out of bed because he was frightened that some of the inexperienced aides would drop him trying to transfer him to his wheelchair. Or they would take hours to complete his morning routine, assuming they could do it at all. On such days, feeling utterly without hope, Steven sometimes even refused his physiotherapy, a sure sign that he was slipping into a black maelstrom of depair. Susannah, however, was always able to get him up and going. He trusted her medical competence and valued her optimistic approach. She gave him hope and the incentive he so desperately needed from his entire staff.

Susannah worried about Steven's mental state. She knew when he told her he was going for a "walk" that he wanted to go alone; she had to let him go by himself. She understood his great need for a few moments of privacy, to be alone outdoors, even if the outdoors was a concrete sidewalk in the middle of the city. She wanted him to know that she had confidence in him and his ability to do certain things on his own without being shadowed every second of his day. Still, she worried constantly every time he rounded a corner that took him out of her sight. He would be gone for a half-hour, once for forty-five minutes, and she would be anxious the whole time. Despite these fears, Susannah knew that she had to let him have his solitary walks. Denied them, she worried that his depression would lead him to seriously consider suicide. Her instincts were right. During that period, Steven did contemplate the ways in which he, despite his inability to move, might end his life, and with it his misery.

Steven's apartment didn't have a wheelchair-accessible bathroom, so he wasn't able to get into it. As a result, he always had to be bathed in bed. While some of his attendants were not skilled in this practice, Susannah was an expert. Using an inflatable sink, rather like a small swimming pool, which had a hose for draining the water into a catch basin, she gently bathed Steven. She soaped him and scrubbed him, pouring water from a pitcher over him until he was clean and refreshed. This expertise and tender care not only created a comfort level with her, but gave him confidence that such care was possible.

The two bonded, and over time this bond expanded beyond caregiver and client into a friendship that has endured.

At one point, staffing shortages were so severe that Steven had only two attendants, each working a twelve-hour shift. Such was their dedication and professional commitment that, despite the long hours, they kept him functioning well. Susannah was one of the two.

Later she was joined by two others who provided reliable and competent care, nursing student Brenda Gadsby and physiotherapy student Sarah Biggs. At last, Steven's situation began to improve.

More than a decade later, Susannah is still with Steven. "She was a ray of sunshine in my gray and gloomy days," he says. "Right from the beginning, Susannah was capable and committed to my well-being, and she still is a very important support for me. There are now several attendants who have been with me for years and they are like family to me. They can anticipate my needs before I mention them, and like old married couples we can finish each other's sentences. They have given me back my freedom."

Some of the attendants in those early days, however, were truly awful. Steven discovered that one had been stealing from him, using his bank cards to withdraw money for herself. Despite knowing this, because there was no other caregiver available, Steven had no choice but to keep using her as his attendant until she could be replaced. He knew he couldn't let her know that he knew she was stealing from him, and he didn't dare confront her because he had no ability to defend himself if she turned on him and became dangerous. After three long weeks, to Steven's immense relief, the matter was resolved. As it turned out, the woman was not only a thief, but had a record of identity theft, as well as alternate identities. She had conned her employers into believing she had a reputable record of service. Though the woman was apprehended and about $200 of Steven's money was returned, the stressful incident underscored his vulnerability.

Steven never blamed Gentle Touch for his home care problems. It did the best it could within the available financial parameters. Steven is convinced he was a financial burden for the company, yet it never gave up trying to make things work for him. "Despite all the difficulties and disappointments that first year," he says, "without Sharon and her company, I would have been institutionalized. She gave me a chance and that's what I needed to get me going." Sadly, a year after Steven had moved on to other caregivers, Sharon died tragically.

✦ ◼ ✦ ◼ ✦

DAVID and Joanne Fletcher believe the opportunity to manage his own affairs gave their son the confidence he needed to function effectively and to contribute to his community in a meaningful way. "This program," says David, "helps take pressure off the hospitals, and makes inclusiveness real. In many cases it can also be less expensive. Despite how hard it was to get started, it was absolutely the best decision for Steven."

Proof that self-managed care was the right decision was driven home when Steven managed to take his first trial trip away from the apartment and stay overnight in hotels. On April 4, 1997, Susannah travelled with Steven as Gordon Fletcher drove them all to Minneapolis to see the engineering building at the University of Minnesota. The trial trip went smoothly, and Susannah, sitting in the back of the van with Steven so that she could care for him, felt that the trip had been a real confidence booster. Steven now felt certain he could travel and, with competent aides and the right equipment in tow, could manage his health care routines safely in a hotel setting.

Later that summer, Susannah and Brenda Gadsby accompanied Steven and Claire Vivier, whose romantic relationship was steadily evolving into a close and comfortable friendship, on a short trip to the Rockies.

Claire, who was living in Alberta to complete a work term, and Steven both loved the majesty of the mountains and the trip gave them the setting and privacy they needed. Susannah's sensitivity was essential at this time. "When we went to Minneapolis," she recalls, "I participated with the fellows in most of the activities. But the trip with Claire was different. Steven needed medical staff to be near, in case we were needed, but for this trip we stayed out of the way as much as we could, and tried not to intrude upon the time Claire and Steven had together."

The highlight of the trip was Steven and Claire's chance to explore the Athabasca Glacier and ferry to the top of a mountain, just like other tourists. In an amazing example of accessibility, the glacier buggies were designed to accomodate wheelchairs. Though to this day Steven has difficulty with "accessible" taxi vehicles in Ottawa, getting to the top of a glacier in Alberta posed no problems. The ability to get around on this trip made him feel less constrained and strengthened his will to overcome other obstacles.

With Claire at Athabasca Glacier.

XIV

Battles On and Off Campus

Steven was anxious to get on with life. And that meant going back to university and enrolling in the MBA program. But, to do so, he had to write and pass the General Masters Admissions Test or GMAT. This exam was offered four times a year, and Steven was eager to sit for it as soon as possible. That first opportunity was March 1997, a year and two months after his accident.

As with almost everything else he tried, it was a mission fraught with challenges. Though his family, as always, supported his decision, his doctors wanted him to take a neuropath test to make sure he had no brain damage before he launched himself into complicated endeavours. With good intentions, they suggested that perhaps he should just take a year off and better adjust to his new life first.

Loath to let anything interfere with the GMAT, Steven successfully stalled on the neuropath test and doggedly pushed on. He called the people in the United States who administer the exams to discuss his particular circumstances, indicating his intention to enter the MBA program. They were initially hesitant when they realized Steven was a high-level quadriplegic and might need special accommodating to get through the test. Steven was told that they did not know of anyone else in his position who had taken the exam, and the authorities weren't sure whether such a person could, in fact, do so. As a result, they told him they would turn his application down if he applied.

Taking the response as merely an initial reaction, Steven pressed his case. The second, third and fourth responses were similar; the answer continued to be "no". Eventually, however, the reaction changed from a flat "no" to "if we did let you take the exam, we're not convinced that you could pass it." In the end, the response was, "Just exactly what accommodations would we need to make, to let you take this exam?" Permission was given for Steven to write the exam scheduled for March 1997.

Steven then had to determine what accommodations he would need to take the GMAT. There were only two. He needed a scribe to take down his answers, which he planned to dictate. And he needed extra time, because his process for answering questions would be slower than most. Diagrams would have to be described verbally for the scribe to draw, for example, because he could not draw them himself. These accommodations were easily granted.

By the time approval was granted and he was registered, time was limited for Steven to work out the logistics of the exercise. How would he study, for example? Or get his work done? After identifying the problems he faced, Steven went about solving them one by one.

With financial help from Manitoba Public Insurance, Steven hired a student to help him study. This could have been tedious, as Steven couldn't so much as turn a page and had to explain precisely what he wanted to do. However, the student helper, a bright young woman, quickly became familiar with mathematical expressions and the nature of the exam. Her assistance was exactly what he required.

Steven had to learn how to learn all over again, something that many disabled people must do. It is a serious and difficult challenge. He had previously been a visual learner, not an aural one. He was accustomed to putting his thoughts and diagrams on paper and studying those images to secure them firmly in his mind. Now, those days were gone. Steven could only progress with his GMAT preparation when an able-bodied individual was present to assist. His health care attendants were always available, but they could do no more than turn the pages of his textbooks. Looking back, Steven believes "it was survival" that allowed him to quickly develop a new form of learning.

Even today, ten years later, with a specialized computer at his desk and a Blackberry in his pocket, much of Steven's learned material is still acquired and retained through memorization, since it is not always possible for him to record notes and key messages in a timely fashion.

Exam day arrived. Though he was tired and not feeling well, he was ready and eager to take the test. As a procedural requirement, he had to use a scribe he didn't know to write the exam. Steven had been assured that the scribe was conversant with the nature of the exam and would know what he was doing. However, as the exam got underway, Steven discovered to his horror that the scribe didn't know how to draw perpendicular lines, how to express division algebraically, or even understand how to put mathematical expressions on paper.

At one point when Steven dictated "alpha", the scribe asked how to spell it. Steven replied, "You don't spell it. It's a symbol; you have to draw it." The scribe then asked how to draw it. Steven took a deep breath—or at least as deep a breath as he was able to take—and said calmly, "You draw a little fish and make it swimming to your left."

Looking back, he recalls, "Not for the first time, I marvelled at how my world had changed." Today, Steven can see humour in many things that didn't seem at all funny at the time. Taking the GMAT exam was one of those. At the time, it was intensely frustrating because he knew he only had one kick at the cat, and his time was being eaten up in describing how to draw the most elementary diagrams so that his scribe could put them on paper.

The examiners did give him extra time, for which he was grateful. By the time he had finished explaining what the various symbols, drawings and shapes should look like, and verbally editing as he went along, he had needed it. A rapid reader, he made up some of the lost time in the reading comprehension section of the exam, and to his relief the scribe was quick and accurate in taking down language dictation.

Steven passed the exam with flying colours, which is why he can look back with humour at the things that went wrong. Getting a good score on his GMAT made him ever more confident that, despite obstacles, he could compete and prevail. (He never did take the neuropath test to find out if he had any brain damage.) He started immediately to prepare for university classes.

In May 1997, he received the letter confirming his acceptance into the MBA program at the University of Manitoba. Jen Paterson was visiting him when the letter arrived, and he asked her to open it. She was just as nervous as he was, and after she pulled the letter from its envelope and held it for him to see, he asked her to read it with him.

Being accepted into grad studies was a high point in a year-and-a-half of low points and it gave him some much needed confidence, as well as hope for the future. But as always, the next step presented new challenges. How would he get to the university? How would he do assignments? How would he keep up in a class of bright, able-bodied people? If the list of problems seemed endless, Steven's approach to problem solving was every bit as resolute: examine the obstacles blocking the way and seek reasonable solutions to overcome them. As he says, "The way to eat an elephant is to take one bite at a time."

XV

Aides and Anguish

Being paralysed from the neck down involves far more than just not being able to move or feel anything; a C4 quadriplegic's life is constantly at risk because of a long list of serious threats. One of the worst is autonomic dysreflexia, every quadriplegic's dread. It occurs when the body reacts to a sensation, but can't identify it because of the disconnection between brain and body. It could be anything from a mosquito bite or a pressure sore to a bowel blockage or an over-filled bladder. The body reacts to the unidentified stimuli by dramatically increasing blood pressure, sending it soaring. The victim experiences an intense, throbbing headache and excessive perspiration above his or her sensation level. Unless dealt with immediately, autonomic dysreflexia can trigger a stroke, inflict brain damage or lead to death. After Steven's accident, it didn't take much to trigger the symptoms of autonomic dysreflexia, but with time, experience and skilled attendants, these attacks are no longer the problem they once were.

Autonomic dysreflexia is not the only danger Steven faces. Because he has no sense of touch below his neck, he is very susceptible to pressure sores or decubitus ulcers. These injuries to the skin and underlying tissue develop when the blood flow carrying essential nutrients and oxygen to the skin is cut off, causing the tissue under the skin to die. In order to keep the blood properly circulating, a person's body position must be constantly changed. In healthy bodies, messages from nerves in the skin are sent through the spinal cord to the brain to indicate discomfort and the need to move. The brain then issues a command for the body to shift positions, even while sleeping.

A person with a spinal cord injury, however, will not be aware that his or her tissue is beginning to break down, since the messages are blocked at the level of injury and never reach the brain. Immobile, the body weight then stops the blood flow, rather like a large rock on a garden hose will effectively stop the flow of water through it.

Pressure sores can never be taken lightly. If the wound is on one of the body's main pressure points such as the buttocks, a small wound can expand quickly over the course of a day. These vicious sores can eat right through to the bone, causing infection that can lead to amputation and even death, as one did for the late Christopher Reeve. Even when properly treated, pressure sores can become severely infected and this infection can lead to a heart attack or coma.

Even a wrinkle on a cushion can cause pressure sores and other problems, and bedsores can keep patients in hospital for years. Steven has special air-filled cushions and an air-loss sleeping mattress to protect his skin and keep sores from forming. He has also been blessed by nature with "good" skin that is holding up well under his circumstances.

Still, he must be constantly vigilant. His specialized wheelchair continuously tilts and rocks to keep him from having too much pressure on any one point of his body for a prolonged period of time. His attendant moves his arms every so often to stretch his shoulders. Steven bemoans the fact that some patients are denied cushions or proper chairs because of a few hundred dollars. "They suffer," he says. "They end up having extended stays in hospital, and maybe die there, because money isn't available for them to acquire the equipment that could help them. It's not right."

Loss of sensation also means that Steven could be cut, burned or severely frostbitten without being aware of it until someone else notices the consequences. If cuts are not noticed and treated right away, they could trigger the autonomic symptoms described earlier. All sorts of other risks are also associated with seemingly small injuries.

For most of us, taking a deep breath is easy, and we can more or less take our ability to do this for granted. Steven, however, does not breathe well, since normal breathing and cough reflexes are not preserved after a C4 spinal cord break. He lived on a ventilator for a long time while he took intensive respiratory therapy to train his neck and upper diaphragm to expand so that air can rush in to his lungs. When he takes a deep breath, his abdomen swells out because he has no muscle tone. Long months of respiratory therapy now allow him to live without the ventilator, but that does not mean that his breathing is strong. Because he has no control over his abdominal muscles, he can't cough without assistance. This inability to cough is another serious concern for high-level quadriplegics because coughing removes dust, mucus and saliva from the lungs. Without this cleansing ability, infections occur, leading to pneumonia.

When he needs to cough, his health care attendant must push hard on Steven's abdominal wall to emulate the body's normal function. As long as someone who knows how to perform this task is on hand, coughing is not a serious concern. However, if there's no one available who is trained to perform an assisted cough maneuver, it quickly becomes a serious concern. Inhaling air is fundamental to life and choking can lead to death.

Steven has an indwelling catheter to drain his urine. A long tube inserted into the bladder through the urethra, the indwelling catheter remains in the body, held in the bladder by a small saline-filled balloon. This catheter drains urine from the bladder into an external bladder bag taped to the body. The bag is regularly emptied by the health care attendant, who must ensure that the outlet valve is cleaned and free from infection. The drainage bag must always stay lower than the bladder to prevent a back flow of urine.

It takes a skilled health care provider to attend to the various tasks associated with indwelling catheters. Scrupulous attention to cleanliness is mandatory and routine care must include daily cleansing. Indwelling catheters are usually replaced about once a month, depending on individual medical protocols. If the catheter is clogged, or has become painful or infected, it may require immediate replacement. Changing it needs to be done with great care. Even with skilled attention, the patient is highly susceptible to a variety of complications.

These complications include bladder, kidney and urinary tract infections, blood infections or septicemia, skin breakdown, bladder stones and blood in the urine or hematuria. The bladder can spasm, requiring irrigation of the catheter, a procedure that requires training and expertise. Even a kink in the external catheter line can cause a serious obstruction preventing the flow of urine from the bladder, which could become overfilled as a result, possibly triggering autonomic dysreflexia. Bladder cancer can also develop after many years of catheterization.

These are not insignificant complications and Steven needs well-trained attendants. He also needs them to understand why it is important to put him through nightly range-of-motion exercises for his legs and arms. Without them, he could develop heterotropic ossification, in which bone grows in the joints because they aren't being used or moved enough. Without the exercises, Steven's muscles can atrophy, wither and shrink, since movement stimulates blood circulation. It is imperative that the exercises be done—and done well—by someone who understands their purpose.

Steven's body does not control its own temperature, as normal people's bodies do. A normal, healthy human is able to maintain a constant body temperature of approximately 37°C, despite the temperature of the surrounding environment.

To maintain this, the body sends signals through the spinal cord telling the brain when the body is overheating or becoming cold. The brain then sends signals back down the spinal cord ordering the body to make necessary adjustments to maintain normal temperature. When they are cold, normal people shiver, put on warmer clothing or move to a warmer spot. When they are hot, they perspire, have a cool shower or move to somewhere cooler. Steven's body does not shiver or perspire below the neck, because it does not feel temperature changes. When outside in temperatures over 32°C, his body temperature begins to rise. Similarly, when the temperature drops, his body becomes cold and hypothermia can result. In essence, his body tends to take on the ambient temperature of his environment. Steven once described it as being "a bit like being a lizard".

The regular bowel routines that quadriplegics must endure are essential to maintaining good health. A blocked bowel, or a bowel infection, can cause anatomic symptoms, and become a serious threat to life. As a result, the bowel routines that Steven hated so much in the hospital have to be continued at home, another reason skilled attendants are essential.

Quadriplegics are subject to muscle spasms, especially at night. In an able-bodied person, when a stimulus to the skin is sensed, the brain determines whether or not it is dangerous. A dangerous stimulant, such as a flame, results in a reflex action—in this case jerking away from the flame. If the brain decides that the stimulant, such as cool water, is not dangerous, the brain will send a signal down the spinal cord ordering the body to cancel the natural reflex action. In a person with a spinal cord injury, however, the brain cannot perform this task below the level of the injury to the spine. Spasms and contractions cannot be ordered to stop, and any time the body is stimulated below the level of injury, the stimulation can trigger reflex actions, allowing muscle spasms and contractions to occur. Steven's spasms are controlled by a variety of medications, which are administered by a qualified attendant.

Because he is unable to be physically active, Steven no longer puts his weight on the bones in his legs and other places in his body. Normally, the force bearing down on bones lets them build and retain mass. This keeps bones strong and healthy. Without weight or pressure bearing down on them, bones deteriorate, becoming more porous, increasingly fragile and easily broken. This condition is called osteoporosis, a bone-thinning disease to which quadriplegics are susceptible. Steven works to hold off the thinning of his bones through exercise, medication and diet.

Steven likens his quadriplegia to being trapped in a conscious world without a body; on those occasions when his body does come into play, it's usually a major inconvenience. He needs dependable health care, and in his first year in the community he was often worried that he wouldn't be able to find it. He was subjected to health care aides who didn't even know how to do a bed bath properly. If they did attempt one, it took three hours instead of twenty minutes. Steven's desire to be clean at all times was for more than personal grooming purposes. Cleanliness was necessary for his health, and he wanted to be sure his attendants all realized that.

Sometimes the staff sent to him couldn't get him out of bed. Professionals use a technique to lift "dead" weight, and when inexperienced personnel precariously hoisted him, he was terrified by the risk of falling. A fractured hip could prove deadly.

Some of the inept aides had been hired for their ability to tend to simple personal care needs. They had no specialized medical training. The result was a high turnover of staff as scores of attendants came and went.

As frustrated as he was by the inconsistency and ineptitude, Steven understood why it was happening. Attendants were paid the same wage to tend to an otherwise healthy person with a broken leg, as they were to tend to Steven. What was the incentive to take him on if an attendant could find an easier assignment?

Sometimes aides wouldn't show up for their shift, and a stranger he'd never seen before would be sent over to watch him. Of the many challenges he faced as a quadriplegic, worries about the quality of his health care were high on the list, adding a psychological burden to the physical ones he had to endure. While depression is a common affliction among people who have become catastrophically injured, Steven, feeling increasingly isolated, abandoned and afraid, slipped into a deepening sadness that threatened to overcome him completely. He knew he was existing very much below any quality of life worth living. As things got worse, getting out of that life seemed a rational thing to do. As he began to fantasize about possible ways to die, Steven realized that improving his circumstances was critical. Susannah Mah's entrance into his life, with her compassion and competency, was literally lifesaving.

Meanwhile, at university, Steven set about to charting a course for himself. As with everything, it was difficult. And, as with everything, he refused to concede defeat. At his first class, the professor gave students a reading assignment, which Steven immediately did. The next day the professor threw a timed quiz on the assigned reading material. The answers to the quiz questions were to be put on a multiple-choice form using an IBM bubble sheet. Steven was still struggling at that time with a high turnover in aides. The aides, as part of their duties, used their hands to do the things that Steven would otherwise use his own hands to do—writing, for example. Unfortunately, his attendant that day was a new one who had never seen a bubble sheet. Steven spent the first fifteen minutes of the forty-minute test explaining how to fill in the bubble sheets. In the end, to Steven's mortification, the professor had to come over and physically demonstrate how to fill in Steven's answers.

"Omigosh," he recalls thinking, "This is just my first week and already I'm needing extra help." The professors, however, understood his situation. "They were accommodating without pity," says Steven, which he greatly appreciated. He went through the test in the time remaining and answered all the questions as fast as he could. The attendant also worked as fast as she could. Steven didn't have time to check his responses, but passed the test with an above-average mark of seventy-eight per cent.

It was encouraging. Maybe he could do this after all. Unfortunately, however, he couldn't always get to class. During the first session, when he was having trouble with aides, they couldn't always get him out of bed in the morning. In fact, much of the time that fall, he was left in bed for the whole day. If he got to class twice a week, he felt fortunate.

When he did get to class, he didn't use a tape recorder. He just listened, read the textbook and did the assignments. Sometimes he would ask his aide to jot some particular note down, but he didn't ask the aides to try and take notes of the lectures because they were health care attendants, not experts in the courses he was taking. He didn't expect them to have to take detailed notes on complicated subjects outside their experience. After lectures, he would go home and read the texts. His papers, assignments and exams were dictated to an experienced scribe (he had learned from his GMAT experience to test the nature of his scribes), and so he got through the first year.

Before long, Steven became adept at using a computer wearing a "head mouse", an infrared remote that looks like a silver jewel about the size of a small button. The head mouse adheres to the middle of Steven's forehead, equidistant from each eye. By looking at the screen, he can direct signals from the mouse to the computer. With almost imperceptible head movements, he operates his computer swiftly and expertly.

When Steven forgets to remove his head mouse before going out, as he sometimes does, some have asked if it is a new technological medical device. Some think that perhaps he belongs to a new age religion. Others try not to look at it when talking to Steven, or take surreptitious looks at it when they think he's not paying attention. Most people quietly accept it as a personal eccentricity. Small children, however, often come right out and ask, "What's that funny silver thing stuck on your forehead?" And it was a little disconcerting for one caller, when talking to Steven on the phone, to hear his attendant's voice in the background saying, "Wait a minute, Steven, I have to take the mouse off your head ...".

Though he was making progress, Steven often felt like he was stuck in a quagmire. It seemed to take forever to move obstacles out of his way and some days he felt as though he had gone one step forward and four steps back. Though often discouraged, he plowed forward, forcing himself to carry on even when it was difficult to feel motivated. Prior to his accident, he had accomplished things quickly and easily. Now, wanting to return to his usual fast pace, dealing with bureaucrats and their systems nearly drove him to distraction. So while he studied at university, he simultaneously fought one bureaucratic battle after another in his quest for independence.

One of his earliest identified needs was for vehicular transportation. Ordinary cars or vans are not equipped to handle Steven's large, heavy, specialized wheelchair. After much persuasion, MPI provided Steven with a customized van that accommodated his chair and allowed him to travel safely from one place to another.

The next step in ensuring his safety was to convince MPI of the need to have a back-up heater in the van. David Fletcher was particularly persistent in his efforts to persuade the insurance company that such protection was necessary, and he did a lot of the legwork required to win that particular battle.

It was not an easy victory. With its eye always on setting precedents, MPI was reluctant to install any kind of back-up propane heater. David had to educate the decision-makers at the insurance company about the tendency for high-level quadriplegics to take on the ambient temperature of their external environment. He pointed out that if the vehicle stalled and its heater failed, Steven would be at serious risk. In Manitoba, even able-bodied people can die from exposure inside a stalled vehicle out on the winter prairie. Steven would not last long in a stalled car during Manitoba's long, cold winters. If the car's engine shut down, a back-up heater would keep the air in his van at a consistently safe temperature, keeping hypothermia at bay.

Despite these rationales, MPI said "no" to the heater. Steven appealed. MPI continued to refuse the back-up heater—until the day before the appeal hearing. The Fletchers began to suspect that one of MPI's tactics was to keep saying "no" until people were worn down and gave up. Not many claimants carry their pleas all the way to the MPI review tribunal. Many can't afford the legal costs, others question the bias of an internal appeal, while still others are simply too discouraged to continue fighting the system. While stalling techniques may be used to discourage other claimants, the Fletchers never gave up. The day before Steven was to present his case, MPI relented. A propane heater was installed in his van.

Getting the heater was a big win and bolstered his spirits. On those "one-step-forward, four-steps-back" days, he would mentally list his successes. Getting back into the community was absolutely critical, doing well on his GMAT exam under difficult circumstances was incredibly encouraging, and returning to university was an essential step in preparing for his future. All these successes could have gone the other way. Steven takes justifiable pride in the fact that when doing the MBA program, he never took an extension to complete assignments or projects and always wrote the exams on the same day as the rest of the students. Other students might find excuses for not meeting deadlines, but Steven never sought to excuse himself and succeeded on the normal timelines. His commitment to live a normal life and succeed in an able-bodied world was genuine and determined.

Today his situation is infinitely better, yet some things await resolution. Among these are the costs associated with providing a high standard of medical care; he is still battling MPI over some of these items.

XVI

Aides and Accolades

Steven began searching for a house as soon as he moved into the apartment. Because he had special requirements and little money, the search was difficult and time-consuming, but eventually he found a house that was made-to-measure for his needs. On a quiet tree-lined street near the University of Manitoba, a bungalow that had been owned by a wheelchair-using employee of the Canadian Paraplegic Association came up for sale. The house had been completely renovated to meet the accessibility requirements of its owner, and Steven moved quickly to make a deal.

The annual income replacement he received from Manitoba Public Insurance was pegged at the annual salary he had been earning at the time of his accident, about $50,000. That wasn't the amount of money he received of course, because MPI takes the gross amount, and subtracts from it the federal and provincial taxes that Steven would have paid. MPI then provides ninety per cent of the net after tax, so the actual annual income Steven received from MPI was around $29,000. He was also eligible for Canada Pension Plan (CPP) disability, which he received, but MPI then reduced his income replacement by the amount of the CPP benefit.

Steven found this very frustrating. The extra money from CPP each month would have been extraordinarily helpful in making ends meet, but only MPI received the benefit. To make things worse, the CPP portion of the income replacement is taxable, which further reduced the net income. The annual salary he was earning as a young professional of twenty-three, just beginning his career, would most certainly have increased substantially as time progressed. In fact, the new job he would have started, had he not been injured, virtually guaranteed that his earnings would increase, but the insurance company refused to take his potential earnings into account. Nonetheless, with his income replacement as a base, Steven managed to gather the money for a down payment and took out a mortgage. In November 1998, nearly three years after his accident, he moved into his new home.

Living in his own house made a huge difference to his life. At last, he could have a proper shower! That first full shower was heavenly, a gift for which he was truly grateful. While he couldn't feel the water on his body, he could feel it pouring over his head and neck and he could hear it continuing down his torso and legs, splashing and bubbling like a gentle waterfall in the forest.

In the hospital, having a shower involved transferring him to a waterproof stretcher and taking him down to a special tiled shower room. There he would lie naked on the stretcher as nursing aides washed him with a hand-held shower. The water flowed over him and down a drain in the tile floor. In his apartment, he had bed baths using wet cloths and the portable inflatable sink. In his house, however, Steven's attendant places a mesh Hoyer body sling in his wheelchair and sits him on it. He then wheels himself into the spacious bathroom right off his bedroom. There, his Hoyer sling is attached to a track in the ceiling and he is lifted into the shower and plsaced on a shower chair. The chair has holes in it to allow water to access all parts of his skin, and for drainage. His attendant soaps and rinses him, towels him dry and then reverses the process of moving him.

In the house, there is also adequate and workable space for his attendant and equipment. There is comfortable privacy when Steven requires it. He is no longer dependent on a functioning elevator and he has a quiet green yard to sit in, where he can feel the breezes and the sunshine on his face, and drink in the outdoor fragrances. Here, with his health care aides, his life has a remarkable degree of normalcy.

✦ ◼ ✦ ◼ ✦

IN bygone days, people in Steven's circumstances were cared for at home, which was the only available option. The quality of their care was sometimes, but not always, good; sometimes it was abusive. "Invalids", as they were called, were frequently parked to await the inevitable end of their unheralded existences. More recently, institutional living, with its multitude of benefits, has been a godsend for many patients and families, and the only choice for people with certain disabilities. Today, professional home health care attendants have made it possible for anyone, even a high-level quadriplegic, to live fully in society, offering both their talents and their productivity to their communities. This is the case with Steven. Many health care attendants have worked for him over the years, and many of them have been truly incredible. It is fitting and appropriate to pay tribute to them in this book. Three specific attendants, representing various stages of Steven's reintegration into society, have been selected as examples of the many who have made a crucial difference in his life.

◆ ✖ ◆ ✖ ◆

SUSANNAH Mah has already been introduced. She has been with Steven since he first left hospital and has been part of the evolution of his care and his progress. Her early days with him were critical to his emotional and physical survival. Her calm and professional presence, particularly during the stressful transition period from the hospital to self-managed home care made her a key figure in his life.

Susannah eventually took a leave of absence from her work with Steven when she became pregnant. She returned as a nurse-manager in the fall of 2004, after becoming a mother and obtaining a university degree in nursing.

For Steven, she manages staffing and nursing care, interviewing and training attendants to ensure that they are proficient in catheterization, aware of autonomic symptoms and so on. She instructs his staff on what to do and she teaches them why these things must be done.

For example, Steven must be turned throughout the night to prevent pressure sores from forming. He is frequently awakened by random muscle spasms, or because he finds himself in discomfort because he is lying on a bent ear or some pulled hair. His attendant looks after these discomforts. Steven sleeps in the nude so that his attendants can move him with greater ease and to prevent his clothing from forming crease marks on his skin.

Susannah also makes sure that attendants know how to use their own bodies correctly when lifting Steven. When his attendant wakes him, Steven is placed on his back and given a bed bath. After a night

Susannah Mah at Lake Louise,
where she accompanied Steven in 1998.

bowel routine, he is hoisted into the shower. He has only one attendant
with him at a time, and yet each can lift him alone, with seemingly
little effort. This six-foot-four-inch, 200-pound man's dead weight is
lifted, not just by his husky male attendants, but also by his smaller-
framed female ones, and placed, correctly positioned, in his chair.
Their techniques for doing this are practised, sure and very impressive.

Steven is moved from bed to chair—or chair to chair—using a
"pivot transfer". Using this technique, even the smallest and lightest
of Steven's attendants can move him. Putting Steven into a sitting
position, the attendant squats in front of him and embraces him
around his torso. Then, pivoting on one foot, grasping Steven tightly,
he or she spins a quarter turn and places him into the new location.
The first time I saw Melissa Anderson, another of his aides, do this,
I was transfixed. Despite her delicate appearance, she must have the
strength of ten men, I thought. But not so, I learned. It's all in the
technique.

Susannah Mah doesn't work regular shifts any more, but comes
in the early mornings or evenings as required to tend to Steven's medical

needs. She has travelled with him to Montreal, Toronto, Vancouver and the US. "Travelling with Steven by plane is quite an experience," she acknowledges, "and in the beginning it could become quite nerve-wracking. But he has overcome each hurdle as it appeared, and he manages to get where he needs to go."

Susannah also serves as a back-up attendant for emergencies, and is prepared to help on weekends if someone is away. She recalls the time that James Montgomery, a health care attendant who shares Steven's passion for the wilderness, became stranded in the Whiteshell widerness area. James had been hiking the Mantario Trail, an area with which Steven was intimately familiar, when a violent thunderstorm wiped out the pit trail he was following. Realizing he would be seriously delayed in getting to his shift with Steven, and that a reliable substitute for his services was needed immediately, James swam across a wind-ravaged lake to an inhabited area. Drenched and dripping, he walked to a nearby cabin and knocked on a stranger's door to ask to use the phone to call Susannah. She took his shift until he could return.

Not all requests for back-up help come as the result of such dramatic circumstances, but as Susannah points out, James and the rest of the Fletcher team are devoted to Steven. They will go that extra mile for him, even if it takes them across rough water.

As nursing manager, Susannah works closely with James Montgomery, who does the overall scheduling, organizing and management of Steven's care. The two interact through email or phone calls, and in a regular in-depth staff meeting that occurs once every couple of months. "James makes my job easy," Susannah says, "and he creates a positive ambience for the whole team. Steven himself is now busy, productive and committed to making a positive difference in the world. Things are not perfect of course, and we still have a long way to go, but Steven is a long way away from the horribly depressing days we lived through when he was newly out of the hospital. It is so good to hear him laugh now."

Melissa Anderson (now Thiessen) is the health care attendant who aided Steven as he stepped into the wider public world. Talented and committed, Melissa grew up in Winnipeg. Like Steven, she was active in sports and is a skilled swimmer. Again, like Steven, family camping trips were an integral part of her youth and she loves being outdoors in a natural setting. Music is also a significant factor in her life; when she was young she sang in one of Winnipeg's most prestigious choirs and played in local bands.

Before she came to Steven, Melissa spent two years in Christian missionary work overseas, particularly in Africa. She spent time as well in India, staying at the Mother Theresa homes. She eventually led Christian teams from South Africa to both India and Africa. "At the Mother Theresa homes in India," says Melissa, "I think I really learned about putting others' needs before mine, letting my wants go for a time and focusing on others. My faith gives me courage to believe that God has called us all to do something great for His glory."

Returning from overseas, Melissa went to work for the health care company that manages Steven's case. When asked to work full time with him, she initially considered the assignment as just a job, tending to her client's medical and personal needs. However, as time progressed, she began to recognize it as more of a calling. When she was asked to travel with Steven to Ottawa and enter Parliament by his side, she spent time talking to her parents, her boyfriend (who is now her husband) and praying. "When I decided to go with Steven, I felt at peace with the decision," she says.

Melissa was the first non-elected person in Canada's history allowed to sit on the benches on the floor of the Chamber with the Members of Parliament while the House of Commons is in session. As such, she has entered the annals of history.

Though she had never been terribly interested in politics, being with Steven was a crash course in parliamentary procedure. "I went from not knowing much about politics to having a pretty good grasp of it. I can honestly say I like politics now."

Melissa seldom talks about herself, but when asked about Steven, she has a good deal to say. Working with him has taught her patience and humility. "I am a strong-willed, independent person. I have had to learn again and again to put my needs and desires on the back burner and focus on Steven's needs."

A good example is her role in meetings with Steven. "Steven's role is to be front and center, doing the things he needs to do; mine is to be his shadow. Part of that role is to sit quietly and help when asked, or when I notice a need that must be addressed. I think it helped that I had worked with Steven for a couple of years before heading to Ottawa. As a health care attendant, I had long understood the necessity for complete client confidentiality and discretion, but basically he and I were just comfortable with each other and our respective roles."

Melissa's unusual position in Parliament allowed her to see the political process intimately. Not only did she accompany Steven to the House of Commons Chamber, and to standing committee meetings,

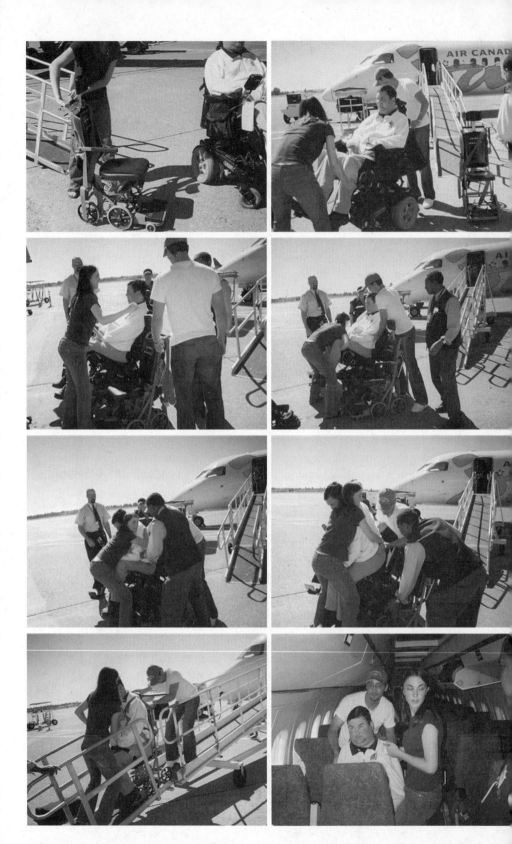

she also attended Conservative caucus meetings and shadow cabinet meetings with him as well. Melissa gained the respect and confidence of everyone she touched, from Conservative Leader Stephen Harper, to opposition members and employees of the House of Commons.

Perhaps most important to today's smoothly functioning "Team Fletcher" is James Montgomery. James attended Canadian University College in Lacombe, Alberta, an accredited liberal arts institution that stresses Christian commitment. At Lacombe, James took a general program of studies, along with some outdoor survival courses. He became involved with the Lacombe Action Group, which worked with both mentally and physically handicapped individuals, and found that he enjoyed these activities.

James became employed by a firm that provides assistance to handicapped clients. He had been working with brain-injured clients when Steven Fletcher invited him for an interview for possible employment as a full-time attendant. James knew of Steven, and was interested in meeting him, though he did not follow politics closely and had no party affiliation.

"Despite that," James recalls, "I had a strong feeling that this guy was for real. I had seen him on TV and I could tell when he was being interviewed that he meant business and knew what he believed in."

Their meeting was a good one. At the end of the interview, Steven hired James, and the two young men began a mutually satisfying working relationship that has deepened over the years into a sincere and caring friendship.

James Montgomery believes that he was called to work with Steven Fletcher. "Everything in my life seems to have been to prepare me to understand and serve Steven," he says. "The only thing that I had not done was to become politically active, but even that seems to have been a plus, because I can stay calm in the middle of a political storm, which Steven's attendants need to be able to do."

Initially, James worked Steven's night shift on weekends (Friday, Saturday and Sunday) because he had returned to university full time to obtain a kinesiology and applied health bachelor's degree. The combination of studying during the week and caring for Steven on the weekends at night worked well.

The first thing that James noticed about Steven's house was the giant Post-it notes all over the place—on walls, windows, cupboards,

Left: Travelling by plane, which Steven does regularly, requires specialized techniques and teamwork. His attendants make it look almost easy.

easel boards and even on doors. "When I say giant, I mean it," he says. "The notes were about two feet square and they were everywhere, as if some deranged interior decorater had gone wild wallpapering the house."

Steven explained to his puzzled aide that he was in the middle of an election campaign, and his house was the temporary campaign headquarters. His strategy was posted on the walls so that the campaign team could review it easily. "You see, James," Steven told him, "if you want to take over the world, the first thing you need to do is get a whole bunch of giant Post-it notes." And thus James began his training in how to care for Steven Fletcher.

James was fascinated with all this activity. He wasn't at all familiar with the political issues that seemed to surround his new client, so Steven advised James to begin reading the newspapers and other writings to get a more thorough perspective about the kind of activities in which he was engaged.

It was the beginning of James's political education. In 2004, James was with Steven as he went campaigning door-to-door. "It was both exciting and stimulating," he says, "to the point that even though I wasn't on duty election night, I went over to election headquarters anyway, because I just had to be there when the results came in. I knew better than most people how hard Steven had worked to win."

In 2005, James was a full-time university student during the day and a weekend aide for Steven on weekends. Melissa Anderson was the main health care attendant in Ottawa, sitting in the House of Commons with Steven each day that the House was in session. James occasionally went to Ottawa if Steven had to remain there on the weekends, and about once a month flew to Ottawa with Steven. James enjoyed travelling with him. "During my first year with Steven, I met both the prime minister [then Paul Martin] and the Opposition leader [then Stephen Harper] in the same evening. It occurred to me that that was a rare opportunity for any Canadian citizen."

In the summer of 2005, James and Melissa were "crazy busy", as James puts it, visiting hospitals with Steven throughout southern Ontario as part of Steven's role as health critic for the Official Opposition. Due to a staff shortage, James and Melissa were virtually the only two attendants available that summer, and they travelled constantly with Steven, who was taking his role as Opposition health critic to heart. He was relentless in his pursuit of knowledge about the delivery of health care in Canada. Accompanying Steven on his many trips, James and Melissa added to their own base of medical

Teamwork: Steven in Parliament, with James Montgomery at his side.

knowledge as Steven explored hospitals and the work that went on within their walls. His goal was to become familiar with the subtle nuances of hospital policies and to make comparisons between institutions to discover what worked best for patients.

James was amazed at the depth of Steven's knowledge and the questions he asked medical staff. He was equally amazed at how eager they seemed to be to share their ideas. "He was usually able to inspire them to open up and really talk about the future of health care in Canada," James says. "They seemed willing to trust him, I think because they knew he was sincerely interested in improving things."

Melissa planned to be married at summer's end in 2005 and

wanted to stay in Winnipeg with her husband, rather than spending so much time in Ottawa. Finding a suitable replacement for her in the House of Commons would not be easy, however.

After much discussion, the team decided to hire a health care attendant who actually lived in Ottawa to attend to Steven during the day on Parliament Hill and in the House of Commons, while two Manitoba-based attendants would alternate (one week on and one week off) doing night duty in Ottawa. Kristy Osmond was hired in the fall of 2005 as the Ottawa health care attendant, taking Melissa's position in the House of Commons. Kristy's twelve-hour day shift includes House duty. It's a heavy routine and she handles it well. Jenny Siepman alternates with James, travelling to Ottawa to do Steven's night shift. Sarah McDougall and Ashleigh Kraiynk are also qualified to travel with Steven and are frequently en route with their client.

"Travelling as a health care attendant is not like being a tourist," says James, for what most attendants remember from each trip is not the scenery, but the position of the big wheelchair.

In addition to his biweekly stints in Ottawa, James manages Steven's care. This includes duties and responsibilities from interviewing prospective employees to creating a short list for Steven to consider, and working with Susannah Mah to ensure that medical personnel are properly trained, to scheduling the aides' shifts and organizing the diverse aspects of Steven's care. Considering Steven's busy schedule, in which unexpected events and meetings are always cropping up, keeping the health care supervision on schedule is a logistical nightmare.

James sets Steven's schedule and staff assignments two months in advance, but Steven's need to travel means that frequent shift adjustments must be made after the initial schedule is created. "When you are told that Steven has to be in Toronto tomorrow morning for an important meeting, it's often necessary to switch shifts between an attendant who travels and one who doesn't," explains James, "and that sometimes means that my own personal schedule gets changed as well. I may have to trade shifts with the scheduled aide if a sudden trip comes up and that person isn't one of the ones who has the specific skills required for travelling with Steven. Transferring him to an airplane seat is quite a different task than a regular transfer, for example, and it is somewhat awkward to do Steven's daily physical routines in the ordinary beds found in hotels, rather than in his own special bed, which has mechanical functions to allow it to rise, lower and tilt. There are so many modifications to his care delivery that need to be made when travelling with Steven that sometimes I have to go with him myself if an unexpected trip comes up."

In addition to assigning shifts, James has to ensure that the activities and events at the legislative and constiuency offices are coordinated with everything else. Among other duties, he also does most of the flight booking for travelling. Handling the itinerary is a big enough job for any MP's itinerary coordinator, but having to make as a priority the health and well-being of the MP at the same time can make the task, as James says in his understated way, "quite frustrating".

James gets Steven in and out of bed, goes through his regular body care routines with him, showers him, puts his body through the range of motion and stretching exercises, and tends to all his physical needs. "My degree in kinesiology and applied health has taught me how muscles work and enabled me to easily put Steven through the regime set up for him by the hospital physiotherapists, and my knowledge of health care allows me to catheterize and so on, but my other more ordinary services are essential for an enhanced quality of life. I dial the phone, drive the van, cook the meals, change the bedding and feed Steven his meals. But I would never dare to think or make decisions for him! He is extremely able in that regard."

That the schedule runs as smoothly as it does, is due to the remarkable dedication of the team of attendants. "We have been able to hire incredible people," James says. "They have stuck with us despite the erratic schedules and having to function so often in the public eye. They are discreet and unobtrusive, and have as their sole mission the goal of continually improving the care they give to Steven. As a group we're like a family, and as individuals we're an extension of Steven. We are his arms and legs, his hands and fingers. We don't run his life. We help him to run it for himself. If you can imagine that Steven's brain signal could be sent to my workable arm instead of his own non-workable one, then you'll better understand how, as attendants, we try to respond to Steven's needs."

James had a vision for the aides who worked for Steven; they would become a team dedicated to Steven, not for money or glory, but to deliver a consistently high standard of care. "Thanks to Steven's leadership, that vision has come to be. Steven's attendants no longer see themselves as individuals working alone at a job. We have become Team Fletcher, and we try to help each other out as much as we can, because we're focused on our mission."

Above: With Jenny Siepman and Ashleigh Krainyk at Niagara Falls. Rght: Melissa Thiessen and Steven take in a Seattle Mariners game. Below: Steven and Kristy Osmond on Parliament Hill, against a backdrop of the gorgeous Ottawa River.

XVII

Educating Others

After speaking to a school class recently, Steven reflected on how things have changed since he first began talking to students in 1998. At that time, a friend's mother persuaded him to address students at River Heights Junior High School in Winnipeg. She thought his story would be thought provoking and educational. Steven agreed to the request, mainly because he didn't want to disappoint his friend. And though he found it hard to talk publicly about his quadriplegia, he was aware the students were keenly interested in what he had to say. Until then, he had preferred to try to ignore his quadriplegia, hoping that others would too. He felt that if everyone ignored his paralysis and nobody talked about it, it was almost as though it didn't exist. It allowed him to feel somewhat normal.

In reality, in the beginning, he often felt self-conscious about being completely immobile, about the size and weight of his wheelchair, and about his ever-present attendant. It was a long time before he had the courage to be seen being fed in public.

However, once he began explaining his situation to others, he came to recognize that his quadriplegia is a part of him that others are curious about, and that most people want to try to understand it. This is not necessarily because of a bizarre or ghoulish motivation, but rather because dealing with high-level quadriplegia is outside almost everyone's experience and they're at a loss as to how to conduct themselves. They don't realize the full extent to which a human body can be affected by a catastrophic spinal cord injury. For example, because Steven can't feel anything below his neck, a tap on his arm won't get

Above: Interested students question Steven,
and right, he shows off his chair.

his attention. He found his audiences wanted to know more about the many other protocols or sensitivities people need to consider. What actions or words would be considered courteous and what might be considered rude, and why?

After his election, Steven was taking his family through the House of Commons when, in the Chamber, a hapless senator extended his hand to shake Steven's and then, embarrassed when he realized that Steven couldn't move his arm or hand, ended up patting Steven on the head, a gesture interpreted by some to be condescending. The senator simply didn't know how to handle the situation.

In a similar vein, Steven can recount stories about people who talk VERY LOUDLY AND SLOWLY to him, because he's in a wheelchair. Waiters who ask Steven's dining companions, "And what does he want to eat?" have a similar problem. They simply don't know what to do.

People often become nervous when they're unsure what to do. They like to understand what's going on around them; it helps them be comfortable and confident. And for the most part, people want to behave appropriately and sensitively with others, and appreciate having useful information to guide them through situations that are new to them. Steven suggests that when able-bodied people are unsure what to do, they should simply ask the disabled person what's appropriate.

As a result, Steven is in a unique position to help educate others about spinal cord injuries and he realizes the importance of doing so. "I didn't set out to become a poster boy for the severely disabled," he says, "but it seems I'm kind of filling that role whether I want to or not, so I accept it as a good thing that will help build public awareness about quadriplegia. We now have the ability to save the lives of many people who used to die from catastrophic injuries, and it's time that we learn how to help these people become productive and contributing members of society. We can't just warehouse them in institutions to wait out the rest of their lives watching TV or being visited by groups of volunteer entertainers. The first thing we can do is to make sure our society understands the limitations of an individual's disability and then look to the very real abilities the individual retains."

Despite his initial discomfort, Steven has learned to talk about his situation to audiences with some degree of ease and humour. It always seems to him, though, that he is describing someone else rather than himself. When he sees himself in a mirror or a windowpane, he still can't believe it's his image he is seeing because he imagines himself very differently. He still thinks of himself as his previous self, the mining engineer climbing over rocks, the canoeist paddling furiously over rapids, the tall man striding along a path. When he sees the image of his current self, immobilized in a motorized chair, he's still startled.

Ten years after his accident, Steven attended a local hockey game and ran into a former high school classmate whose son was on one of the teams. When Steven asked his old friend what she had been doing in the years since graduation, she replied almost apologetically that she had not done anything spectacular, that she and her husband just had regular sorts of jobs and pretty ordinary lives, with three kids and a house in the suburbs. Steven told her that that sounded like a perfect life, and he meant it.

"That was the way I had wanted to live out my Canadian Dream," he says. "People see themselves as leading so-called 'average' or 'normal' lives without knowing that that's the greatest way to be able to live. Life abundant is all wrapped up in the everyday things so many of us take for granted—having kids, cutting the grass. Such everyday ordinary things are wonderful, and they are spectacular in their own right."

XVIII

Wind over Water

Having paddled through rapids that were more like waterfalls and thrilled to icy spray on his face, Steven missed the exhilaration of wind racing over water and waves rolling beneath him. Paddling was out of the question, but he longed to be on the water.

As a graduate engineer, he had worked in the underground research facility at Atomic Energy of Canada, at Pinawa, Manitoba, a town with excellent rowing facilities. Steven had enthusiastically taken up rowing while he was there, and had intended to add rowing to his list of regular activities as time went on. Then, with the accident, rowing became out of the question. Still, he longed for the water.

"Steven was never meant to be an observer," says his father. "When he was a boy, he and his friends and siblings went out to an area on the Whitemouth River called Farmers' Rapids. There, the young people would take their canoes down the rapids and portage their way back. They did this over and over again, laughing and splashing and having a wonderful time. After his accident, Steven returned to the Whitemouth and watched from his wheelchair while other kids paddled, as he had once done. It was hard to see him sitting there, but as always, instead of moaning about it, he looked for some way to get back into the game."

When Steven learned about "sip-and-puff" sailing technology being used to allow quadriplegics to sail independently, he was understandably intrigued. To get back on the water he decided to learn to sail. Taking to the water at the Fort Whyte Centre (now called Fort Whyte Alive), a nature reserve on Winnipeg's outskirts, he learned the techniques he needed to become a sailor.

Steven operates a sailboat by sipping and puffing into a straw. The straw operates a computer, the computer operates a motor and the motor operates winches that control the sails and rudder. Sailing effectively using this technique requires an understanding of the sip-and-puff technology, as well as the knowledge required by all sailors of the effects of winds and currents on the direction of sails and the rudder. Sip-and-puff technology uses a pulley system. When the sailor sips, the computer and winches bring in the sails, while puffing or blowing into a tube unfurls them. Biting switches the mechanism to the oars. With control over the oars and the sails, the sailor can handle the whole boat. It's every bit as difficult as it sounds.

Steven barely had the essentials of sailing mastered when he decided to compete in the Falcon Lake Spring Classic, a sailing race held annually in Manitoba's Whiteshell region. The classic included all classes of yachts and sailboats, and though it was not designed as a race for the disabled, anyone wishing to participate was welcome. For Steven, the lure of a race was irresistible.

Steven's boat was set rather sensitively for safety, so it wouldn't tip. The safety setting was necessary under the circumstances, but it meant that he couldn't steer his boat in a straight line. He was strapped into his boat so that he wouldn't fall over, and went wildly sipping and puffing away in a concerted effort to make speed. The others were way ahead of him, but still he persevered. His goal, if he could not win, was to cross the finish line and know that he had traversed the route correctly and safely.

He was amazed to discover when he finally got to the finish line, which every other participant had already crossed, that he had won the race. He was presented with a huge trophy, far bigger, he says, than the trophies given to kayak and canoe race winners. When he showed the trophy to his father all he would say was, "Sailing rules are not intuitive."

It turned out that the other boats were all sailing at a similar speed and therefore within easy viewing distance of each other. The front-runner missed going around one of the required markers, and the other boats trailing behind him stayed in his wake and missed the marker as well. They were too preoccupied with catching him to realize they were all off course.

Steven, so far behind that he couldn't see the others or follow their faulty route, went around all the required markers shown on the race course map, which he had memorized before the race began. The

Steven learned sip-and-puff sailing techniques on the placid lake at Fort Whyte Alive in Winnipeg, a watery environment quite different than that he discovered off the shores of Vancouver.

others, having all been disqualified by playing follow-the-leader, stood and watched while Steven Fletcher, the only sailor to legitimately finish the course, was presented with the huge first-place trophy.

Once again, Steven learned that staying the course and persevering could result in an unpredictable victory, even against able-bodied competition and more experienced opponents.

It was a different story when, in September 2001, he competed in the Mobility Cup Sailing Regatta in Victoria, on the cold waves of the ocean. In sailing, when the wind comes from a certain direction onto a boat, that boat has the right of way over other boats being hit by wind approaching them from another direction. In an ocean race, where the start line is long, the paths of the boats can therefore cross as they head out to sea. In this case, for Steven, most of the other boats had the right of way. This meant that if Steven hit or bumped any of them he would be the one at fault, and he would be penalized. Still he was loath to give way if he could avoid it and he began weighing the odds of crossing in front of the line without actually colliding.

Since the BC regatta was for disabled sailors, another person had to be in each boat for safety reasons, in case there was a serious problem. That person, seeing his set jaw and determined face, started yelling, "Don't try to cross his path, Steven! You shouldn't do this!"

Steven did it, of course, crossing the finish line before the other boats arrived, with the guy in the back yelling, "Brilliant, Steven! Brilliant! Way to go!"

Steven placed high in the standings, in part by tacking left on that first race. After the tallies of all the races were done, he had finished first among the quadriplegic racers, and was awarded the 2001 Sam Sullivan Trophy, named after the disabled individual who had helped found the Disabled Sailing Association of North America. Sullivan was someone with whom Steven would come to share many interests, and once again, the wind over the water splashed an icy, intoxicating spray on Steven's face.

Steven won the Sam Sullivan Trophy a second time in 2004, when the international competition was held at Pelican Lake, near Ninette, Manitoba. By this time he was a Member of Parliament, so his sailing prowess attracted a fair bit of media attention.

He was delighted and honoured when the Disabled Sailing Association of Alberta, which hosted the 2005 Mobility Cup, appointed him honorary chair of that event. That year, the event drew participants from Canada, the US, the UK, Australia and Japan.

Through their interest in sports, Steven and Sam Sullivan have become close enough that Steven travelled to Vancouver in 2005 to help Sam in his successful mayoralty campaign. The two have much in common. Both were athletic young men prior to the accidents that left them disabled. Sam broke his neck in a skiing accident at the age of nineteen, and, while not as severely damaged as Steven, had to fight hard to be reintegrated into mainstream society. Like Steven, he met head-on the challenges he faced to live an independent life. He supported the community living movement that sought to de-institutionalize people with disabilities and was determined to do as much by himself and for himself as possible. His determination has lead to personal success and innovative help for others.

Sam and Steven, along with Congressman Jim Langevin of Rhode Island, Representative Tom Kennedy of the Massachusetts Legislature, and Tim Louis, a former Vancouver city councillor, were the founding members of the Disability Caucus, a forum that brings politicians with disabilities together to discuss disability issues and to encourage more people with disabilities to enter elected public office. While Steven is the most severely disabled of the group, the members share common frustrations and problems. The caucus provides a forum for sharing concerns and ideas that benefit not just the members, but others as well.

In August 2006, Steven Fletcher and Sam Sullivan ventured up the 760-metre trail to British Columbia's Burgess Shale in the Canadian Rockies. With the help of their "sherpa" volunteers and Trail Rider equipment designed by Sullivan and Paul Cermak, a volunteer engineer with the Tetra Society of North America that produces innovative assistance devices for disabled people, Sam made it to the top and Steven part way. Like a cross between a wheelbarrow and a rickshaw, the Trail Rider (which sometimes sits in a corner of his constituency office and often provokes visitor curiosity) is an innovative one-wheeled all-terrain vehicle, low slung and lightweight. It enables even those with severe disabilities to travel through remote wilderness areas.

The volunteers who help guide the Trail Rider are called sherpas, after the renowned Himalayan mountaineers. Over the past century, real Sherpas have assisted and guided adventurers in thousands of expeditions. It was a Sherpa mountaineer, Tenzing Norgay, who climbed Mount Everest with the late Sir Edmund Hilary in 1953. By choosing to call their Trail Rider volunteers sherpas, Sam and Steven honour both their remarkable namesakes, as well as the volunteers.

"I have to congratulate Mayor Sullivan for making it all the way up to the Burgess Shale and for recruiting what appeared to be the

Summer outings in the Trail Rider, like this one on a path to Old Pinawa Dam, keep Steven in touch with the Canadian Shield.

entire cast of the Sly Stallone movie *Cliffhanger* for his sherpa team," Steven joked. "My team (sister Julia, brother-in-law Steve, Jenny and James) did a great job, but I may have to look into where Sam recruited his team when I attempt this again."

"[The climb to the Burgess Shale] is no walk in Assiniboine Park," he continued, referring to Winnipeg's large and lovely (but admittedly flat) city park. "Hiking up the side of a mountain is serious business. That's why, once we started to run into trouble, I decided that the Canadian Rockies are a great place to apply a prudent 'conservative' approach and we headed back down the mountain."

XIX

Taking Such Measures

In Manitoba, vehicle insurance is underwritten by the provincial government through its Crown corporation, the Manitoba Public Insurance Corporation, called MPIC, MPI or Autopac by its customers. The governing party of the day does not run the corporation directly. Indeed, governing politicians are inclined to make much of the "arm's length" distance between government and its Crown corporations. The public, however, could be forgiven if it notes that ministers and premiers, through a variety of influences, can apply pressures on Crown corporations. For example, the premier and his ministers make the laws and the regulations under which MPI operates. More significantly, the majority of the members of the board of directors controlling MPI are political appointees, who retain their positions at the pleasure of the government in power. The provincial government also has the ultimate authority to sell the corporation and disband the board.

One could reasonably conclude, then, that the MPI board and its senior bureaucracy would have at least a passing interest in trying to do what they believe the government would like to see happen. One could also safely assume that there would be many ways for the government's desires to become known to MPI's officers.

MPI's philosophy is laudable. Its goals and mission statement are among the most progressive offered by any insurance company in Canada. For Steven Fletcher, the most important of those statements was MPI's commitment to try to restore vehicular accident victims to a life that is as close as possible to what they could have had, had they not been injured. Specifically, citizens injured by automobiles are entitled to various forms of compensation, with all hospital and medical expenses to be borne by MPI. In addition, MPI is responsible for expenses directly attributable to the victim's injuries.

Section 138 of the Manitoba Public Insurance Corporation's Act requires that MPI "take such measures which are necessary and advisable to contribute to the rehabilitation of a victim to lessen the disability resulting in bodily injury and to facilitate the victim's return to a normal life or reintegration into society."

To accomplish these objectives MPIC may "provide the victim with funds for occupational, educational or vocational rehabilitation that is consistent with the victim's occupation before the accident and his or her skills and abilities after the accident." The regulation further specifies that the objective in this section is to return the victim, as much as possible, to his or her condition before the accident. The intent behind this regulation was to enable the insurance company to authorize funds to meet unexpected expenses claimed by specific individuals to ensure that the goals and objectives of the corporation would be met. These were promising and encouraging words to the recently paralysed Steven Fletcher.

True to its mandate, MPI initially assigned Steven a particularly understanding and effective counsellor, Sue McCutcheon, who worked hard to fulfill the corporation's objectives. She encouraged Steven and wholeheartedly supported him in his efforts to become a contributing member of society, in keeping with MPI's policy statements.

Accordingly, at the expense of MPI under the statutes and regulations governing the payments of benefits to an insured person, Steven decided to continue his pursuit of his MBA degree and returned to university to do so. The insurance company's support was essential to this process, and MPI followed through on its commitments in a thorough and encouraging fashion.

Steven's subsequent record of academic achievement in obtaining his MBA not only increased his opportunities for employment, but also verified the wisdom of MPI's mandate and action. The logic was unassailable. After all, if Steven, with his added education, could become employed and earn a good salary, MPI would benefit along with Steven.

In keeping with his bent for public service, while obtaining his masters degree, Steven ran to become president of the University of Manitoba Students' Union or UMSU. He was elected and then re-elected for a second term, again with the enthusiastic support of MPI.

Steven had read and understood all the provisions available to him through his insurer, and was not shy about requesting them. His health care attendant became increasingly important to him as he became more independent. Attending classes, travelling to meetings, being constantly on the go, meant that his health care attendants needed to travel with him. MPI had no difficulty with this. Providing that his trips were reasonable and purposeful, the corporation agreed that it would cover the cost of his attendant's travel as provided for under Section 138 of the MPIC Act.

Under these circumstances, Steven travelled to St John's, Newfoundland, as president of UMSU, to attend a meeting of the Canadian Alliance of Student Associations. He also travelled to Victoria, BC, to compete in an international sailing regatta for disabled sailors and, as indicated previously, won. MPI not only willingly covered his health care attendant's travel costs, it also sent him a note of congratulations on his victory.

Steven's trip to Victoria was the first time he had met quadriplegics who had done meaningful things with their lives, who had become successful in a professional sense. Just as inspiring, he met those who had succeeded in their personal lives, who had married and even had families.

The Manitoba New Democratic Party was in power when Steven decided, in April 2000, to present a brief containing recommendations he felt might be useful to Becky Barrett, the NDP minister responsible for MPIC. Former NDP cabinet minister Sam Uskiw, who supported Steven's perspectives, and Steven's father were in attendance at this meeting. Though the brief was general in nature and did not relate specifically to his case, by this time Steven had acquired a reputation as a strong and effective activist; as a result, the meeting provided the minister with the opportunity to observe this young man in person and assess his potential.

Shortly after Steven's meeting with the minister, Charles Adler, a well-known journalist and radio talk show host, wrote a column indicating that Steven Fletcher would be seeking the Manitoba Progressive Conservative nomination in the Manitoba constituency of Tuxedo. The by-election had been set for the fall of 2000, and Steven, who was raised in Tuxedo and knew the area well, had been persuaded to seek the PC nomination.

Almost immediately after the Adler column appeared, Becky Barrett issued a ministerial inquiry to MPIC asking for details of Steven Fletcher's case. As noted above, cabinet ministers are not to interfere in any way with the workings of Crown corporations. The minister's job is to recommend legislative changes to the act governing the Crown corporation for which he or she is responsible, and to appoint the board of directors, which then assumes responsibility for the running of the corporation. In all other aspects, the minister must have a strictly hands-off approach, so that Crown corporations, once established, can run independently without political interference from government MLAs.

The ministerial inquiry, sent to Sue McCutcheon, asked how much Steven Fletcher's care was costing the corporation. Further, it questioned the legality of corporation financing of certain of those costs. Responses were sent back to the minister, prompting further inquiries. As the inquiries continued, McCutcheon suggested that she would need a team of assistants to help her handle them.

These requests from a minister for information on a specific claimant could not be missed by the senior staff at MPI. The minister wanted to know how much Steven Fletcher's education was costing. She wanted details of his expenses. Steven began to ask himself why. He knew that claimants' files are strictly confidential and are not to be revealed to anyone except the case workers handling them. The minister is not allowed to seek information from any claimant's file unless that claimant gives her permission to do so. Ministers who ask for information to which they are not entitled put Crown corporation staff in a terribly awkward position. How do they respond? What do the pointed questions imply? Were they doing something wrong? In October 2000, a few months after the first ministerial inquiry, Sue McCutcheon, Steven's supportive case worker, was transferred by her supervisor to another position within the corporation and Chris Beck was assigned to Steven's case.

Steven found that with the new case officer, who told him he was receiving instructions from "above", the attitude of MPI staff toward his care had altered dramatically. He felt he was no longer being seen as a claimant entitled to service, but rather as an adversary seeking more than his due.

About the same time that McCutcheon was transferred, Steven lost the Tuxedo nomination to Heather Stefanson who went on to win the by-election the following year. Nevertheless, Steven had made a name for himself during the nomination process; people were fascinated and eager to see more of him. And together, Heather and Steven gave the riding a youthful shot in the arm and substantially increased the party membership; they were widely applauded for their efforts.

As a result of the profile he'd attained through the nomination process, party members began to push for Steven to seek the party presidency. After consideration, and despite his heavy schedule, he decided to accept the challenge, and began to campaign.

A year later, in November 2001, Steven was elected president of the Manitoba PC Party. This new position necessitated trips to rural constituencies around the province to attend meetings and conferences. As he had before, Steven asked MPI to finance his attendant's travel costs, just as it had when he made trips as president of UMSU or as an athletic competitor in international competitions. Now, however, these travel requests were denied. Given that he could not travel without a health care aide, MPI's refusal essentially denied Steven the wherewithal to leave the city of Winnipeg.

It was beginning to become apparent to Steven's friends and supporters, both in and out of the political arena, that MPI was attempting to prevent him from embarking on a career in politics. A July 2002 memo from Chris Beck to Jack Zacharias, CEO of MPIC, states in part:

> We are unable to support Mr. Fletcher in his political goals for the following reasons: There is no reasonable timeline or certainty that Mr. Fletcher will ever be an elected official.

> Should Mr. Fletcher become an elected official there is no guarantee that he will be re-elected as his fate is in the hands of the electorate.

In fact, Steven had not asked for support for his "political goals", though, as will be seen, he was subsequently elected and then re-elected "at the hands of the electorate".

Beck further stated in his memo: "The Masters of Business Administration program would never have been considered in our vocational plan as it is not a prerequisite to a political career." While having an MBA is obviously an advantage for people seeking to govern, having such a degree is also an advantage in many other careers. Steven did not have a political career in mind when he entered the MBA program. Did the minister's frequent inquiries cause the bureaucrats to change from being helpful to hostile, from being advocates to adversaries? Steven's family in particular was concerned that MPI's sudden and otherwise inexplicable decisions to reduce and restrict his insurance benefits were designed specifically to prevent him from advancing his party's cause, as well as his own potential political career. In short, it seemed that MPI had enthusiastically supported Steven's efforts to become a meaningful contributor to society, until he entered party politics and chose to run for a party that at the time formed the province's Official Opposition.

Don't Be Too Successful

According to the MPI mandate, education is part of patient rehabilitation. This mandate had been enthusiastically endorsed in Steven's case, and he had been grateful for it. It was surprising, then, to hear MPI president Jack Zacharias admit, in the presence of Steven's lawyer, that MPI had agreed to fund Steven's return to university for his MBA because the decisionmakers had believed he would not succeed. They expected that he would have to drop out before completing his studies. In effect, the corporation would have been seen to be doing its part to meet Steven's educational aspirations, without having to go beyond an initial funding commitment.

"No one," said Zacharias, "really thought he could actually do it."

As the case became more complex, Sidney Green, a prominent Winnipeg lawyer, whose own political career had been both colourful and effective, became Steven's legal counsel. This was significant, not just because Green was an articulate, witty and entertaining speaker, noted for his ability to recognize and clearly point out any emperor's nudity, but also because he had been a cabinet minister in the NDP government under Premier Ed Schreyer in the 1970s, and later leader of the Progressive Party of Manitoba. Both of Green's personal political affiliations had been adversarial to Manitoba's Progressive Conservative Party. A further irony was the presence of Sam Uskiw, who also came to Steven's defense.

Uskiw, a Manitoba lawyer and an NDP cabinet minister in the 1970s and 1980s, had been commissioned by the Manitoba government under Conservative Premier Gary Filmon, to examine the no-fault public insurance program established by the province in the mid-1990s. Uskiw's review was to determine whether or not MPI was meeting the objectives of the new legislation. As part of a legislated review, the commission was asked to study the main objectives of the plan, one of which was "increasing the amount of money available to compensate seriously injured accident victims for economic loss." In 1998, when Uskiw completed his review, he reported that the no-fault legislation was working well overall, but he had identified more than fifty recommendations that he believed would improve MPI's performance and make no-fault legislation work as intended by the act. The majority of the recommendations were immediately implemented, but the government was defeated before any other changes could be made.

At least one of these recommendations would have made a big difference for Steven, had the government acted upon it—a recommendation that it be mandatory that MPI pay for legal costs for MPI claimants, just as it does for itself, to balance the fairness of hearings before internal MPI reviews, appeals and court cases.

Uskiw went to bat for Steven on the contentious caregiver issue, arguing that MPI should pay for trained professional caregivers to accompany the victim regardless of the claimant's location. The issue was eventually settled in Steven's favour (though Steven has since returned to court to force a reluctant MPI to comply with this decision, which at the time of this writing had not been done). Uskiw observed that MPI was eager to collect premiums from car owners, but reluctant to pay out claims if those same car owners happened to be in an expensive accident. It appeared to him that MPI was more concerned with its bottom line than with satisfying the claimant. Uskiw was once told by another individual studying the MPI performance that if MPI could keep cutting the benefits to the insured, it could consistently keep premiums low and most people would like that— unless or until they became disabled in a serious accident. Addressing MPI's concerns over premiums, Uskiw pointed out that rates would not have risen one iota in meeting Steven's needs, because his costs were negligible as a percentage of budget.

Green felt, as did most, that MPI initially fulfilled its obligations to Steven Fletcher in a satisfactory and exemplary manner. "Ultimately," he said, "it was a case of the corporation becoming embarrassed by its own success. The complications came because no one expected that Steven could accomplish what he did. With each successful achievement, Steven kept costing the insurance company more and more money. As he began to move out into the world, his identified needs and subsequent demands on the corporation kept getting higher and higher.

"Initially MPI trumpeted Steven's success, sending him letters of congratulation and generally encouraging him to keep progressing. Here was a splendid example of how MPI was helping to restore a man, who couldn't even move a finger, to full participation in society. If ever a case presented an opportunity to boast about the effectiveness of public no-fault insurance, this case was it."

The positive encouragement and support didn't last, however, and there are many observers, including friends, politicians and advocates for the disabled, who feel that partisan politics caused a dramatic shift in the way in which Steven's claim was being handled. Certainly Steven and his family felt an immediate change in attitude from MPI decision makers as soon as his political aspirations became known.

Steven's twenty-four-hour, round-the-clock need for assistance is a matter of life and death, not comfort or convenience. This care can be provided in a hospital, a personal care facility, or in the community. Wherever he is, there will be a medical cost. Steven believed that the insurance policy should pay that cost, no matter where he happened to be, because this is medical care, not personal home assistance. While he cannot vacuum, prepare meals or feed himself (and all these things need to be done for him), his attendants are not personal home assistants. They are essential health care workers, who are there because of his quadriplegic condition and varied medical needs.

When Steven submitted requests for health care attendant travel costs, as he had previously done, so that his attendant could accompany him on trips to constituency meetings in rural Manitoba, MPI suddenly reversed its pattern of assistance and said no. It gave as its reason that it was not authorized by legislation to approve such expenses.

Steven decided to appeal this decision to the internal government Automobile Injuries Appeal Commission (AICAC), set up to examine contentious MPI decisions. The commission was authorized to determine whether the decision in question was legal, and whether it was wise or fair. At the time of Steven's appeal, Yvonne Tavares presided over the commission.

Sid Green argued on Steven's behalf that to deny him the presence of his health care attendants because he was travelling outside Winnipeg, violated the intent of the legislation, specifically Section 138. MPI insisted that it couldn't provide travel for Steven's attendant because his attendants basically provided only personal home care assistance, and such costs were capped.

After hearing the arguments, the commission agreed with Green that Steven's attendants were not personal home care assistants, but rather medically trained aides, with a duty to provide health care to their patient. It further agreed that MPI could indeed legally grant Steven's request to have his attendant travel costs paid when he had to go out of town. Such a matter, the commission ruled, was well within the purview and mandate of MPI.

However, exercising its discretion, the commission denied Steven's application, on the grounds that he really didn't need to travel because he didn't need to be president of the Progressive Conservative Party.

It was, as Sid Green put it, "the stupidest decision I've ever heard in my life."

Speaking on behalf of the commission, Tavares dashed hopes for restoration of Steven's travelling ability when she concluded that, while the commission agreed with his counsel on the matter of legality, in her opinion, MPI was not compelled to assist Steven just because it had the legislated ability to do so. Though this comment might have been seen as logical under different circumstances, in this case MPI had offered as its original reason for turning down Steven's requests the fact that it was not authorized by legislation to approve such expenses.

One would presume that having been told that the decision-makers at MPI could in fact legally grant the request, they now had reason to do so or, to put it another way, they no longer had reason not to do so. The decision was directly contrary to the statement of MPIC CEO Jack Zacharias, who had said, "We would if we could."

As Green worked to secure Steven's due, he kept coming back to the basic problem—MPI never expected that it would encounter a high-level quadriplegic like Steven Fletcher who so greatly exceeded its expectations. In other words, MPI had not anticipated that a Manitoba motor vehicle accident victim could live through a C4 spinal cord break and be capable of re-entry into society to such a degree that regular assistance under Section 138 of the act would actually be required. The law itself, however, was written to address just such anomalies. And it was important that MPI recognize this fact.

No-fault insurance, while benefitting single vehicle accident victims, also restricts their ability to sue the insurance corporation for anything other than the violation of the Manitoba Automobile Insurance Act. The advantage of this stipulation is that it prevents the frivolous and costly lawsuits that have sent insurance rates soaring in other jurisdictions. The disadvantage is that under such a restriction, things such as pain and suffering are not grounds for an appeal. Failing to abide by the prescribed rules and regulations of the act would be, however.

With this understanding, and convinced that their argument for appeal was sound, Steven and Sid Green went first to the Court of Queen's Bench, where they were unsuccessful, and then to the Manitoba Court of Appeal. Their application was denied at that stage because the decision under dispute did not involve a matter of law, but only of discretion in the law's application.

Green filed a separate suit to the Manitoba Court of Appeal regarding the "perceived reasonable apprehension of bias" evidenced by Tavares, whom they had discovered was an NDP supporter and contributor. Because of the MPIC Act's stipulations, this suit could not be about the rightness or wrongness of the MPI decision to deny travelling ability to Steven Fletcher. It was rather about the perceived inherent bias of the presiding chair of the appeals commission. However, the Manitoba Court of Appeal felt that even though Tavares was a financial backer of the NDP, bias could not be clearly proven.

Frustrated but determined, Green asked leave to carry Steven's case forward to the Supreme Court of Canada. The case involved a political question, given that Steven Fletcher was the president of the main opposition to the governing party and Tavares was a financial contributor to the party in power. The question therefore became: "Was there a reasonable apprehension of bias given the fact that Ms. Tavares, the chair of the commission, was a financial contributor to the NDP?" The Supreme Court, busy with numerous charter challenges and rulings on sensitive and controversial government issues such as same-sex marriage, refused to hear Steven's case.

By this time, however, Steven had learned of the ongoing ministerial inquiry into his case. On his behalf, Green immediately filed suit against the minister and MPIC for abuse of statutory authority, and remarkably quickly, the lawsuit was resolved. In his argument prepared for Queen's Bench, however, referred to above, Green pointed out that "it would be reasonable to conclude that the Ministerial Inquiry had its effect on MPIC ... the Ministerial Inquiry concerned itself with the costs being expended on Mr. Fletcher's case ... [which] had not been an issue prior to the Ministerial Inquiry."

On July 9, 2003, MPI issued Steven with a "two-year determination process", despite recommendations to the contrary supplied by experts in the field, including its own consulting psychologist, Moira Somers. She wrote to caseworker Chris Beck on July 25, 2003, saying:

> Had someone forewarned me that I should one day find myself in the position of having to explain to an insurance company why somebody with C4 quadriplegia should not be put through the usual determination process, I would not have believed it. Nevertheless finding myself in this position, I will attempt to address the salient points of our discussion and your letters.
>
> MPI is aware that Mr. Fletcher, like all C4 quads, requires total assistance with respect to bowel and bladder functions, bed mobility, transfers, pressure relief and re-positioning, eating, dressing, grooming, bathing, transportation and home-making. At the risk of sounding facile, I must ask you: How much more disabled can a person be?
>
> MPI has many claimants that who have been declared vocationally disabled for far less compelling reasons that are present before you in the current case.

Under the two-year determination process, Steven was told that he was employable and if he did not find permanent employment within a two-year period, he would be subjected to a cancellation of his income assistance. In other words, this completely paralysed man would either find a job or have no income whatsoever.

Steven had been preparing himself for a career that would make maximum use of his knowledge, training and experience. Under this devastating pressure from MPI, however, he felt there would be no time for an appropriate career to evolve. As an engineer with an MBA, and a natural leader with an intimate knowledge of the Canadian health care system, he felt he could make a significant contribution to society by becoming a lawyer. It was a career to which he believed he was well suited and which could possibly be self-sustaining, with potential to establish his own firm and reach out to attract corporate clients who could benefit from his unique background and education. As a result, he had decided to enroll in law school. MPIC, however, refused any financial support for this next step toward ultimate independence.

As Sid Green pointed out, "The evidence is clear that prior to his accident, Mr. Fletcher was an individual who aggressively and positively sought to improve his condition of life while making a substantial contribution to the society in which he lived. There was every reason to expect that from his history he would attain high levels of achievement in whatever field of endeavor he applied himself to. His achievements were sustained in the academic, social, athletic and public service arenas."

These were exactly the qualifications, Green also said, that were "virtually ideal for someone who wished to pursue a political career." Any career that involved travel of any sort would still require the insurance company to cover his medical attendant care costs.

Faced with having his income cut off, Steven once again battled depression and additional stress, and was once again made acutely aware how helpless he was. With great desire and mighty effort, he was doing all that he could to prepare himself for meaningful employment. The thought that his insurance income might be eliminated was terrifying.

On September 11, 2003, the statement of claim suing the minister and MPIC for abuse of statutory authority was internally reviewed. A week later, on September 19th, MPIC set aside its order for a two-year determination process for Steven. To say he was greatly relieved would be a massive understatement!

However, the scare he'd had made him ever more motivated to work to ensure that citizens were respected and well served by their governments. When the Conservatives nominated him as their candidate for the next federal election, he was eager to meet the challenge.

In June 2004, he was elected to the House of Commons as the Conservative MP for Charleswood-St. James-Assiniboia, a victory that necessitated a great deal of travel back and forth to the nation's capital, and yet more requests to MPI to allow his attendants to travel with him. Initially, all these requests were routinely denied.

Never people to give up, Steven and Sid Green returned to the appeals commission to launch another appeal. This time, under another presiding officer, the appeal was decided in Steven's favour. Even MPI's financial obligation to the federal House of Commons was identified; the House of Commons was to be reimbursed by MPI for any monies it might have expended on Steven's behalf that were, in effect, MPI's responsibility. This would cover the money the House of Commons had advanced to Steven during his time of need.

Media reports indicated that this was a clear victory for the young MP. And Green and Steven were in good spirits, heartened by the overall direction that MPI was being shown from the appeals commission, and confident that their remaining concerns would be addressed over time. Advocates for the disabled and other claimants who had felt themselves badly treated by MPI sent congratulations to Steven's office.

As Green says, however, MPI still didn't seem to get it. It continued to argue that Steven's health care was really personal home care assistance, and that home care expenses were capped at a specific dollar amount. MPI simply refused to accept what the appeals commission was telling it. By refusing to allow Steven's health care attendants to travel with him, MPI was essentially attempting to confine Steven to Winnipeg. It would not cover his necessary health expenses when he ventured beyond the perimeter of the city, despite MPI's own mission statement.

"So," said Sid Green, "the appeals commission tells MPI, 'You can say yes' and MPI replies, 'We can't say yes.' Can't they hear?"

Although Green's legal services concluded with the completion of the appeal, he could not suppress his astonishment when the minister announced in 2001 that MPI had recorded a massive surplus and she planned to give twenty million dollars to the University of Manitoba. "How stupid is that?" he fumed. "If MPI has all that money, how about spending it where it should be spent ... on the vehicle accident victims who have specific identified legal claims?"

XXI

If You Think ...

Incensed that NDP cabinet minister Becky Barrett would be "donating" some $20 million from MPI's surplus to the University of Manitoba, Steven lambasted the NDP. He was in the unique position of being both president of the university's student body and an unsatisfied MPI claimant. Among other things, he wrote an article in *The Manitoban*, the university's newspaper, asking why Manitoba's public insurance company was giving large sums of money from its huge surplus to outside organizations, instead of using it to benefit insured vehicle accident victims? The article (which appears in its entirety in Appendix B) appeared on January 10, 2001, and said in part:

> Over the past couple of months, Manitoba Public Insurance has received much publicity. It has enjoyed a $100-million surplus this year, largely due to the investment income and windfall in revenue because of new car sales.
> The question for MPI now is what to do with all this money?
> MPI and the provincial government decided a one-time rate reduction for motorists and a donation of $20 million to university infrastructure would be a great way to spend the money. This donation to post-secondary educational institutions was met with public outrage.
> Why should automobile ratepayers subsidize university infrastructure?

Explaining that the public outcry had prompted the government to reverse its decision and instead rebate its insured customers, Steven went on to outline why he believed this politically expedient decision to rebate was not a wise one.

> I believe MPI must focus on the insurance-benefits side of the equation. If there is extra money, it should first go to improve benefits.
>
> Two of the founding principles of MPI are to restore an individual's quality of life as much as is practical to the level it was before the accident and to compensate individuals for economic loss due to the accident.

Summarizing his personal experience following his horrific accident, he wrote: "I feel MPI fails on both counts. My belief is that everyone should be concerned about this, since [an accident] can happen to anyone."

He then went on to outline some of the financial implications for accident victims in a series of scenarios, explaining:

> If you think you can sustain a serious injury and then work to offset the costs of your injury, you are wrong. MPI will claw back almost every nickel you earn from your income replacement. It is actually possible to lose financially if you return to work under the current MPI scheme.
>
> If you think the Canadian Pension Plan will save you, you are wrong. MPI claws back the CPP benefits from your income replacement as well, even though CPP is contributed to separately and is a completely independent plan.
>
> If you think you can get private insurance as a young person to help cover the costs, you are probably wrong. Very few young people qualify or can afford to buy insurance to protect themselves from these types of accidents.
>
> If you think you can hire a lawyer to sue MPI, you are wrong. Under the current no-fault system, you cannot sue MPI or anyone else if it is an automobile accident. [Under the previous system, which used tort law, there were many scenarios where suing wouldn't help either. But that's another story.
>
> If you think you can appeal decisions made by MPI, it is difficult. To appeal a decision you need a lawyer. Even if

you are successful with your appeal (and I have been), you still lose money to lawyer fees, which can be substantial.

MPI will not reimburse you for lawyer expenses, even if you are successful. To make appeals even more unfair, MPI has several floors full of lawyers ... all of them ready to fight appeals. In essence, your insurance dollars go to lawyers paid to fight against you! You are paying both for your lawyer and for their lawyers.

There are some very important positive aspects to the MPI coverage. MPI does help with vocational rehabilitation, physical rehabilitation, and medical expenses such as equipment and medication.

The no-fault system has tremendous potential, but the substantial problems with MPI coverage need to be fixed.

I have been lobbying for changes to MPI legislation and policies since my accident five years ago on January 11, 1996. My experience with MPI is what first drew me into politics. Before my accident, I did not give much thought to these types of issues. Yet since my accident, my eyes have been opened wide and I have realized the injustices in our medical system and our insurance coverage.

I am determined to contribute to making MPI and other types of insurance fair and equitable. For years I was told there wasn't enough money. My feelings of disgust resurfaced after the recent announcement by MPI of donations and rate cuts.

MPI policies are also particularly harsh on young people. I never thought my position as UMSU president and my experiences would intersect, but here we are.

Steven concluded: "if the government is serious about funding University infrastructure, then it should do so itself."

Years after his accident, Steven Fletcher is still battling Manitoba Public Insurance for funding to live a normal life and the right to be in politics. He says, "On the one hand we 'save' or extend the lives of individuals and then we do not provide the resources to help these individuals, young or old, to have a reasonable quality of life. This contradiction is what initiated my first major political initiatives. In particular, I focused on Manitoba Public Insurance to ensure that they meet their mission statement: 'Bring the quality of life of a victim as much as practical to the level it was before the accident.'"

During his battle, Steven was most upset with the internal corporation memos Steven obtained through Freedom of Information legislation. Particularly offensive was a memo from claims supervisor Chris Beck, which read in part, "It was felt that Steven's political career could not assure sustainable long term employment ... and that we had a right to explore other options [for a career for Steven]."

In the same memo, Beck states, "What is even more concerning from a cost and reinsurance perspective is the result should Steven be elected to Parliament. We would have no way of predicting what our costs would be and we would clearly have no mitigation of our IRI [Income Replacement Indemnity] exposure."

This attitude was also apparent in a review decision of Sept 13, 2004, in which MPI underscored its refusal to allow the necessary health care aide funding that would enable Steven to leave Winnipeg, even to earn a livelihood. "If Mr. Fletcher is indeed capable of holding remunerative employment as an MP," reads the decision, "then he is certainly capable of holding remunerative employment here in Winnipeg."

Steven recalls the revealing and rather astonishing comment made by Beck when Steven asked why some key MPI decisions about him were not on record in his file. Beck said that there were no records of these decisions because they were made orally at the management committee meetings.

When asked by Steven how he knew that the intent of the decisions was correct, Beck said that he was very confident that the intent was being followed based on the conversations around the water cooler. Such an admission by a claims supervisor was shocking. The strategy seemed designed to avoid leaving a paper trail that might expose the rationale for certain decisions through freedom of information inquiries.

As outlined earlier, Steven's health care attendants, with MPI's support and encouragement, had previously accompanied him wherever he went, but when he was about to begin travelling as a member of the PC Party, the rules changed. He received a letter from Beck stating that MPI had reviewed the costs of his attendants and as a result, "MPI would no longer consider additional Health Care Attendant expenses as they relates to your duties as President of the PC Party or your future political endeavours."

Many people understood what Steven was facing and did their best to help and encourage him through his long dispute with the Manitoba Public Insurance Corporation. Among those was Steven's uncle, John Hobbs, a lawyer who kept in constant contact with the

Fletchers from his home in Regina, giving advice, guidance and comfort as needed. None of the Fletcher family had extensive experience dealing with the massive bureaucratic system in which they were now embroiled, and the resulting trauma made it hard for them to concentrate on the technicalities and logistics of its long-term challenges. John proved to be a good guide, explaining how complex government systems worked, and how to cut through the tangle of red tape that enveloped them from so many different jurisdictions. Managing the problems with health care and insurance adjusters was a large and difficult task, and those were just two of the many authorities that would impact Steven's post-accident life.

As a government minister under Premier Gary Filmon during the 1990s, I found that large government bureaucracies are set up to deal with mandated issues in a cost-efficient, standardized way. Rules and regulations are established to make sure that abuses of the system are minimized, and that no one client will be given an advantage over another. Many observers believe that the formulas for delivering services make everyone equal at the lowest common denominator. It's true that over the years, Canadian society has developed a unique culture, one which has many good attributes. However, this culture has also encouraged the development of swollen, inward-looking bureaucracies. The civil service often has more power than the people's elected representatives.

I recall one parliamentary old-timer telling me, "Think of the Legislative Assembly as a large balloon filled with water, with busy ants running around on its surface. The water inside is the civil service, and the ants are the elected politicians. The ants run around for a period of time, making only the smallest of dints as they try to change the shape of the balloon. Then they are plucked off and discarded and a whole bunch of new ants jump on the balloon and bounce up and down on the surface in different places than their predecsessors. But the water inside the balloon just stays there, knowing that the ants are simply annoyances that will soon be gone, and it can fill back out to the shape it was."

His analogy contains a germ of a truth that Steven had encountered: bureaucracies have a nasty potential for morphing into systems that have as their main goal the need to sustain and protect themselves.

In systems designed to serve the largest number of people at the lowest possible cost, exceptions are hard to deal with—they throw the system out of whack and upset routine delivery. Rules often have only one interpretation and allow only one course of action.

Making decisions, no matter how sensible, that have the potential to be precedent setting, is seen as dangerous; it could lead to higher, more expensive, standards for service. Government workers on the front lines are afraid to take risks. What if they make the wrong decisions? Who will get the blame? They become slaves of the rules and regulations that protect them from having to make judgements or that prevent them from seeing the real person with the real need in front of them. Because they expect people to follow the rules, they feel personally threatened if someone interprets the rules differently.

John Hobbs recalled the Milgram experiments of the early 1960s, which revealed that an average, presumably normal, group of ordinary citizens would willingly inflict painful, even harmful and potentially fatal electric shocks on innocent victims if ordered to do so by an authority figure. Dr. Stanley Milgram, then a professor at Yale University, set up a series of simple experiments to find out if individuals would comply with commands from authorities if those commands violated their own morals. He was trying to figure out why so many Nazis, such as Adolf Eichmann, believed that they were justified in their inhumane actions because they were "just following orders."

In Milgram's experiments, an individual was strapped into what appeared to be an electric chair, and hooked up to many wires. A volunteer subject was brought into the room and was told that he or she was part of an experiment to discover whether learning could be enhanced if the would-be learner was punished for making mistakes. The subject was instructed to adminster a shock, by pressing a lever on a machine, to the individual in the chair (the learner) each time that person gave the wrong answer to a question. The subject was further told that each time a shock was administered, its intensity would by rise by fifteen volts, gradually increasing from fifteen to 450 volts, as the number of errors increased. The volunteer subject was then given a forty-five volt electric shock to demonstrate what the learner would feel when being jolted with electricity after just two errors.

In reality, the hapless learner was an actor and no electricity actually flowed from the subject's lever. The actor deliberately made mistake after mistake, resulting in the subject sending shock after shock to the "victim" across the room. As the surge of electricity supposedly increased with each error, the actor would begin to evidence signs of pain. When the learner began to moan and then scream, most subjects would hesitate, but were ordered to continue.

The results were, pardon the pun, shocking. A majority of the subjects, fully sixty-five per cent, continued to obey to the end—

believing they were delivering 450-volt shocks—simply because the experimenter commanded them to do so.

Milgram and his successors carried out many variations of this intitial experiment. Among their observations were two that John Hobbs pointed out could be applied to many large bureacracies. If the subject could see or hear the victim, compliance with the orders given by the authorities decreased; it was clear that the subject was less likely to cause pain when looking the victim in the eyes. If, on the other hand, the subject could not see or hear the victim, compliance with the orders given by the authorities increased; it was apparent that the subject was more likely to inflict pain when unable to see the results of it. In both situations, however, ordinary people, feeling no animosity or hostility, carried out actions foreign to basic universal standards of morality simply because they had been ordered to.

"When people think of themselves as merely instruments for 'just following orders' they become dehumanized," Hobbs says. "They don't have to take responsibility for their own actions. They can say 'Don't blame me. I just work here,' or 'Sorry, sir, it's not my fault, we've always done it this way.' When that happens, a shift in morality occurs, and individual compassion and understanding take second place to blind adherence to an unquestioned authority. Timidity and compliance replace courage and initiative."

Like some of the "victims" in the Milgram experiments, Steven Fletcher was neither seen nor heard, at least in the beginning. Bureaucrats at MPI and in the health care system who made decisions that negatively impacted him couldn't see him struggle or suffer. They never experienced first-hand the results of their decisions.

Commenting on MPI's decision to refuse Steven the cost of modifying a van so that he could have personal transportation, Hobbs said, "Everyone was stunned at the refusal, especially when they told Steven that he should take public transportation instead. How they thought he could he get his big specialized chair into any public conveyance was beyond us. Here they were encouraging Steven on the one hand to get a job, and on the other hand they were making it nearly impossible for him to leave his home. They just couldn't see what this young man was up against. It was as if they were blind. A man from Mars on his first visit to planet Earth, standing in a room with a group of physically handicapped humans, would point to Steven as the one person in the room who was so severely impaired that he absolutely needed a modified van to go places."

In a submission to MPI, Steven wrote "The unreasonableness

of MPI's arguments is beyond belief. MPI's lawyer said that I did not need a vehicle for schooling, work, networking or socializing because I could use email instead. The MPI lawyer argued that because I was educated, I would always be able to anticipate when I would be subject to life-threatening medical conditions and so I would always be able to get back to my residence in time to be worked on. I do not see why I should even have to counter such ridiculous arguments."

As Steven continued to challenge the system, he wasn't acting according to expectations. Hobbs says, "The bureaucrats couldn't fathom the idea that Steven intended to live, not in an institution, not in a group home for the handicapped, but on his own, in a place of his choosing immediately upon leaving the hospital. He refused to lower his expectations to fit the bureaucratic model, refused to live his life at the lowest cost to the insurance company. He wasn't behaving the way the book said he should.

"Steven's continued insistence that the conditions outlined in Section 138 of the Public Insurance Act of Manitoba were being incorrectly interpreted was a source of extreme frustration for those at MPI," Hobbs says. "It was almost incomprehensible to them that Steven would want to do the things he was trying to do. He drove them crazy.

"MPI is still continually playing catch-up with a man who continues to surprise them and exceed their expectations. No matter where it puts the marker down, he passes it. Who would have believed that he could do all these things?"

In reality, despite their high-toned mission statements, both the public insurance and health care sytems expected Steven to live at the lowest cost to them. Their expectations that Steven, at age twenty-three, would willingly allow himself to be confined to a personal care home for the rest of his life were shattered when he refused to be institutionalized.

The problem," says Hobbs, "was that the systems he was dealing with had not contemplated someone like Steven Fletcher. Exceptional individuals are often perplexed by the treatment they receive from systems that do not operate with them in mind. That's not to say that those systems weren't designed to accommodate the exceptional. They were. They just don't always operate that way because most people don't expect to receive more than the bare minimum. They may try fruitlessly for awhile to change the status quo, but most people ultimately give up, wearily muttering old saws such as 'You can't fight City Hall.' It requires too much effort, too much energy and often too much money to do battle with the authorities when you're already beaten down. Authorities say 'no' and then make you spend a year and a half going through appeal processes that you hope will force them to say 'yes'. Most people are too tired or confused to continue with what amounts to a reverse onus process. Authorities seem to count on this fatigue factor taking over."

Steven, however, wouldn't conform.

"Steven," Hobbs says, "was not one who was perplexed. He recognized immediately that the bureaucracy he had to deal with didn't always make right or timely decisions. Their reactions were always budget driven, not service oriented, as their mandates required. Crown corporations must always be responsible with premium payers' money, but they need to remember that being responsible includes operating according to their prime objectives. If high-ranking bureaucrats could see and appreciate the consequences of some of their decisions, they would surely come to different conclusions. But because the systems are so huge, no one within them is directly accountable. Steven believed that the government bureaucrats needed a lot of help to learn how to come to the right decision in a timely manner."

"Actually," Hobbs adds, "Steven could have been a great poster boy for MPI. If MPI had learned to become partners with this unique and extraordinary individual, if it saw him as a man who was going to go where no one with his kind of injury had gone before, the company could have shared the credit for proving that societal reintegration of the catastrophically injured was possible. MPI could have shown that it was reasonable and realistic to assist determined individuals to become productive and that providing equipment and services as permitted in the Manitoba Public Insurance Act was not a waste of money, but rather a wise investment."

Instead, MPI underestimated the power of the human spirit. Rather than see that spirit, the company was aware only of the cost of maintaining the damaged body. MPI complained that it cost more money to look after Steven than any of its other claimants. Of course Steven was the most costly accident victim. He is completely paralysed from the neck down and requires round-the-clock medical care. How many people so severely injured would even survive such an trauma, let alone attempt to become self-sufficient? But Steven never asked for anything the act didn't allow. As he told the *Winnipeg Free Press* in January 1999: "I'm not fighting with MPI. I'm just helping it fulfill its mandate."

The problem wasn't Steven. The problem was an adversarial

culture in which each accident victim was seen as a potential fraud. This culture is being forced to change, but it still holds vestiges of what John Hobbs calls "the historical conflict of interest between the insurer and the insured."

As a Crown corporation, Manitoba Public Insurance holds a monopoly on vehicle insurance. It is intended to be self-sufficient, but is freed from the need to make a profit. The reason MPI is not profit driven is so that it can remove the conflict of interest between insurer and insured, and concentrate instead on consumer protection and service.

✦ ◼ ✦ ◼ ✦

STEVEN won his case. On March 9, 2006, the senior legal counsel for the House of Commons wrote a memo to his colleagues. "I am greatly pleased," the memo read, "to be able to inform you that the Manitoba Automobile Insurance Compensation Appeal Commission, having heard Mr. Fletcher's appeal from the earlier decision of the MPIC Internal Review Officer, has upheld almost in totality Mr. Fletcher's claims for continuation of MPIC coverage and has thereby overturned the lower ruling."

Though Steven won his case, MPI has, at the time of writing, yet to comply with the decision, and Steven must still advocate for himself and fight for his benefits. Fighting MPI means that he is really fighting the bastion of ratepayer-funded lawyers and bureaucrats who work to ensure that MPI pays out as little as possible to accident victims. It's an ironic battle, since, as Steven points out, his insurance payments pay the insurance company's lawyers to fight the appeals he makes against the company. It is a sad truth that many accident victims give up their appeal battles because they simply cannot afford to hire lawyers to match the legal strength of MPI. That fight can become overwhelming.

"People can spend a whole lifetime focused on fighting the insurance company and never win," says Steven. "In the meantime, they miss experiencing the rest of the life they have, or go broke. No wonder so many give up."

But Steven never quit. His victory will help other vehicular accident victims be seen as more than expensive burdens to the insurance companies that must settle their claims.

Adds John Hobbs: "The story here is about overcoming the world, breaking new ground, redefining expectations and showing everyone that high-level quadriplegics are more capable than society and Crown corporations would have ever believed. Because of his extraordinary abilities, Steven is opening doors for other catastrophically injured people, in much the same way that the great baseball player, Jackie Robinson, opened doors for black athletes following him. The story here is that society will have to get ready for fuller participation from individuals who were once shunned. And it's a positive story, full of hope."

XXII

Soul Searching

Some people set out to have a career in politics. They plan and prepare for years to get themselves elected. All their activities and personal contacts are selected with that one goal in mind—to get elected. They generally try to avoid controversy, making them, by default, supporters of the status quo.

Others run because of concern about a specific issue or a desire for a change in government direction. These people interrupt the planned flow of their lives and careers to become candidates. Because they believe they can make a difference, they are not generally supportive of the status quo.

Some candidates have deep-seated convictions and a strong desire to serve according to those convictions. Others simply like the idea of holding power and obtaining the perks and privileges that accompany being elected to a high position. I have noted that politicians in both these categories are capable of performing well for their constituents. Being sincere and committed doesn't necessarily mean being competent, and being self-centered doesn't necessarily mean being incompetent.

Some belong to a political party because they believe in its stated philosophy and they will be reasonably consistent in their approach to decision making.

Others "party shop" for the best deal for themselves as candidates, seeking a safe riding, a senior position, or a post-election reward. These people will join the party that benefits them the most, and are tempted to switch allegiance if the personal benefits become greater elsewhere. They are not always consistent in their approach to decision-making. Still others become involved in a cause, with no political allegiance, and find themselves drawn to a particular party as issues related to that cause arise.

There are many reasons for entering the fray, but my observation is that the best candidates for election at any level are ones who have a clearly defined value system, a reason for running, and courage to do what they believe to be right. While never seeking to be deliberately put at a personal disadvantage, the best candidates will see their own personal interests as secondary to that of their duty to serve with integrity. Contrary to public opinion, such altruism still does exist among politicians in Canada, and when it's discovered, it's like finding gold.

In Steven Fletcher's case, his ancestry reveals a family history of patriotism and service that promoted an altruistic approach to life. His paternal grandfather had served in the British Colonial Service. His father, David, learned self-control and personal discipline as a result of this British heritage. One of his ancestors, Colonel Patrick Mackellar, was a British army engineer who was with General Wolfe at the battle on the Plains of Abraham.

David's father and grandfather were both engineers. His father worked on telecommunications for the pipelines in the Middle East, in Iraq and in other countries; then, during his colonial service, he was sent to Malaya, where he met his wife.

David's parents were married in the Anglican Cathedral in Singapore. When the Japanese invaded Malaya during World War II. they lost all their worldly possessions. David's parents were on leave in Australia, visiting some of his mother's relatives, when the Japanese entered the war and David's father immediately volunteered to go back to Malaya to fight. He arrived in Singapore just as it fell to the enemy and spent the next four years in a prisoner of war camp, and labouring on the Burma-Siam railway. Imprisoned and starved, he survived the terrible ordeal, which many did not.

David and his mother, meanwhile, travelled to New Zealand to live out the rest of the war; for more than four years they didn't know if David's father was dead or alive. When he eventually returned home, it was clear the war had taken a huge toll on him. The tortures and horrors he had lived through had affected him greatly, and would affect his family.

David's father returned to work in Malaya, but David, at the age of seven, was sent to a boarding school in New Zealand, where he remained for the rest of his childhood and teenage years. Though David went back to Malaya to visit his family on holidays, he spent little time with his family. Later, he went on to university in Christchurch, New Zealand, worked briefly in England and finally came to Canada where he met Joanne.

After they were married and began to plan a family, his boarding school experience made him determined to keep his children with him. "Boarding schools are pretty tough places," he says. "I always said I would never send *my* kids to boarding school. I always said that I would spend as much time as I possibly could with my kids. I would never send them away."

While David is a first-generation Canadian, Joanne Fletcher's ancestors have been in Canada for eight generations. Scottish Presbyterians from Islay, Scotland, and the Isle of Skye, they came to Canada in the mid-1800s to farm in southern Ontario and Québec.

Joanne's father, one of seven siblings, joined the Royal Canadian Mounted Police and was stationed in Whitehorse, in the Yukon, during World War II, in order to assist the Americans in their duties there. Retiring from the RCMP, Joanne's father joined TransCanada Pipeline as the line was being laid across Canada. As it had during his years as a Mountie, his work focused on the country's needs and a vision for its future.

The family eventually moved to Winnipeg. There, years later, Joanne and David met while taking skiing lessons. In David, Joanne found an ideal mate, a professional man with a high code of conduct and a sense of the world around him.

As the son of parents with an ancestral history of patriotism and service to others, Steven has a deep appreciation for Canada. Given this, his decision to run for elected office seemed natural.

Even during his school years, his interest in the democratic process was evident. In Grades 10 and 11, he was awarded his school's citizenship award. In Grade 12, he was elected school president, selected for the model parliament and was active in a wide variety of school activities.

Steven's natural leanings were conservative, and politically, he was attracted to the Progressive Conservative Party. By the time he was twenty, however, it was clear to him that the federal PC Party was on its last legs. Like so many provincial Progressive Conservatives at that time, he was frustrated by federal politics. He had supported the PC candidate in the federal election of 1988, but he was disappointed with her performance in Ottawa.

In the federal election of 1993, he switched his vote to Mark Hughes, who was running for the relatively new Reform Party. He considered Hughes, who held degrees in agriculture and theology, to be a credible and intelligent candidate, and the Reform Party the only alternative to the floundering PCs. Hughes didn't win. The Liberal candidate did, but Hughes came in second and beat the incumbent Progressive Conservative by a comfortable margin. Today, Hughes is the lead pastor at one of Winnipeg's largest churches. The election that year was eventful, with more than half of the Canadian electorate switching parties from the 1988 election. For the PCs, the handwriting was on the wall.

Recognizing, as many did, that Liberal candidates across the nation were being elected because conservative thinkers were splitting their votes between PC and Reform candidates, Steven began to promote union in conservative ranks. His concern was that Canada might descend into a one-party state with a series of small ineffective fringe parties, each working at cross-purposes with the others. He believed that Canada, like all Western democracies, needed a strong opposition to serve as a watchdog on government and to be a government-in-waiting as an alternative choice for the electorate. In the meantime, he was worried that the Liberals would have a free ride in Ottawa for a long time, which would not be good for either them or the nation.

In 1997, after he was released from the hospital, Steven felt that he wanted to contribute to society, as well as receive benefits from it. He decided to volunteer to help in local government constituency offices. Despite his quadriplegia, he felt there was a lot he could do to help, the simplest and most obvious being his ability to use the telephone. His MP at the time was a veteran Liberal, Lloyd Axworthy, and Steven went to his Winnipeg office, offering to serve as a community volunteer. Axworthy never got back to him. Perhaps the fact that Steven wasn't a member of the Liberal Party had something to do with it. Nevertheless, the Liberals passed up the one opportunity they had to woo Steven Fletcher to their side.

In that first year out of hospital, because of his ongoing need for medical care, Steven became deeply affected by the rumours about the future of Canadian health care if the "scary" right wing was ever elected to govern. The scare tactics had an impact. In 1997, the year after his accident, despite his conservative leanings, Steven voted Liberal.

Looking back, he says, "After calming down and doing my research I came to my senses, and recognized that the Liberals were actually a big part of our health care problem. Certainly their solutions were not those that I believed would improve our situation. As a patient who had learned a lot about our health system, and as someone who was dependent on it for my every need, I began to do in-depth studies of the legislation that concerned Canada's health care system, and those of other countries as well. As my knowledge grew so did my attraction to those political parties that reflected my conclusions about what direction Canada needed to go. And it sure wasn't in the direction that the Liberals were leading us."

This didn't mean he was about to cast his support impulsively behind the federal PCs. He was still very uneasy about the future of the party and concerned that it was becoming elitist and "too red" to provide a home for centre to center-right thinkers. He began a quiet personal exploration into the various political options for himself and for his country. "I want the future to be good because I intend to spend a lot of time in it," he said, and picking up on the slogan being used by young conservatives in the '90s: "We are the future and the future is now."

When he was elected president of UMSU, Steven was also elected to the board of the Canadian Alliance of Student Associations, which gave him occasion to travel to Ottawa. (This was before MPI became concerned that allowing Steven to travel might enhance the potential of a political career for him.)

In Ottawa, in 1999, he met with then Finance Minister Paul Martin. Steven recalls being guided to the minister's office through much security to be greeted by Martin relaxing in his chair with his feet on the desk. Steven spoke about a number of issues of concern to university students. Martin listened and explained that much of what Steven was concerned about fell under provincial jurisdiction. (The provincial ministers, on the other hand, had always explained to the students that they couldn't accomplish much because the federal government had decreased transfer payments for post-secondary education.) The next time the two men would meet would be on the floor of the House of Commons five years later. Paul Martin was by then prime minister and Steven an MP.

In 2000, Steven once again travelled to Ottawa to make his pitch for the universities. By then he was being wooed to run federally for the PC Party in Winnipeg. Hearing that Steven was going to Ottawa, PC organizers arranged for a meeting between Steven and Joe Clark, former prime minister and then Progressive Conservative leader.

"Having grown up hearing Joe Clark's name almost continuously and seeing him on TV, it was good to meet him in person," said Steven. "We had a positive meeting, and later, during a private conversation, he asked me to consider running as a Progressive Conservative. It was both flattering and humbling, but I couldn't accept the invitation. I was focused on provincial politics. Whatever the answer to the request would eventually be, I could not consider leaving Manitoba under any circumstances while I was still so busy on campus. I said 'Thanks, but no thanks,' and put the offer out of my mind.

"Joe and the federal Conservatives approached me again in Winnipeg, after I had sought and lost the Manitoba Progressive Conservative nomination in Tuxedo, and repeated the request, this time specifying Charleswood-St. James-Assiniboia as a seat for me. By then I knew that I could not accept the federal PCs as my political choice. I declined, politely, and with respect, because the offer was sincere and because I was saddened that this grand old party no longer held the appeal that it should have held for me and for many other young adults.

"Joe couldn't see the need to unite the right and bring the whole spectrum of conservative thinkers back into the same party. This was a priority of mine, but he reacted emotionally to any thought of such a union, showing, I felt, more venom than vision. He refused to accept the fact that Canadians didn't seem to want the PCs anymore. He was angry with the Reform Party for 'stealing conservative votes' and blamed 'them' for the decline in Tory fortunes. I didn't think he could see the bigger picture that could be painted for the conservative movement. He was, unfortunately, out of tune with the people he wanted to attract to his side. In Joe I saw a diehard Tory refusing to change, even while living in an era that has constant and unrelenting change as its hallmark."

Steven eventually joined the newly formed Canadian Alliance, which was born out of an initiative launched in 2000 by the Reform Party and several provincial Tory parties to negotiate a merger with the Progressive Conservative Party of Canada. Some conservatives believed that as long as both Reform and PC parties existed, there would continue to be a divided and therefore ineffective conservative movement in Canada. After much meeting and analysis, the Reform Party members voted to disband. The federal Progressive Conservatives, however, refused to do so. A party such as theirs, they felt, was so much a part of Canadian history that it could not seriously consider relinquishing its rightful place on the political platform. They rebuffed any initiative to unite the right.

The Canadian Alliance existed for only three years, from 2000 to 2003, but in that short time it served as the Official Opposition in the Canadian House of Commons, second in power and strength only to the governing Liberals.

"But as conservatives," Steven observes, "with two federal conservative parties still in existence, we were still splitting our votes all over the place, and of course by doing so, all we were doing was letting the Liberals win seats. 'United we stand, divided we fall,' Aesop said 2,500 years ago. Too bad we still hadn't learned the lesson he was trying to teach."

Though Steven didn't realize it at the time, his frustration over the division among conservative thinkers on the national scene would eventually lead him into federal politics. The route to Ottawa, however, was a circuitous one.

XXIII

Entering the Fray

S teven's interest in campus politics was sparked by his brother Gordon, who, as president of the engineering faculty student body, had become concerned about the performance of the University of Manitoba Students' Union. Together, they discussed the voting structure at the union's general public meetings, which made it easy for very small numbers of people with special interests to determine polices and practices, and the union's finances, which had been in the red for a generation. Though it was unheard of for someone to run for student president without first going through the UMSU ranks, Steven and Gordon decided, with virtually no prior discussion between them, to throw their hats into the ring as presidential and vice-presidential candidates respectively. They were confident that they stood a good chance of winning if they campaigned well.

They did.

The brothers approached the election in a typical engineering manner. They analyzed results from past elections, segmented the student population into faculties and interests and geared their messaging accordingly. Realizing they were running in a left-of-centre environment, they deliberately used orange as their campaign colour. They assumed that at least some of the left-of-centre voters would vote by the colour of the campaign posters, while those more conservative in their approach to life might be more likely to vote on the content of the campaign platform.

Because UMSU election campaigning was not allowed before a set starting date, and knowing they needed a strong campaign to

promoting a united campus
maximizing student potential
a foundation for individual success
www.stevenfletcher.com

Vote for
Steven Fletcher UMSU PRESIDENT
Gordon Fletcher UMSU VICE-PRESIDENT
February 9 & 10

financial accessibility
physical accessibility | bringing umsu to you
social accessibility

Common Sense

improving our reputation
across the nation

The Fletcher brothers took the U of M by storm.

increase their profile, Gordon and Steven planned to be first out of the starting gate the minute the official campaign began. The Fletchers had their posters made and picked choice locations for them well ahead of time. The night before the election campaign was to begin, volunteers with ladders took the posters and stationed themselves at the selected locations, waiting for the clock to signal midnight. At one minute past midnight on the opening day of the campaign, in a well-coordinated exercise, Fletcher posters were put up in forty prime locations, and dozens of secondary locations as well. It was estimated that they had covered the whole campus in less then twenty minutes, leaving few—if any—good locations for opposition posters. It was a stunning beginning. The display of signs first thing in the morning was an attention-getter on campus.

Determined to get their message out, Steven and Gordon embarked on a rigorous speaking schedule. Their goal was that, between the two of them, they would make a two-minute speech in front of every class across campus. Gordon would "do" two classes at 8:30 and 9:30 a.m. and every hour thereafter. Between these classes, Gordon tended to his own studies. Steven, who had just bought his accessible house in Fort Garry, close to the university campus, woke at 6:00 a.m. and his health care attendants began the laborious and time-consuming task of preparing him for the day. It was usually between 10 and 10:30 a.m. before Steven joined Gordon on campus. For the rest of the day both of them spoke to classes, while attempting to stay on top of their own courses.

Each day, Gordon arrived at the university at 7:30 a.m. and swept the campus to check that the signs were still in place and in good repair. If there were any problems, he contacted a sign crew volunteer to attend to the problem.

It turned into a ferocious campaign. Emotions were intense among the four slates. Before the ballots were even counted, candidates began challenging the legitimacy of the vote based on perceived campaign anomalies. As a result, the ballots were locked up until an elections appeals tribunal, chaired by a Liberal lawyer, could determine if there had been any infractions of the election process.

The tribunal ruled there were none. Five days later, the ballots were counted and the two brothers became president and vice-president of the University of Manitoba Students' Union.

The following year, not being finished with all he had set out to accomplish, and still a student at the university, Steven decided to defy the odds and seek an unprecedented second term as UMSU president.

If the first contest had been heated, the second was hotter still. But Steven prevailed. Steven remained in office as president and continued revamping and reorganizing the way things were done. He points with satisfaction to his accomplishments, chief among them being bringing UMSU out of debt for the first time in twenty-five years.

If one is amazed that Steven Fletcher could accomplish all that while adjusting to living as a quadriplegic, one will be even more amazed to recognize that his campus politics did not slow him down in any way while acquiring his MBA. Steven did not miss a single assignment, or seek any special favours in his studies. He completed his MBA course work right on schedule in 2001.

XXIV

Putting on a Label

In 1999, Gary Filmon announced he would be retiring from politics. A popular Manitoba premier who had led his provincial PC Party to victory in three successive elections, he and his government had just been defeated by the NDP. After twenty-four years in politics, Filmon felt it was an appropriate time for him to resign from the provincial legislature, and for the party to select a new leader.

Filmon had represented the constituency of Tuxedo, a pleasant, properous urban riding in southwestern Winnipeg that includes a portion of Charleswood. So strong was conservative support in the riding that it was often said the person who won the party nomination in Tuxedo would be sure to win the seat at election time.

Steven had grown up in the area and his family home was there. The unexpected political opportunity created by Filmon's retirement made Steven think. Perhaps all the things he had learned through his ordeals—his intimate knowledge of the public health care system being the most obvious—could be used to make government work better for the people it was meant to serve. Certainly the philosophy of the provincial PC Party (not to be confused with its federal counterpart) attracted him more than any other. Always a believer that most people, given a chance, would choose to be self-sufficient rather than needy, Steven wanted a government that would seek to inspire individual independence rather than foster dependency.

Here, he thought, was an opportunity to participate fully, to make a meaningful contribution; here his ability would be the thing that counted most. After some consideration, and with the backing of a group of residents, Steven decided to seek the nomination in Tuxedo.

Steven's adversaries at the university set upon him like a pack of starving wolves when they heard he was going to seek a partisan nomination. An UMSU president should not have any political affiliations, they said, demanding that Steven step down as student body president immediately. Steven argued that UMSU's by-laws did not prevent him from participating in provincial politics.

The Manitoban, the campus newspaper, had a field day running critical comments about Steven's political ambitions. Under the headline "Student coalition targets Fletcher", the October 4, 2000 edition reported, "an alliance of students has launched a campus-wide venture to remove UMSU president Steven Fletcher from office." A group calling itself "Umsuwatch" began to circulate a petition. If it got 5,000 signatures, it could force the implementation of a by-law that would impeach the UMSU president.

Before long a second coalition of students was formed, calling itself the "Friends of Steven Fletcher committee". The FOSF began circulating a flyer in response to the petition, inviting students to get both sides of the story before signing any petition and including clarification of specific items raised by Umsuwatch. In *The Manitoban*, Steven defended his record of achievement by saying that under his watch UMSU had moved to a surplus budget for the first time in twenty years, that competition among businesses at University Centre (the student union building) had brought better services and reduced prices, and that funding to social programs had increased.

Umsuwatch was unable to obtain the required number of signatures to impeach Steven, but nonetheless presented the 1,000 it had obtained to Steven, who indicated that he had no plans to step down. He would fulfill his term as UMSU president and seek the provincial PC nomination in Tuxedo. "And perhaps," he added, "I might also seek a third term as UMSU president."

Steven's entrance into the Tuxedo provincial nomination process also startled other observers. Many Progressive Conservatives expected that Heather Stefanson, a thirty-four-year-old with a long political heritage and impressive credentials, would be acclaimed as the Tuxedo candidate. Instead, it was now a contest, and not everyone was happy about it. A coronation is always easier on the nerves.

Stefanson's family had a long history in the constituency. Her father, Hugh McDonald, had grown up in one of the first homes built in Tuxedo. With a degree in political studies, Heather had worked during the 1990s as a special assistant in the Prime Minister's Office, as special assistant to federal agriculture minister Charlie Mayer and as executive assistant to provincial minister Clayton Manness. Her husband, Jason Stefanson, is a nephew of Eric Stefanson, a respected provincial cabinet minister whose reputation for integrity and decency had made him first choice for party leader to replace Filmon. He had declined, but the Stefanson name nevertheless carried considerable weight.

With all parties seeking promising female politicians, Heather Stefanson seemed an ideal candidate. Steven would have to work hard to win the nomination.

He called together his supporters, including me, with Max Goldack, an experienced political campaigner, chairing his nomination campaign. In Steven's living room, over endless cups of coffee and far too many donuts, we laid out our campaign and went to work.

As the night for the nomination meeting approached, we recognized the race was going to be tight. Both candidates had accumulated credible support. It would all come down, as it always does, to how many supporters showed up to vote for their candidate.

When we got to the meeting place on nomination night, my heart sank. The hallway at the front of the building could not accommodate Steven's oversized chair. He would have to enter at the back of the hall, which he did. But that was not where the voters were. The voters entered at the front, where Heather was greeting them with a friendly smile and warm handshake.

Steven's team, of course, was at the front door handing out material and buttons, but it wasn't the same as having the candidate there.

Of more concern, voters were being directed to a side room where they could vote in advance if they didn't wish to stay for the meeting. The rules previously specified that voting could not take place until candidates had been officially nominated and speeches had taken place, but that had recently changed. Agreed to by managers and returning officers, it was something that couldn't be undone. We had been hoping, however, that Steven's speech would attract the few undecided voters in the room and help put him over the top. Advance voting took away that slight edge, and we needed every vote we could find.

We carried on. Heather was introduced and nominated by the president of the local association. This was not normal protocol, for presidents usually remained neutral, but it was a powerful signal to the audience. Heather's speech to the crowd was well delivered, professional and gracious. The applause was enthusiastic. Her performance had been flawless.

181

Throughout, I had been watching the speaker's platform with dread. The platform was very high, square in shape, and the ramp for Steven was set at an impossibly steep angle. *He'll never make it up,* I thought, *not with a mechanized chair that weighs almost 500 pounds.*

When he was called upon to speak, I watched as Steven approached the platform, eying the ramp and doing mental mathematics. He felt there was a chance he could make it up, so he took that chance. Halfway up, however, his chair slowed to a stop and began to roll backwards. Campaign workers rushed to his aid and with difficulty got him going again and pushed him to the top. The platform itself was simply a square stand that wasn't really designed to accommodate more than a couple of people and a podium. Steven's chair took up the entire space. He was so precariously perched that I was now afraid he might roll over the edge. Despite these distractions, he didn't bat an eye. He gave a passionate, powerful speech that caught many listeners off guard.

As the audience rose to give him a standing ovation, a man behind us said, "My God, it's a good thing Heather's people got us to vote for her before this guy spoke." I exchanged glances with Joy Smith, the MLA for Fort Garry and a staunch Fletcher supporter. She grinned like a kid. "We've got to tell Steven that one," she murmured.

Stefanson won the PC nomination for Tuxedo that night, but the party was a winner too. Because the contested nomination was taking place in the former premier's riding, there was increased media coverage and an increased membership for the local association, particularly among young people. Hundreds of Tuxedo residents had joined the party so they could participate in the selection of a new candidate.

Heather Stefanson and Steven Fletcher entered the competition as acquaintances and ended it as friends, a testament to their ability to work together for unity and strength within the party. Heather went on to become the MLA for Tuxedo and has earned herself a solid reputation in both the legislature and in the constituency. Steven took the things he had learned from this first foray into party politics and applied them with considerable success to his subsequent campaigns. He went on to become the Member of Parliament for the riding that includes Tuxedo, and today enjoys an excellent working relationship with Stefanson.

XXV

Plunging In Wheels First

Steven's campaign in Tuxedo had stimulated his interest in the future of the PC Party of Manitoba. He wanted to contribute to its growth and prominence in the province, and help prepare it for an eventual return to government. Mentioning this to Stuart Murray, who became leader of the Manitoba PCs in November 2000, he learned that the party president was planning to step down, which would likely create openings on the board of directors. Murray suggested to Steven that he might consider letting his name stand for a position on the board.

Having been bitten by the political bug, Steven was willing and eager to run for the president's position. He had ideas for the party, and directions in which he felt it should be heading. After determining that he had a strong degree of support, particularly among the solid, hard-working volunteers outside of the party hierarchy and seldom in the limelight, he plunged wheels first into uncharted waters.

As with his university experience, he quickly found that there were some who frowned on anyone running for the presidency without first "paying their dues" by serving on the executive as a table officer. These people felt Steven was overreaching himself and should not be on the ballot. Despite this, he carried on.

Again, I was part of Steven's campaign team, and this one was a lot of fun. He discussed the pros and cons of party philosophy and policies with members, and it was clear that they were longing for such introspection. Members wanted to know how society could progress positively into the future without losing the good things of the past. These discussions were right up Steven's alley. The answers all lay in sustainable development, balance, analysis and planning. Like those of former Manitoba Premier Gary Filmon, who was also an engineer, Steven's problem solving and deductive reasoning abilities were highly honed. Engineers, I have noticed, have a logical way of thinking that's refreshing in the often fuzzy and fluffy realm of political thought.

Being president of a party involves much more than clear political thought, however. The fact that Steven was studying for an MBA was regarded as particularly beneficial for the party's board of directors, since rebuilding the party called for strong management skills.

The 2001 board election took place during the annual general meeting of the Progressive Conservative Party of Manitoba in Brandon in November. After the party's defeat in the 1999 election, the presidential campaign proved a welcome and healthy challenge for members and created some badly needed energy. Steven's supporters enthusiastically handed out buttons and brochures, hung posters and generally promoted "their guy" for the presidency. His carefully organized and energetic campaign was stimulating and rejuvenating for the party and it demonstrated more than the strength of his support. It showed clearly that Steven wanted to do the job.

The other presidential candidate, Bob McGregor, was a backroom strategist who had served on the party executive. A radio broadcaster, he had a poised, professional demeanor and strong backing from many in the party hierarchy. He was expected to win.

Steven, however, had natural charm and unbridled passion that had the potential to ignite the membership. He wanted to set people on fire and send them out to the public burning with enthusiasm.

He had been told that each candidate would be given ten minutes to address the assembly before the voting. This was confirmed with the organizers, and on that basis, Steven prepared his speech.

Unlike other speakers, Steven doesn't take notes to the platform. Since he can not turn pages, and because podiums are a hindrance, he relies on his memory for public speaking. He has a remarkable ability to do this, which predates his accident. For his speech to the assembly, he timed his delivery to about nine minutes, giving him a minute of wiggle-room, in case he needed it.

Steven was the first speaker. As he was about to roll on to the platform, the presiding official announced that each candidate would be given five minutes to speak. Steven and I exchanged horrified glances. He turned to the official and said, "You mean ten, don't you?"

re-elect

Steven Fletcher
for PC Manitoba President

"The PC Party of Manitoba has an honorable history and a promising future. By focusing on our core values, grassroots support and along with our MLA's record we will lay the foundation for future success."

Steven Fletcher

Integrity Hardworking Experienced Accessible
proven record

Top: The Fletcher family in March 2000.
Bottom: Steven's campaign poster when he ran for president of the Manitoba Progressive Conservative Party in 2001.

"No," was the response, "You have five minutes and then the bell will ring and the microphone will be cut off."

Steven had already been introduced and the audience was waiting. While I protested vigorously to the officials that the speakers had been told they would be given ten minutes, not five, Steven began his speech.

For most people caught in such circumstances, the solution to shortening the speech would be to simply pull some pages out of it and ad lib a new sentence to join the remaining pages together in a way that sounded logical. Since most practiced speakers know how long it takes them to deliver a page of type, this isn't as hard as it sounds. If it had been me, delivering about one page a minute, I would simply have pulled five pages from my speech, retaining the ones that contained my most important points.

For Steven, all that rearranging had to be done mentally, to fit the new time limit. He had no pages to pull. Moreover, all the points in his speech led to a single conclusion, and that conclusion needed all the points to make sense. The ending of his speech, in my opinion, was the best part of it, and I was fearful that the bell would cut it off halfway through.

Steven pulled it off. His speech was masterful. It was seamless, each point following another in logical succession, and concluding with the climactic ending he had planned. Even I, who had timed the speech at least a dozen times, could not tell where he had cut it. The speech was good, but it was Steven's ability to stay calm and in control, to go through the mental gymnastics required to cut that speech in half on the spot in front of hundreds of people that impressed me most.

"Hey," he said afterward, "I've been through worse things than that." I had to acknowledge that was true.

Nonetheless, Steven's lips tightened and his eyes narrowed when his opponent took eight minutes to deliver his speech, and the officials didn't ring the bell. Perhaps they had figured out that the candidates had been told their speaking time limit was ten minutes after all, and decided to correct their mistake before the second candidate spoke. I will never know for sure, because Steven told me, in very clear language, not to complain. Sensing that he was beginning to outperform his mentors, and developing a political maturity of his own, I shut up.

When the votes were counted, Steven Fletcher had been elected president of the PC Party of Manitoba, the youngest person to hold the office, and the first with quadriplegia.

One of the first obstacles Steven faced was the inaccessibility of the party headquarters at Weir House, a turn-of-the-century mansion located on Kennedy Street in Winnipeg across the street from the Manitoba Legislative Building and the lieutenant governor's residence. The house had been donated to the party decades before and had just undergone approximately $200,000 worth of renovations. Gracious and historic, Weir House is not without flaws. There is no parking for visitors, and the building itself, while charming, can be a hot, stuffy warren of narrow staircases and crowded rooms. The main entrance has a beautiful door and portico, but it's more than a metre above the sidewalk and is reached by a flight of steep concrete stairs.

In short, if you're in a wheelchair, you can't get in; and if you could get in, you couldn't get round the hallway corners or use the staircases to reach the meeting rooms. There are no ramps, and there is no elevator. There is no parking place that would allow a specialized van to open its side ramps to accommodate an oversized electric wheelchair.

The party found itself with a president who couldn't get in to party headquarters. At least in the short term, meetings would have to be held elsewhere, with papers and files transported from Weir House to the meeting locations. So Steven began to conduct the business of the party from his home, which suited him just fine, especially during the winter months.

The problem of Weir House was a real one, however. Steven felt strongly that whether or not the president was wheelchair bound, party headquarters must be accessible to all. Everyone agreed. "Of course, of course," they all said, but building ramps to enter Weir House was next to impossible because the house was massive and there was little space between the structure, the public sidewalk and neighbouring dwellings. And once inside, then what? The only way an elevator could be installed was to gut rooms on all floors, which meant costly structural changes that the party could not afford.

The obvious solution was to sell Weir House, or rent it out and get new headquarters. But the building's historic status, its enduring link to the party, and the recent renovations proved strong counterarguments. Despite press attention that threw a spotlight on the accessibility issue and caused some friction within the party, the problem remains to this day. Still a rabbit warren, Weir House continues to be owned by the party, but almost all functions and meetings are held elsewhere.

However, Steven was gratified some years later when the Parliament of Canada quickly and willingly authorized some changes to the Parliament Building to make it wheelchair accessible for MPs. "It's something," he was told, "that we should have done years ago."

Making Weir House accessible was less important to Steven than other work that faced him. The party, for instance, needed to raise funds. Steven challenged members to raise money themselves and not leave it all to others. To set an example, he promised to raise

$3,000 himself by a certain date, and did it. His belief that he has to push himself as hard as, or harder than he pushes others is a fundamental part of his character, and he inspires others to produce.

Any political party, even at the best of times, faces factions within. Following its fall from power in 1999, the Manitoba PC Party was feeling the additional stress of moving from government to opposition. Not only had the party suffered electoral defeat, but it had a new and untested leader in Stuart Murray, who was under the microscope both publicly and internally. Everyone blamed everyone else for everything. Such tension is not uncommon for a party that has gone through massive changes. And the task of restoring the party to a strong, confident and unified force, as one member observed, "was not one for the faint-hearted".

Steven's heart was not faint. A strong leader, he handled internal disputes adroitly and firmly, faced external controversial issues calmly and honestly, and always sought to promote his conservative philosophy. Because he was not afraid to take a stand, he earned the respect of many. For the same reason, he also frustrated, and sometimes angered, those who disagreed with him. As one dissenter grudgingly acknowledged, "Well at least no one can accuse Fletcher of being weak or wishy-washy."

It was a busy and challenging year and at the end of it, Steven was asked to run for a second term in order to continue the work he'd begun. He didn't hesitate. He felt the party was healthier and more confident, but that there was still much to do before it would be fully competitive once more. He needed little persuading to roll back into the ring.

At the 2003 AGM, he again sought the presidency. And again, he faced Bob McGregor. At the last minute, however, McGregor announced that he was withdrawing from consideration, and Steven was acclaimed president. It was a vote of confidence, evidence of the membership's faith in his abilities.

"Let me share a story with you," he said to the convention delegates in an acceptance speech punctuated with cheers and ending with a standing ovation. "On the back of the brochure that I have provided each of you there are two pictures. One is of me on top of a mountain. If someone told me a year ago that this summer that I would be able to go on a hiking trip up a mountain I would have said, 'That is impossible.' With innovative equipment, dedicated volunteers and determination, I climbed that mountain. The impossible can be made possible."

XXVI

Heading for the Hill

Sooner than expected, Steven found himself climbing a political mountain that, for excitement and challenge, rivalled the ascent to the Burgess Shale. There was a difference, however. In mountain climbing, people pull together; in politics, sometimes it seems they pull one another apart. Elements of both were evident in Steven's next attempt to scale new heights.

He began his career in federal politics in an era of dramatic partisan change. The conservative movement in Canada was emerging from a decade-long internal battle, which he felt strongly had to end.

In 1984, Brian Mulroney had led the federal Progressive Conservatives to their biggest election victory in Canadian history, with a majority government of 211 seats. Having come into power with a huge mandate, Mulroney enjoyed an initial surge of popularity and admiration. By 1993, however, when he announced his retirement from politics and his resignation as prime minister and PC leader, his popularity had plummeted. He left behind him a party in conflict and disarray, and the conservative movement in Canada at a crossroads.

In those years, Western Canadians, particularly, had grown intensely frustrated with what they perceived as the federal government's Eastern Canadian bias. More than disappointed with the Mulroney government, a minority agitated for Western separation from Canada; others decided to found a new party as an alternative to the PCs. Formed in Winnipeg, on October 30, 1987, it called itself the Reform Party of Canada and adopted the slogan, "The West Wants In". The new party's first leader was Preston Manning, son of

Alberta's former Social Credit premier, Earnest Manning. From 1987 to 1993, the Reform Party grew, establishing itself as a significant political force in the West.

In 1993, Mulroney resigned as leader of his party. Kim Campbell, his minister of Justice, was elected leader and on June 25, 1993, became Canada's first female prime minister. She inherited a party in shreds, however, and was unable to repair the damage in the four months before the next federal election. On October 25th, Canadians soundly rejected the PC Party. Reduced to two members—neither of them from the West—the PCs did not even qualify for official party status. Some quipped that when the Conservative MPs went out to dinner, the maître d' would ask politely, "Good evening, madame, monsieur. Will this be for a party of two?"

Elsie Wayne and Jean Charest, the two elected, carried the remnant of the Progressive Conservative banner in Canada's Parliament and had to watch with dismay while fifty-two newly elected Reform MPs—all from the West—took their seats in the House of Commons. Jean Charest took over the leadership from Kim Campbell and was officially elected PC Party leader in 1995.

Liberal leader Jean Chrétien became prime minister and the Liberals formed a majority government. They would remain in government for the next thirteen years. During this time, most conservatives realized that their opposition votes were being split among too many parties, but no one party was willing to merge with another to present a unified alternative.

In the 1997 election, Reform won an additional eight seats and became Canada's Official Opposition. It did not, however, win any seats in the East. The PCs managed to elect twenty MPs and returned to official party status, but it was cold comfort. Any hopes they harboured for having any significant influence in Parliament were crushed. The Progressive Conservatives remained a rump party, of little but historical consequence.

Anyone trying to follow the Canadian political scene during the turn of the new century might have been forgiven for being confused. Things were chaotic. People moved back and forth between parties like butterflies among flowers, trying in vain to decide where to land. Only the Liberals were happy with this political mayhem. Taking advantage of all the divisions and resultant vote splitting that had become the hallmarks of conservatism in Canada, they were able to maintain power without accountability.

In 1993, to the dismay of the rest of Canada, a newly formed

Québec separatist party, the Bloc Québécois, had garnered enough support to form the country's official opposition. The irony of a party with a mandate to break up Canada becoming Her Majesty's Loyal Opposition and the second-most powerful party in the nation was not lost on most Canadians. Those who were concerned there were too many opposition parties to effectively hold government to account began to investigate ways to reintroduce a balance of power in Ottawa.

Governments require a government-in-waiting sitting in opposition to give them a strong incentive to behave. Without such opposition, corruption can occur. Scandals rocked the Liberal government and its support began to slide.

In 1998, with the blessing of his fellow Conservatives, Jean Charest had moved to provincial politics to fight against the Québec separatist movement as leader of the Liberal Party in that province. For a second time, Joe Clark became leader of the PC Party.

In September 1998, Preston Manning, finally recognizing that conservatives must no longer be divided, initiated what was termed the "United Alternative", a movement to bring together conservative thinkers from all political backgrounds in an effort to "unite the right" and put an end to the vote splitting that was keeping the Liberals in power. After many meetings and two United Alternative conventions, a constitution was formulated and the Canadian Reform Conservative Alliance, better known as the Canadian Alliance, was voted into existence. On March 25, 2000, members of the Reform Party voted ninety-two per cent in favour of dissolving their party and adopting the constitution of the new political party.

The Canadian Alliance hoped to bring all conservatives into its tent, but while many PC members had switched hats and joined the new party, the Progressive Conservative Party itself refused to be part of the united right.

The first leader of the Canadian Alliance was former Alberta treasurer Stockwell Day. A capable politician who had performed well in the Alberta Legislature, Day had a rough ride in Ottawa. The media tormented him mercilessly because of his straight-laced ways, and those who had supported Manning for the leadership resented Day filling the role. Internal disputes and dissension were common and, at one point, several Alliance members joined with the twelve-member Progressive Conservative caucus for a period of time. Day called for a leadership vote to resolve the matter and in March 2002, economist Stephen Harper was elected leader of the Canadian Alliance.

In the November 28, 2000 election, the Canadian Alliance won sixty-six seats, including two in rural Ontario. The PCs lost seats, dropping to twelve from the twenty they had won three years before. In 2002, Joe Clark announced his resignation as leader of the PC Party. The following May, Peter MacKay replaced him.

In Manitoba, the provincial PCs began to distance themselves from the federal Tories after the Reform Party came into being in 1987. The federal PC Party grew so unpopular in the West that Manitoba Tories were ripping up their party cards because the cards included memberships in both provincial and federal parties. Suffering declining support, the provincial party decided that its members did not have to automatically be federal PCs. This decision allowed Manitobans of any federal persuasion to become members of the Manitoba PCs. Before long, people who voted federally for a variety of parties—even Liberals—were attending meetings of provincial Tories. The move, however, strengthened the provincial party and encouraged a wider diversity of people to enter the local conservative tent. The provincial PCs prospered, even as the federal PCs became a party of two.

With the creation of the federal Reform Party as a right-of-center alternative to the federal PC Party, many federal Conservatives began to shift their allegiance. Not surprisingly, this caused concern among old-time Tories, who feared that the Reform Party would continue to grow at their expense. And that, in fact, is what happened. In a few short years the Reform Party became a powerful force, while the Progressive Conservatives dropped steeply in public support.

With the dissolution of the Reform Party with its "Blue" Tory label, many of the center and centre-left "Red" Tories moved their party affiliations over to the more moderate Canadian Alliance. As a result, the party began to grow in size and influence. It was at this juncture that Steven Fletcher agreed to let his name stand in nomination as a federal candidate for the Canadian Alliance for Charleswood-St. James-Assiniboia.

As president of the Manitoba PC Party, he had ties with people who belonged to a variety of federal parties and he entered the nomination contest stating that his goal was to unite like-minded people behind a single candidate. Old-school federal PCs, who couldn't bear the thought of working with the Canadian Alliance, were infuriated. Steven wasn't just any candidate. He was the high-profile president of the Manitoba Progressive Conservative Party.

In the process of letting his name stand, Steven met with the leaders of the riding's Canadian Alliance Association, John and Donna Alexander, a couple who had lived through many years of changes in boundaries, party labels, structures and alliances before becoming members of the local Canadian Alliance Association. In 2003, John, retired from a career in the Canadian Armed Forces, was elected president of the Charleswood-St. James-Assiniboia Canadian Alliance Association. Donna, a former junior high school teacher with finely honed communication skills, was elected to chair the candidate selection committee, in preparation for the next federal election. Together, the Alexanders were a force to be reckoned with. They were dedicated to their cause and were expert campaigners for it.

In their official capacities as leaders in the local Alliance Association, Donna and John made an appointment to meet with Steven at his house to discuss his possible candidacy. David Fletcher joined Steven, and the four of them spent an afternoon together talking. As Donna became increasingly convinced that Steven would be an excellent candidate, she asked what, if any, limitations his quadriplegia might place upon his ability to travel. "I remember asking Steven if he was physically capable of doing the job—not questioning his intelligence in any way, but needing to know the impact of the physical demands that would be made of him, particularly the frequency of flying and travel in general. And Steven laughed and said, 'I can do anything if I need to.' I was absolutely blown away by his confidence. I knew with certainty that nothing would hold him back."

At one point during the meeting, the group took a break. Donna and John went outside and had, as John says, "a little quiet chit-chat. We said to each other, "Who is this guy? Can he possibly do this?" They were impressed with his intellect and knowledge, his determination and his style, but they weren't absolutely sure about the impact of his physical condition. Donna looked ahead to a possible success at the polls and wondered if Steven's election could cause difficulties for the House of Commons.

"That, of course," John replied, "wouldn't be our problem. It would be the Speaker's problem." But because Steven seemed to have a great deal to offer Parliament and the country, the Alexanders decided it was important to carry on exploring his merits as a potential candidate.

At the end of the meeting there were no doubts left in their minds: Steven would be an excellent candidate for the Canadian Alliance. Steven had passed the first hurdle, and would be allowed to continue through the rest of the selection process.

Talking about their conversation with Steven on the way home from the interview, both Donna and John found themselves with tears in their eyes. They had not expected that he would move them so profoundly. They agreed that it would be very gratifying if he was elected and could say, "Mr. Speaker, I rise in the House today ..." His presence would be a profound example, they believed, because his quadriplegia would be incidental; it would not be a reason for electing him.

"We were so touched," Donna says, "and impressed. We had a nephew, Donald, who because of a swimming accident had become a paraplegic. He committed suicide because he didn't want to live in that state. I knew that if Steven had been running for Parliament when Donald was still alive, it would have been very encouraging for Donald to see that were no limits to what you could do. I remember thinking that this would be one of the most wonderful things that I could be involved in if Steven became our nominee—getting Steven elected to Parliament not just for his sake, but for the sake of citizens all over the world. You didn't have to be disabled to be encouraged by his courage. He was so young and so brave."

The process for selecting candidates to stand for a Canadian Alliance nomination was long and arduous. There were five people on Donna Alexander's selection committee and they met with as many people as they could, whom they thought would be excellent representatives, even if they had not joined the Alliance. Finally, they winnowed it down to two individuals—Steven and Don Murdock, a salesperson for the Chapel Lawn Memorial Gardens, who, through his wife Karen and her parents, had deep roots in the constituency.

Meanwhile, the Progressive Conservative Party of Canada was on its last legs and emotions were high, with ardent members of the PCs arguing that the only way to "unite the right" was for everyone politically right of centre to join the federal Progressive Conservatives and restore the historic status quo. This atmosphere affected Steven during the nomination process in the Charleswood-St. James-Assiniboia riding, where many PC stalwarts lashed out at him in a variety of ways.

For example, in an April 19, 2003 letter to Steven, longtime Winnipeg city councillor for St. James Jae Eadie expressed "great disgust" with him for seeking the nomination while in office as president of the PC Party of Manitoba—a clear indication, he continued, that Steven was not a "True Tory." Accusing the Alliance (which he consistently called the "Reform Party") of having as its "single purpose in life ... to destroy the Progressive Conservative Party", he called for Steven's resignation as president of the provincial Tories.

Disappointed with the tone of Eadie's letter, Steven countered with his own. "The Manitoba PC party is separate from any of the federal parties," he pointed out. "Party members, board members, MLAs and any party officials are free to join any party they wish federally.

"You may," he added, "also want to reflect on why the federal Progressive Conservatives only won 2 seats in the 1993 election and why the federal Progressive Conservatives have struggled to keep official party status ever since. ... My goal is not to destroy any party but to create an alternative to the governing Liberals that can implement compassionate, conservative values."

Jae Eadie was not alone in opposing Steven. Others also attacked him, but the electorate had the last word. Steven won the Canadian Alliance nomination. However, a short time later when the Progressive Conservative and Canadian Alliance parties combined to form the Conservative Party of Canada, Steven found himself facing the nomination process all over again.

XXVII

Like-minded People

Winning the Canadian Alliance nomination was no cakewalk. The eligible voters divided themselves into two camps almost immediately. Steven's strongly stated goal of uniting like-minded people behind a single candidate while being president of the Manitoba Progressive Conservative Party made him an instant target for those who didn't want the PCs drawn into the Alliance tent.

He began his campaign by bringing together family and friends who lived in the riding of Charleswood–St. James–Assiniboia. This initial pool in turn solicited additional support for his candidacy, selling as many memberships as they could to people who wanted to have him as their MP. Many of the meetings with Steven's volunteers occurred around the ping-pong table at his home. There was much "pinging" and "ponging" during the strategy meetings, and always food and laughter. The nomination campaign began in April 2003 and was slated to run until September 2003, ending with the nomination meeting.

Throughout Steven's career, the Fletcher family has always played a key role in supporting his bids and nominations. His political campaigns were in many ways reminiscent of their canoe trips of the past; their destination was set; they would conquer long portages, harsh weather, swamps, insects and uncertainty along the way. Having faced and survived the horrors of Steven's hospital stay, they knew no other challenge could even register on the scale.

Not only was theirs a closely knit family, but each member also had unique talents to lend to the mix. Gordon was a technical wizard who designed and produced brochures and posters that were works of art. Julia's effervescent personality won votes at the doors and on the phones. Was there anybody in the constituency that Joanne didn't know? Steven's mother was adept at identifying the vote and greeting visitors to the office. And David was an excellent strategist and a fine photographer.

Both Steven and his opponent for the nomination, Don Murdock, addressed Canadian Alliance members at the AGM held on May 23, 2003. Equally committed to uniting the right, they offered the membership a choice between two individuals. In addition to their AGM speeches, the candidates participated in two debate nights, one on each side of the Assiniboine River, which divided the constituency of Charleswood–St. James–Assiniboia into its northern and southern parts. As the voting deadline approached, party memberships began to soar.

Constituent Liisa Johnson was typical of the many members who recognized Steven's tenacity and vision. "He ran his campaign in our community as if he was running for prime minister," she said. "He did it well. Everything had to be done and finished properly to the nth degree. I liked that. We saw eye-to-eye."

The nomination meeting had been scheduled to be held at the Assiniboia West Recreation Centre on September 8, 2003. On the night of the meeting, the large multi-purpose room was filled to capacity with voters, as well as observers and members of the media. All recognized that a win for Steven would signal support for the campaign to unite conservatives in one federal party. But it was more than that; besides convincing people of the worth of his ideas, Steven also had to overcome questions and prejudice about his quadriplegia.

Though it's hard to believe that people might vilify someone because of a physical disability, such people were found at the nomination meeting. One man circulated copies of a short nasty note telling members they shouldn't be voting for a cripple. The garbage can quickly filled as people read it, crumpled it and threw it away. Others were sincerely concerned about Steven's ability to do the job, and worried that the physical demands on him would be too great. But when it was announced that he had won the Canadian Alliance nomination, the room erupted in loud sustained applause.

Steven immediately selected his campaign team and went to work to win the riding. Many of the volunteers who had been involved in the nomination contest were active in this next phase of the race. The team members pulled together from Day One and the atmosphere at campaign meetings was optimistic and exciting. John Alexander arranged for the main organizer for the Canadian Alliance to meet with Steven and the team, and thus Doug Finley entered Steven's life. Doug was a straight shooting Scotsman with back room experience from dozens of campaigns in Canada and the United Kingdom. He and Steven hit it off right away.

"Doug was refreshing," says Steven. "He sure wasn't your stereotypical political organizer. He had an amazing ability to cut through the chaff, and he knew how to communicate the big picture succinctly. He really inspired us, and gave us increased confidence." Moreover, Finley had a good feel for the constituency, having lived in Charleswood for about a decade when he was president of Standard Aerospace, which was located in the St. James portion of the riding.

Sitting around the ping pong table in his house with Finley and the team, Steven recalls being momentarily overcome at what they were doing. "There we sat, homemakers, retired people, students, school teachers, tradespeople, neighbours and friends, all focused on choosing our own government, with the opportunity to achieve our goal. There are places in the world where ordinary citizens like us would never be able to even contemplate what we were eagerly hoping to accomplish. We are blessed with the most fundamental of freedoms, the right to govern ourselves. It was awesome."

As it turned out, the nomination meeting held on September 8, 2003 was Steven's first, but it was the last nomination meeting held by the Canadian Alliance in Charleswood–St. James–Assiniboia. Just over a month later, on October 16, in a surprise announcement, the leaders of the Alliance and PC parties—Stephen Harper and Peter MacKay—signed an agreement in principle to merge their parties. Each was to have his full membership vote on whether or not to ratify the agreement.

The PC Party of Canada arranged for a Canada-wide convention, to be held via video-conferencing, to vote on disbanding itself, and on creating a new Conservative Party with former members of the Canadian Alliance. In preparation for this vote, local PC associations met to select delegates to send to the convention, to vote as mandated. In Charleswood–St. James–Assiniboia, local PCs voted overwhelmingly in favour of merging with the Canadian Alliance. On December 9, 2003, they met at the Winnipeg Convention Centre where they connected electronically with other PC conventions across Canada. From the outset, it was clear that the status quo would not prevail. The mood was for merger. When the accountants tallied the votes, the

Progressive Conservative Party of Canada, by a huge majority of its members, had voted to dissolve itself. Similarly, in a "one-member, one-vote" mail-in ballot, the Canadian Alliance voted to dissolve itself.

Both parties ceased to exist. In mid-December 2003, an agreement to create the Conservative Party of Canada was ratified, and later that month the parties officially merged. Former Alliance leader Stephen Harper won the leadership of the new Conservative Party of Canada by a considerable margin.

Creating a new party through amalgamation is not easy. While the majority of members were eager to get on with the merger, some, including Joe Clark, the former PC leader and a former prime minister, could not bear the idea of the demise of their historic party. Others, from the Alliance side, could not bear the idea of working with PCs. Such members were left without a political home as a result of the merger, but a much larger percentage felt they were at last back home with a chance to be a political force in the country.

Steven was satisfied to see the right wing unite, but his feelings were tempered somewhat by the knowledge that he would have to go through a nomination contest all over again; the party he had been elected to represent no longer existed.

The first gathering of the Charleswood–St. James–Assiniboia Conservative Association took place in January 2004, to elect a charter board of directors. The mood of the assembly was initially cordial, but the underlying tension was palpable. As the night went on, tempers sparked and the atmosphere became acrimonious. Prior to its dissolution, the federal PC Party had shrunk to about 150 members in the riding, with only about $500 in the bank. By contrast, the Canadian Alliance had grown to 1,200 members and had $23,000 in the bank. Not surprisingly, former PCs felt they were being dominated.

Having been adversaries, it was difficult for the members of the new party to think of themselves as members of the same group. The former PCs wanted the new board to be composed of equal numbers of both former parties. In other words, they wanted fifteen of the thirty board members to be former PCs. They put forward a list of fifteen names they felt should be chosen. The Alliance argued that there should be no quotas, and in turn put forward a list of thirty names from both former parties for consideration. As well, the list was open to nominations from the floor.

The PCs argued that without a guaranteed fifteen seats at the table for its members, former Alliance members would gain a majority of seats on the board and would vote to elect their former colleagues.

Since there were so many more Alliance members than PCs, they argued, it wouldn't be a fair contest.

The argument was heated. Though it was pointed out that there were no more Alliance or PC members in existence, many people held the old allegiances in their hearts. It would take time for the group to feel that they were members of one family.

When the voting was over, the assembly, without being mandated to do so, had chosen a fairly even number of former PCs and Alliance members for its first board. The first board meeting, to select the executive table officers, was held immediately, in a small room off the main hall of the recreation centre. The hour was late and people were tired. Some board members were upset that they would now have to work with people they didn't like.

Fortunately, Conservative Party headquarters had sent facilitators to chair the first meetings and the election of officers for each new association. Lawyer George Orle, a provincial Progressive Conservative, ran the Charleswood–St. James–Assiniboia meeting, and it began in a reasonably smooth manner, electing John Alexander as president and Linda Martin, a former Tory, as vice-president.

Among many other decisions facing the new party was the matter of choosing a candidate to represent the Conservative Party of Canada in the upcoming federal election. While former Alliance members had previously elected Steven, that decision was now null and void. The former PCs had not found anyone to stand as their candidate prior to the dissolution of the party. Setting a date for a general meeting to vote for a candidate to represent the new party became a contentious issue. Those whose hearts were still with the Tories wanted to delay such a meeting until they could find someone to represent their interests. Others were concerned that delays would cause them to lose campaign momentum; they wanted to get on with things as quickly as possible. As the voting on this and other logistical issues continued, and the night wore on, the meeting became acrimonious. Tempers rose. Old wounds opened. Squabbling over who should get what ensued. John Alexander made a motion that the board adjourn so that members should get some rest and reconvene in a day or two to continue assigning duties. Orle, who was chairing the meeting, disagreed. He said that certain decisions needed to be made that night, and the majority of members was anxious to get things over with and settled. Alexander's motion was defeated. Emotionally drained, weary and frustrated, they toiled on.

Donna Alexander, chosen to be on the candidate selection

committee, urged that a nomination date should be set for as early as possible, preferably by the end of February, so that the new candidate would have time to build a presence and profile in the community. Many agreed, especially former Alliance members who had spent time developing a pre-election campaign (formally referred to as the "pre-writ" period) they had expected to have had underway and building momentum by this time. If someone other than Steven Fletcher became the Conservative candidate, time to promote him or her was running short, since the federal Liberals were expected to soon call an election.

The former PCs argued against an early nomination. They wanted time to find someone to endorse as a candidate, in other words, someone other than Steven, who, without the merger, would have been the Alliance candidate. Many expected that if Steven ran for the nomination in the new party—and he had enthusiastically committed himself to do so—that he would win.

The debate became increasingly heated and people started to lose it. They fought over the nomination date, and the partisan undercurrents were obvious.

John and Donna Alexander went home after the meeting feeling discouraged and disheartened. After a restless night of reflection they reluctantly decided to resign from the board immediately. John felt that there was such division that he would have to spend all his time as a referee and would not be able to help Steven become the candidate, and the area's next MP. He also believed that though he had been elected president, he would never have the full support of the board. He was certain that there would be vocal opposition to him no matter what he did. Such a scenario would be unhealthy for everyone.

For her part, Donna Alexander was worried about her husband's health, since he had already had one heart attack and she knew that excessive stress could induce another. The Alexanders did not take their politics lightly. They could not be casual or untouched by the tension around them. As a result, these two, who had worked so hard to unite the right, resigned from their leadership positions in the new party. Instead, they decided to direct their commitment toward Steven Fletcher.

The Alexanders' memo to executive members outlining their reasons for resigning from the board was a dramatic move and it shook everyone up. But it put the party's future in sharp perspective—it could either stand united or fall. Internecine fighting was the wrong way to go.

Linda Martin, who had been elected vice-president, was suddenly thrust into the presidency; there, her careful adherence to rules helped the executive through its first tense year.

I was a member of the executive, and among those who wanted to get on with the process of selecting a candidate. Like many others, I was concerned that the Liberals would call a snap election and catch the new Conservative Party unprepared. I felt strongly that whoever our candidate would be (and of course I was hoping it would be Steven) should be out on the streets getting his or her name and face and ideas known. To me, there was no reason for delay.

Several board members put forward a motion to spend $5,000 to search for people who would let their names stand to become the party's official candidate, but the motion was voted down. Eventually Don Murdock was persuaded to let his name stand again, and the former Tories were comfortable backing him as their candidate. While he held to a right-wing philosophy and was perhaps not as "red" as the old Tories might have preferred, his federal Alliance affiliation had not been the subject of media attention and his provincial PC profile had been low-key. He did not arouse the same anti-Alliance passion among former federal PCs as did Steven, who had been clearly defined as their adversary.

Two significant items played in Steven's favour, however. One was the new fundraising scheme that limited the amount of spending for nomination campaigns, and the other was that Steven had galvanized the former Alliance base, which was much larger than the former PC base. As the president of the Manitoba PCs, he had also obtained the support of a large number of provincial Progressive Conservatives.

Once again, Steven Fletcher and Don Murdock competed for a federal nomination. While the candidates conducted themselves admirably, hostility between the two factions surfaced throughout the campaign.

The nomination meeting was held in March, and the ballroom at the Holiday Inn West on Portage Avenue was packed with hundreds of voters, observers, political commentators, members of the media and prominent Conservatives from across the country. Long lines of people waiting to register spilled from the ballroom door and down the long hotel corridor. Both candidates acquitted themselves well, and the air of excitement was energizing. The ballots were cast and the crowd listened intently to guest speaker and provincial PC leader Stuart Murray while they were being counted.

In the meantime, in January 2004, Steven had taken the time to sit for the LSAT exam so that he would have the option of attending law school and becoming a lawyer if he didn't win the Conservative nomination. He did well on the exam and was accepted into the University of Manitoba Faculty of Law in February.

He contemplated his future during the long wait for the ballots to be counted. "Ottawa or law school? Ottawa or law school?" he kept murmuring as he wheeled back and forth in his chair in the narrow hallway. The answer eventually came. He was elected to be the first Conservative Party candidate in Charleswood–St. James–Assiniboia.

Liisa Johnson summed up the exercise this way, "Getting the nomination was hard. But we kept working to overcome obstacles until we won. That battle for the nomination toughened us up. The unintended favour that Steven's board member adversaries did for him was to strengthen him for the big race."

Steven, with Prime Minister Stephen Harper, centre, and radio personality Charles Adler. Steven's candidacy was endorsed by Harper prior to the 2004 election.

XXVIII

From the Neck Up

Max Goldack, who had been Steven's campaign manager when he ran for the Tuxedo nomination provincially, became co-chair of the 2004 federal Conservative election campaign in Charleswood–St. James–Assiniboia. Because he had been a prominent federal Progressive Conservative, his presence gave Steven's Conservative campaign credibility for former PCs, some of whom were wavering in their commitment to the united right. Brian Higgins, an experienced and respected campaigner, was the other co-chair. The two men worked hard from the moment they agreed to head the campaign, and by the time the election was called on May 23, 2004, things were well organized and ready to go.

John Harvard, a former broadcaster, had been the Liberal Member of Parliament for the area for sixteen years. First elected in 1988, Harvard would be running for the fourth time in 2004 as the Liberal candidate. Because of his long tenure, most constituents believed he was entrenched and unbeatable. An analysis of previous election results, however, revealed that the combined total of Progressive Conservative and Reform or Alliance votes was consistently higher than the Liberal total. Harvard was aware of this and began campaigning in earnest even before the election was called. Indeed, his campaign team had already booked the billboard space the Conservatives had hoped to obtain.

The Conservatives, for their part, had hauled out as much material as they could find about Harvard's voting record and activities, including a video of him sleeping in the House of Commons, while newly-elected Prime Minister Paul Martin made his inaugural speech. Harvard was unfortunately positioned in the camera's direct line of sight, and while the prime minister made his points with great passion, the viewer couldn't help but see Harvard snoring away. Among the items the Conservatives planned to have playing on a video in the corner of their campaign office was a sleeping John Harvard.

Wheels were turning elsewhere, though, and a series of events in May 2004 changed the political landscape in Charleswood–St. James–Assiniboia considerably.

For more than a year there had been speculation that Winnipeg's mayor, Glen Murray, would run federally. Initially a member of the NDP, over time, Murray had become more closely aligned with the Liberals. By 2004, rumours were rampant that he was looking for a Liberal constituency. Though consistently denying any federal aspirations, the mayor continued to put out feelers to various constituencies. At the same time, he was being wooed as a star candidate by Prime Minister Martin and other prominent Liberals. However, the word on the street was that Murray had three conditions before he would consider running: He wanted what was considered a "safe" Liberal seat; he wanted the nomination process cleared so that he could be acclaimed and not have to face a nomination campaign; and he wanted a guarantee of a senior position in cabinet if elected.

In rapid succession, a series of events fuelled speculation that Murray's conditions had been met. During a prime ministerial visit to Winnipeg shortly before the election call, Murray proclaimed Paul Martin Day. Soon after, in the first week of May, in a surprise announcement, John Harvard announced his immediate resignation from politics. The next day, Murray announced his intention to replace Harvard as the Liberal candidate in Charleswood–St. James –Assiniboia. And, in a totally unexpected move, the prime minister appointed John Harvard as the twenty-third lieutenant governor of Manitoba, to be sworn into office the following month.

Shortly after Harvard's resignation, the Liberal Association in Charleswood–St. James–Assiniboia affirmed Glen Murray's candidacy. Murray, however, had not planned to step down as mayor unless or until he won a seat as MP for the riding. While the City of Winnipeg Act required a mayor to resign if he or she decided to run for a seat in the Manitoba Legislative Assembly, it was silent about a mayor seeking a seat in Parliament. Nevertheless, the public expectation was that politicians should vacate one level of government before seeking to run for another. That Murray didn't, evoked howls of outrage.

On May 11, 2004, Murray gave in to public pressure and announced his resignation as mayor. His supporters consoled themselves that if Murray didn't become an MP—which they felt was highly unlikely—he could always run again for mayor and get his old job back.

That opportunity, however, was soon snatched away. Premier Gary Doer, the NDP premier of Manitoba, perhaps miffed that Murray had shifted from the NDP to the Liberals, set an immediate date for the Winnipeg mayoralty contest—June 22, 2004, which in all likelihood would fall before the federal election. If Murray lost his bid to be an MP, he would not be able to return to being mayor. And indeed, this is exactly what happened. On May 23, 2004, Governor General Adrienne Clarkson, at the prime minister's request, ordered the dissolution of the House of Commons. Canadians would go to the polls on June 28, 2004, six days after Winnipeg's mayoralty vote. For Murray, this confirmed that he could not run for mayor if he lost the federal election. But, of course, he did not expect to lose.

John Harvard's government constituency office, located in a visible and easily accessible location with good parking, would have made an ideal campaign office for Glen Murray. Not many places for rent in the constituency so perfectly met the specific needs of a campaign. But just before the federal election was officially called, someone spotted a moving crew in Harvard's office in the dark of night. That person called John and Donna Alexander, who got up and went over to Harvard's office to see what was going on. Looking through the window, they saw that the office was completely empty. All the furniture and equipment had been removed. The locks had not been tampered with.

Donna promptly sent an email off to popular radio talk-show host Charles Adler, asking if an MP's office wasn't supposed to be kept open to serve the public during an election campaign. She pointed out that John Harvard would not be officially replaced as the MP for Charleswood–St. James–Assiniboia until the election was over. Adler chose Donna's to be the letter of the day and read it aloud over the air. Immediately afterward, everything was moved back in to Harvard's constituency office. It hadn't been empty for even twenty-four hours.

Instead, Murray found an office tucked away in a less visible location. To make his presence known, he erected sandwich-board signs on the city sidewalk, which was against city by-laws. Had he never been the mayor of the city, such a misdemeanor might never have been cause for comment. As it was, his action caught public attention; former mayors are supposed to know the city by-laws.

Worse, Murray's supporters erected hundreds of signs along boule-
vards and on public property, in violation of another bylaw passed
during Murray's tenure as mayor. The media delighted in pointing
out the irony of this, embarrassing Murray and causing him to lose
many hours of valuable campaign time ensuring that the offending
signs were taken down.

The writ was dropped and Steven and his team were off and
running. The naysayers at the Conservative nomination meeting,
who had questioned Steven's ability to knock on doors, would have
benefitted from having been able to fast forward a few months, for
Melissa Anderson, his health care aide, had to don rollerblades to
keep up with him.

Getting around was not a problem for a man with his own
wheels, but as the campaign went on and spring turned to summer,
swarms of mosquitoes were a problem for Steven. He couldn't swat
them. One hot humid day, while canvassing on Roblin Boulevard in
Charleswood, the mosquitoes were particularly unbearable. Steven's
aide kept waving them away, but to no avail. He then tried slapping
and swatting the pesky insects, but hitting his client on the head and
slapping him on the face didn't really enhance the image of either of
them. Besieged, the two of them and a volunteer canvasser eventually
took refuge in a nearby fire station, where they had a pleasant break
communicating with some of Winnipeg's fine firefighters. Steven
didn't gripe about the need to seek shelter. He saw it as yet another
opportunity to meet people and learn from them.

Glen Murray's entrance into the race gave Conservative volunteers an even greater incentive to wrest the seat from the Liberals.
They were offended that Liberals viewed Charleswood–St. James
–Assiniboia as a "safe" seat and that backroom politics had subverted
the democratic process, denying local Liberals a chance to choose
their own candidate. Some of these disgruntled, disenfranchised
Liberals even showed up at the Conservative campaign office and
volunteered to work for Steven.

Nevertheless, the campaign was difficult and the race was tight.
Though Murray's conduct throughout the campaign was considerate
and gentlemanly, some of his supporters began a whisper campaign at
the doors. Afraid to openly condemn someone because of a physical
disability, they adopted a patronizing tone. "It's nice of the Tories
to let the crippled kid have a chance, even though they put him in a
riding they know he can't win," one said to me. Another asked me,
"How would he get to Ottawa? He can't even walk."

Clockwise from upper left: Steven, in front of his campaign office;
visiting a seniors' residence in the riding, and chatting with a
military constituent at a local school ground.

"Probably he'll get there on a plane like everyone else does," was my exasperated reply. "Do you really think other Manitoba MPs walk to Ottawa?"

Initially, Murray's supporters were so sure of victory that they took things for granted. When they finally figured out that the former mayor wasn't going to be a shoo-in, some of them got a little testy. The "crippled kid" was suddenly being taken seriously.

Murray's supporters switched their tactics and began to compare their candidate's long tenure with Steven's relative inexperience as an elected politician. If Fletcher got elected, they said (thus allowing for the possibility), he would just be a backbencher, while Murray was, of course, destined for a senior cabinet position if he and the Liberals won. In response, Steven joked that if people voted for him, they would be guaranteed a front bench MP, because the back benches are not wheelchair accessible. When Steven became an MP, he did indeed have a front bench, though not as a result of accessibility problems. He was assigned a front bench seat because he had been appointed senior health critic for the Official Opposition, which merited a front bench position.

The whisper campaign, which was nebulous and difficult to address, became a source of frustration, however. When one reporter asked Steven why people would vote for an inexperienced quadriplegic rather than a high-profile mayor who was a sure bet for a cabinet post, Steven dryly pointed out that he was paralysed from the neck down, not from the neck up. The response was a bit edgy, but it certainly did address the inherent insensitivity of the whisper campaign.

As the campaign continued, it was evident that Steven was winning the sign war. Fletcher signs hung from apartment balconies, brightened lawns and windows and lent a splash of bright blue to a backdrop of summer colours. Had the political pundits taken a drive through the constituency towards the end of the campaign, they might have altered their predictions about the outcome.

All parties suffered from vandalism·to signs and offices. The Conservatives had more signs than the Liberals, which meant more vandalism to Conservative signs than to Liberal ones, which in turn kept the sign crew constantly on the go. Murray's office had anti-gay graffiti sprayed on the door; as a gay man, Murray found this upsetting. Some voters were bluntly prejudiced. One man told me he thought he'd stay home on election day, because the only choices he felt he had were between a cripple and a queer.

The two factions within the Conservative Party began to

cooperate as they worked to defeat the Liberals. They found the Fletcher campaign headquarters was a great place to hang out. Henry Loewen, a wonderfully enthusiastic campaigner, covered his truck with election signs. He would drive this vehicle up and down the main streets of the constituency as if it was a moving billboard. Liisa Johnson appeared on the scene with her big RV covered with signs and parked it in visible locations wherever she went. Steven's campaign team used this idea, and went a little further. Many volunteers had Fletcher signs that they placed in the windows of their vehicles wherever they parked. Many of these vehicles belonged to former federal PCs who were now committed Conservatives. The federal election became the activity that brought together former adversaries, and displaying a common sign was a way of showing unity. It also meant that Steven's name was getting around—literally.

Not everyone had moved to the new party, however. Steven's campaign suffered a disappointment when Dorothy Dobbie, who had served as Progressive Conservative MP for the riding from 1988 to 1993, and two other high-profile PCs crossed over to the Liberals. Each signed glowing endorsements for Murray and agreed to photos, which were featured prominently on Murray's literature.

As for Steven's own campaign literature, at first he wouldn't let his wheelchair be seen in photographs because he was opposed to letting his handicap influence the outcome of the campaign. He would only use photographs that showed his head and shoulders. But, recalls Liisa Johnson, "he was finally talked into letting us take photos in the park with my small granddaughters and Brian Higgins' little grandson. Those kids were so cute and uninhibited. They played around Steven and climbed on his chair and made their big green plush toy frog talk to him, and laughed when Steven answered the frog. We kept taking pictures and eventually Steven let us use them on his election brochure. His chair was finally seen in the promotional literature, in a natural and easy way."

Still, Steven had made little, if any, mention of his quadriplegia during the 2004 campaign. Many people knew that he was in a wheelchair, but most didn't realize that his body was totally paralysed until they met him in person. Some, who had come to know him only through telephone calls or email exchanges, found meeting him in person a revelation. "Funny," one caller said when she learned he was a quadriplegic, "you don't sound disabled".

"Others were somewhat taken aback and didn't really quite know what to say," Steven recalls, "but after talking for awhile they

It was small children, with their relaxed and uninhibited response to his chair, who convinced Steven to allow it to be photographed for public use.

seemed to forget about my wheelchair, and moved on to discuss the issues that made them supporters in the first place. My ideas were more important to them than my physical challenges, which is the way I wanted it to be." Indeed, by the time the election was over, most voters seemed to have forgotten that Steven was quadriplegic. They were either furious with him or in love with him. There didn't seem to be any middle ground. Steven's fearless championing of his causes, his skill in debating and his deep respect for others won out. He was being judged for his views and not for his physical capabilities.

All through the evening of the election, as the polls came in, the count was close. First Steven would be ahead, then Glen Murray; the lead bounced back and forth like a ping-pong ball. The media, interested in Steven because he was the first profoundly handicapped person to run for a seat in Parliament, now became interested for a more

Steven shares a laugh with with Steven Harper and Stuart Murray, then leader of the Progressive Conservative Party of Manitoba. Below, Steven amidst a blur of signs and activity on election night.

significant reason. It looked as though this young man might actually beat the Liberal star candidate, a man who had sacrificed his prominent position as mayor of Manitoba's capital city, to run in this "safe" Liberal seat. Murray was no longer worried about which cabinet post the prime minister would give him. A career politician, he was now fighting for his political life.

Phone calls started pouring in from across the country, journalists and their equipment filled the office, and we were nearly crowded out as we tried to keep track of the information being relayed to us from polling stations across the constituency.

We weren't even sure if we had won or lost until Murray came in the door to congratulate Steven. Though obviously stunned by the results, knowing he had lost not only the federal election but also his position as mayor, Murray was gracious in defeat. He and Steven wished each other well and Steven's volunteers gave him a round of applause.

Steven had won the 2004 federal election in Charleswood–St. James–Assiniboia by 734 votes, obtaining 44.3 per cent of the vote (against 42.5 per cent for Glen Murray). The volunteers in his campaign office were electrified. The cheering and clapping went on for a long time, as did the party that followed.

Two days later, on June 30, 2004, John Harvard was installed as lieutenant governor of Manitoba.

XXIX

Rolling into History

On October 4, 2004, Steven Fletcher, MP from Charleswood–St. James–Assiniboia, wheeled into the House of Commons Chamber and into the history books. As the 38th Canadian Parliament began its first and only session, he became the first C4 quadriplegic ever elected to Parliament.

The 308 members who took their seats that autumn day were part of a long line of MPs stretching back to the early days of the nation and, like their predecessors, they brought with them the hopes, dreams and aspirations of their constituents. At the opening ceremonies, though, time seemed to stand still. Parliament seemed like a changeless institution. And yet it has changed. Once power was invested in the monarch. Now it is invested in the Commons. Once its members were cut from much the same cloth. Now its members are much more diverse. Steven's presence in the Chamber was testament to the continuing evolution of our national institutions.

Steven had first travelled to Ottawa as an MP in July 2004. Having been so focused on getting elected, he hadn't had much time to think about the logistics of settling into Parliament, nor had he received an orientation to guide him in the execution of his duties.

National and Manitoba media were keen to interview him. His win was one of the biggest upsets in the 2004 federal election, and he was the first profoundly disabled person to be elected to the House of Commons. He also gives a good interview—he's never afraid to voice an opinion—so it was no surprise that in his first few days, Steven couldn't open his mouth without a microphone being thrust in front of it.

He says his first day in Ottawa reminded him of his first day in kindergarten. Many of the newcomers looked a little bit lost. Some looked a bit nervous. All looked excited to one degree or another. Going up Parliament Hill, gaping at the historic buildings, trying to determine where one should go and what one was supposed to do, and locating one's caucus room—all were reasons for people to stop and ask questions of one another. It was the beginning of a long orientation and a process of getting acquainted. Though they would soon be crossing swords in the Chamber, for the first few weeks, the atmosphere was upbeat and friendly.

Eventually, all MPs from all parties were given orientation sessions and books that explained the basics of Parliament Hill. By then Steven had done an orientation of his own and he was already at work.

He had been in the Chamber earlier to help the parliamentary architect plan a proper space for his wheelchair and to show his family the majestic architecture of the room with its rich wood carvings, towering stone arches, stained glass windows and forest green seats. The architect explained to Steven that he would be sitting on the opposition side of the Chamber, next to the throne occupied by the Speaker of the House. He outlined in detail all the modifications that would be completed to accommodate Steven and his personal care attendant. After everything had been summarized, Steven thanked him and said, "You realize all these changes are temporary."

Perplexed, the architect asked why. "Because in a few months the Conservatives will be sitting on the government side of the House and you'll have to create a place for me over there." Then he laughed, and so did the architect, until Steven added with a grin, "and then I will run for Speaker." Knowing that renovating the Speaker's Throne would be a massive undertaking, the architect began to look a little concerned.

Steven enters the Chamber through doors behind the Speaker's chair and positions himself so he can see most of the MPs. When he first sat as an MP, it struck him that they all looked just like the politicians on TV, sitting and waiting for Question Period. Of course, the reason they seemed that way was because that's what they, and he, were. It didn't seem quite real. "It felt," he says, "like I had been zapped into the TV screen during an airing of CPAC [Canadian Public Access Channel] but in 3-D or as a holographic illusion.

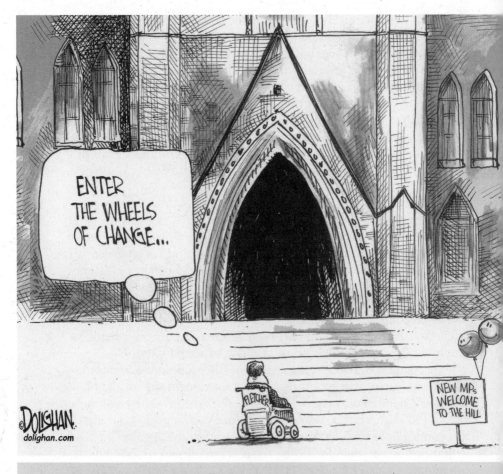

This editorial cartoon ran nationally when Steven first arrived on Parliament Hill in the autumn of 2004.

Nothing, however, could compare to the sense of awe that Steven experienced entering the Green Chamber for the first time as an MP. As the members filed in, Steven felt an almost overwhelming sense of power fill the room. "It was beyond any of my expectations. Two years earlier I would never have thought it was possible. To be in the same room with such powerful people, collectively representing every single Canadian in the country, is thrilling. All Canada sits in the Chamber. I am not 'Steven' there. There I am recognized only as the member from Charleswood–St. James–Assiniboia. I am called by the name of my constituency.

"So many things, from sitting in caucus or in the shadow cabinet to debating bills and meeting delegations, have made me cognizant of the many MPs who have gone before me and who will come after me; all of us part of Canada's history. If I could have pinched myself," he says, "there were times when I would have done so, just to make sure I wasn't dreaming."

Steven was caught off guard when he asked his first question in the House of Commons, for every MP stood spontaneously to give him a loud and prolonged ovation, which echoed through the House. They were applauding his courage and stamina. They knew, as no one else could know, how difficult it is to become elected, and what an honour it is to be chosen. They also knew that his presence among them, as a profoundly disabled person elected for his abilities, was significant. It was the next level of integration, and they supported it. Steven, deeply moved by the tribute, said "Wow," and then pointed out that the Liberal members might not be so happy to have him there once he asked his first question, which he promptly did.

Significantly, his first question heralded his first cause. He asked the minister of Health when he would compensate the excluded victims of the tainted blood scandal, those individuals who had contracted the deadly hepatitis C through contaminated blood transfusions given them by the Canadian health system.

In the summer of 2004, Stephen Harper, leader of the Conservative Party of Canada, had appointed Steven to be senior health critic for the Official Opposition. Given that health care delivery had been one of the biggest issues debated during the election campaign, his appointment, which carried considerable responsibility, was significant. After lobbying for so many years for improvements to the Canadian health care system, Steven was now in a position to actually do something about things he had witnessed or experienced in the years since his accident.

The governing Liberals, under Prime Minister Paul Martin, had made an election promise to fix health care in one generation. Martin had scheduled a meeting of premiers and territorial leaders to discuss this and other health care-related campaign promises.

Steven attended the event and was thunderstruck by how disorganized it was. "Any of the classes in any of the junior high schools in my constituency could have organized an event better than this one," he recalls. A health accord was eventually struck, however, which would transfer $42 billion to the provinces over a ten-year period, with no strings attached. Knowing that the provinces didn't always use health care dollars wisely, Steven had concerns about the "no strings attached" approach.

"Where," he asked, "is the accountability?" He drew the question to the attention of the public and soon MPs were getting phone calls from their constituents. "Where," they asked, "is the accountability?" It seemed clear to Steven that this agreement would be insufficient to meet the needs of Canadians and he advocated improvements.

After many frustrating experiences watching the government sit on meaningful health care reform, Steven had another question for the prime minister. "You say you are going to fix health care in one generation. Can you tell me in which generation that will be?"

◆ ◼ ◆ ◼ ◆

MPs need a place to stay when they are in Ottawa. But Steven needed more than simple accommodation. He needed continuous twenty-four-hour attendant care, accessible housing, medical equipment, and specialized transportation; essentially everything he had in his home in Winnipeg would have to be duplicated in Ottawa. Travel arrangements for his regular flights between the two cities would also have to be organized.

Accessible housing is hard to find at the best of times, and Steven needed it both quickly and close to Parliament Hill. Any dwelling close to the Hill is, naturally, expensive. With a realtor, Steven viewed a number of options, and eventually found and purchased a condo close to the Hill that could accommodate his needs, as well as those of his attendants. The condo required modifications, but it would work.

Ground transportation in Ottawa initially posed a problem. Originally, Steven planned to take his chair with him when he travelled back and forth between his constituency and Parliament. He could do this at first; Air Canada was operating 737 jets on his route, which had cargo holds large enough to accommodate his oversize wheelchair. Unfortunately, the airline soon switched to smaller regional jets. Steven's only option was to purchase a second wheelchair, which remains in Ottawa. This allows him to travel between the two cities with manageable challenges, and reduces the wear on the costly and delicate wheelchair machinery.

When Steven was first elected, he simply rolled his wheelchair from his home in Ottawa to the Parliament Buildings. He enjoyed the outing and found the method worked well—until the snow arrived. Then he quickly learned that maneuvering down the icy, snow-packed Ottawa hills was very different than rolling along the Winnipeg's flat streets and sidewalks.

Third-party accessible transportation was available, but proved to be unreliable because it was so much in demand. Steven endured some horrendously long waits for a handi-cab while his presence was urgently required elsewhere. Eventually, he found a practical solution in the wheelchair-accessible van operated by the House of Commons.

Steven's most important need was continuous twenty-four-hour attendant care. As indicated earlier, Melissa Anderson travelled with him to and from Winnipeg and accompanied him through his parliamentary day. Wherever he went on Parliament Hill, Melissa was at his side. She was given clearance to attend shadow cabinet meetings, national caucus meetings, stakeholder forums and social receptions. Another attendant from Winnipeg was also in Ottawa when Steven was in town. When Melissa's daytime shift was over, the second attendant took over for the evening and overnight. For Melissa, this was a gruelling schedule, as Steven returned to Winnipeg every weekend, but she never complained and was always professional, discreet and gracious.

Though Steven and his friends and family were delighted for Melissa when she married, it meant that she could no longer maintain the hectic travel schedule. But finding a replacement with her strong capabilities was nearly impossible. Finally, Steven decided to hire an Ottawa-based attendant to provide him with care during his days, while a Winnipeg-based attendant travelled with him and managed the evening shifts. His travel schedule is so intense that his attendants' schedules have to be rotated so they can have respite.

Seeking quality attendant care is difficult at the best of times, but it is an extraordinary challenge to find and retain individuals with superior skills, who can not only handle the physical, medical and personal needs of their remarkable client, but who can also manage the social graces, traditions and business acumen required for Ottawa politicking. However, Steven has had incredible success finding and retaining remarkable people to fill what is truly a unique position in Canada.

✦ ✖ ✦ ✖ ✦

AS health critic, Steven faced many issues that had been clamouring for resolution for years. One particularly urgent issue, the subject of his first question in the House, he resolved to bring rapidly to conclusion.

Many Canadians had received blood transfusions infected with the hepatitis C virus in the 1980s and 1990s. The Canadian Red Cross, over which the Canadian government had ultimate authority, acknowledged responsibility for the disaster, and the Liberal government under Prime Minister Jean Chrétien subsequently compensated hepatitis C victims who had received contaminated blood between 1986 and 1990 for their suffering and loss. However, this left no compensation for victims who received transfusions outside this parameter. These terminally ill Canadians were known as the "forgotten victims".

Steven constantly raised the issue in the House, probing and questioning the minister of Health, demanding that the forgotten victims be compensated. He contacted the suffering victims and told decision makers of the misery the disease could inflict.

Through the House of Commons Health Committee, he brought forward a motion demanding that the compensation agreement be revised, and managed to get it passed. On April 20, 2005, the House of Commons supported Steven's motion to pay damages to all hepatitis C victims, including those who had been previously excluded. It was a triumphant moment and he was ecstatic, as were the many victims. They wrote and phoned him expressing their deep gratitude for his persistence.

Among the hundreds of expressions of gratitude that poured into Steven's office was this, from a young wife and mother: "I am a victim of a bad blood transfusion. Blood Services Canada has admitted the Hep C virus that I carry comes from an infected blood transfusion received in April 1991 ... I would like to thank you for being our

Melissa Anderson sits at Steven's side as his fellow MPs applaud his ground-breaking arrival in Parliament.

voice in Ottawa; without it, we would be completely forgotten."

The joy faded with the months however, since the Liberals simply ignored the mandate the government had been given by the House. Steven began to ask questions again, this time to inquire when the government would do the right thing and honour the will of Parliament.

His relentless advocacy on behalf of hepatitis C victims infected by tainted blood was ultimately successful. Within months of the Conservatives forming a government, a $1 billion-dollar compensation package was established for the forgotten victims.

✦ ◼ ✦ ◼ ✦

NOT all the health issues on which Steven worked were inherited, and not all members of opposing parties work in opposition to one another. On one of the flights back to Ottawa from Winnipeg, Steven sat next to Pat Martin, NDP MP for Winnipeg Centre. In conversation, Martin told Steven that he wanted to bring forward a motion that would lead to the eventual banning of trans-fats from Canada's food supply. Martin provided Steven with background material and information about the artificially produced unsaturated fats, which are commonly linked to coronary heart disease and other chronic health problems, and the two of them decided to work together.

The first draft motion Martin showed Steven had NDP approval, but was not acceptable to the Conservatives because it didn't address concerns sure to be raised by many stakeholders, such as industry producers, restaurant owners and international trade bodies. The motion was reworked throughout the night around a table in Steven's office with Pat Martin and NDP House Leader Libby Davis. Steven took the finished product to the Conservative caucus, where it was debated and allowed to go forward to a free vote for Conservatives. The motion passed. Though there was some resistance at the time, it is now generally accepted by the public and other jurisdictions that trans-fats should be reduced as much as possible in the food supply. Steven's ability to work in a non-partisan manner sets an example for others at all levels of government.

When the Liberal government learned that the NDP and the Conservatives had worked together on the motion, a trans-fat task force, co-chaired by the Heart and Stroke Foundation and including all the stakeholders, was created; it was instructed to provide recommendations to the government within a year. After the Conservatives came to power, Health Minister Tony Clement announced in May 2007 that it was Canada's goal to eliminate all presence of trans-fats in the nation's food supply. Clearly, it sometimes pays to spend time with "members opposite".

XXX

Rolling Right On ...

Ethel Hook was one of Steven's constituents and a volunteer for the Canadian Cancer Society. She had written to him as soon as he was elected. Her letter was one of hundreds in four huge boxes that sat in the middle of the floor when Steven moved into his new Winnipeg constituency office in September 2004. At the official opening, Ethel showed up and asked why he hadn't yet replied, making him aware for the first time of the importance of his position and how beneficial it was to listen to constituents. What Ethel was saying made sense. She wanted a well-thought-out national strategy for the prevention and control of cancer. Canada, it turned out, was the only one in a long list of countries not to have such a national strategy. Steven began to research the topic.

Soon after being appointed the opposition's senior health critic, Steven attended a palliative care luncheon in Winnipeg where he met Dr. Dhali Dhaliwal, president and CEO of CancerCare Manitoba, who introduced him to the work of the Council for the Canadian Strategy for Cancer Control, founded in 2002 by some of Canada's most prestigious doctors and scientists, along with cancer survivors, volunteers from the nation's many cancer organizations and representatives from Health Canada (later part of the Public Health Agency of Canada). The council's aim was to bring together the many disparate stakeholders in the cancer field to create a strategy with the goal of reducing the expected number of new cases of cancer, enhancing the quality of life of those living with cancer, and lessening the likelihood of Canadians dying from cancer.

After meeting the council's chair, Dr. Simon Sutcliffe, in Vancouver, Steven intensified his research into the topic, discovering that all cancer stakeholder groups had been lobbying the federal government for the implementation of a national strategy since 1999. They had initially presented the idea to David Dodge, former deputy minister of Health under Prime Minister Jean Chrétien. Dodge had been receptive, and under his successor, Ian Green, an agreement had been signed that stated that the council would be responsible for developing a strategy as well as being the vehicle of its implementation.

When the government established the Public Health Agency of Canada, however, it transferred management of the agreement from Health Canada to the new agency. Subsequently, in an atmosphere of bureaucratic confusion, responsibility for the agreement fell through the cracks. The federal government assured the council it was committed to a national strategy for cancer, but there was little to show for it. Under the Martin government, the agreement began to fall apart.

The cancer community told Steven that the strategy would be included in the Liberal budget of February 2005. However, to their immense disappointment, the budget made no reference to it. Then, at a May 2005 meeting of the council—after nearly six years of growth and advocacy—federal government representatives abstained from approving a business plan for the strategy. It was evident to other council members that the federal government preferred to control any cancer care initiatives on its own, rather than to cede control to an arm's-length group.

The abstention and its rationale angered many in the cancer community, especially those who had been signatories to the original agreements and who had spent thousands of volunteer hours developing a plan that harnessed the very best of Canada's cancer expertise.

Astonished that so much hard work was being set aside without debate, Steven resolved to take immediate steps to force the government to reconsider the merits of the cancer community's plan. After carefully examining it, he was impressed with its thorough analytical base and its innovative governance model. The strategy included a risk-management performance-based framework from the banking industry, established quantifiable goals against which progress could be measured, and incorporated the patient perspective directly into the development of health policy through the establishment of the Canadian Cancer Action Network (CCAN). The plan brought all levels of government, cancer experts, and patient representatives to the decision-making table.

With his extensive personal experience in, and knowledge of, Canada's health care system, and with an MBA and an engineering degree, Steven understood the merits of the business plan and was eager to see it implemented.

In June 2005, the Conservatives had the opportunity to bring forward a supply day motion on any topic they chose. Steven submitted one to the Conservative house leader's office calling on the Liberal government to fully fund and implement the strategy for cancer control, as part of a package that included developing a national strategy for mental health and for cardiovascular illness. Steven's proposed motion was accepted by the Conservatives, and was scheduled for presentation to the House of Commons on June 7, 2005.

Steven had forty-eight hours to prepare for the debate. It was quite an undertaking, for he had received information that Liberal backbenchers had been instructed to vote against the motion. Calling on key advocates in the cancer, mental health and cardiovascular health disciplines, he asked for help to ensure that the House was informed about the issues and that the supply day motion would pass.

Such was the strength of their commitment that many advocates arrived in the Parliament Buildings at seven a.m. on the day of the vote and stayed for the entire day, watching the debate on the television monitor in Steven's office. Some had worked throughout the night before, preparing information for lobbying and debate. Others flew in from across the country. Among the chief stakeholders who took the time and trouble to be in Ottawa for the vote were Dr. Barbara Whylie, CEO of the Canadian Cancer Society and National Cancer Institute of Canada, Dr. Brent Schacter, chair of the Canadian Association of Provincial Cancer Agencies, and Dr. Jo Kennelly, director of scientific advancement and public policy for the National Cancer Institute of Canada.

Throughout the debate, they met with members of all parties, pointing out the various merits of their case, and reminding MPs that since Steven's motion was non-partisan in nature, all those in the Commons should support it. Meanwhile, those in Steven's office kept in touch with constituents in federal ridings across the country. In turn, these constituents, thanks to modern technology, immediately contacted their respective MPs, urging them to vote for the motion. Government backbenchers were besieged by hundreds of phone calls, emails, faxes and visitors from their own ridings.

Kennelly, a key advocate for the cancer strategy, said, "We were part of the debate, even though we were outside the House, and it was an amazing, empowering feeling. We knew we were making a difference, as each MP we contacted began to waver. We had a well-thought-out plan and it had widespread support. We pointed out what cannot be denied—that cancer doesn't discriminate. It can hit us all. There was true-life altruistic politics happening in Steven's office, with all of us crowded there, on our phones and Blackberries, working to convince MPs of the importance of this vote, to help them see that

Above: With Dr. Barbara Whylie, Chief Executive Officer, Canadian Cancer Society; Dr. Simon Sutcliffe, President, British Columbia Cancer Agency, and Esther Green, Chief Nursing Officer, Cancer Care Ontario. Below: Being honoured by Barbara Whylie of the Canadian Cancer Society for Courage and Vision in Public Policy.

lives could be saved, suffering alleviated, and illness prevented if this motion passed."

Initially, Paul Martin's minority government was resistant to the motion, but as the day went on, grassroots democracy began to triumph. The Liberal backbenchers were frazzled. There was no time for the Liberal hierarchy to plan an effective alternative to a negative vote. Finally Steven was informed by "credible sources" that the back-benchers had approached the Liberal Party whip to say that for them to vote against the strategy would be political suicide.

The intensive lobbying effort had been successful. The NDP was greatly supportive of the motion (and had been since the beginning), while the Bloc Québécois was not inclined to support a "national" approach and would therefore vote against the motion. In the end, the Liberals supported the motion and with their votes added to those of the Conservatives and NDP, it carried.

Within days after the passage, however, the government denied access to implementation mechanisms and funding for the strategies. Steven was not pleased. Neither was Stephen Harper, who noted that while the governing Liberals had joined the opposition parties in voting for Steven Fletcher's motion, the Liberals "failed to respect the will of the House of Commons and have provided no further funding for the strategy. [The Liberals] stood and voted for the Conservative motion to support the Canadian Strategy for Cancer Control, but did nothing to make it a reality," said Harper.

About six months after the vote, after Liberal ministers Ujjal Dosanjh and Carolyn Bennett had been subjected to relentless badgering from Steven, Paul Martin introduced a mini-budget, which included support for the Canadian Strategy for Cancer Control. Unfortunately, the support was substantially narrowed and presented without debate. And adding salt to the wound, government support would be for "a" (not "the") cancer strategy, to be implemented by the Ottawa bureaucracy. Martin threw out what is commonly referred to as a "candy scramble"—small bits of inadequate funding for which recipients must search.

In the 2006 general election, the Conservatives' campaign plat-form featured the exact wording of Steven's motion passed by the House of Commons. When the Conservatives formed the govern-ment, the Canadian Cancer Control Strategy was implemented with an investment of $260 million over five years.

In recognition of his work in bringing about the strategy, Steven was awarded the inaugural Award for Outstanding Individual

Leadership and the Courage and Leadership Award by the National Cancer Leadership Forum, the umbrella organization for all cancer groups in the country, including the Canadian Cancer Society, Canadian Breast Cancer Society, and many others. The award was presented at the NCLF 2006 forum, which was attended by key decision-makers in the cancer community, including Health Minister Tony Clement.

Steven was heralded as the catalyst for this initiative by cancer organizations across Canada, since he had effectively pressured, pushed and promoted the initiative. However, while he may have been the catalyst in Ottawa, it was his willingness to listen to and learn from local constituents and people in the field—the grassroots of Canada—that ended in such positive results for the nation.

Steven's determination to succeed was a huge factor in the ultimate victory for health advocates. As Dr. Kennelly reflects, "It is absolutely clear to those of us who watched this political drama unfold, that without the stubborn refusal of this young parliamentarian to accept 'no' for an answer, such a significant health strategy would not have become reality."

The Conservative government also followed through on Steven's motion with the creation of a working group for cardiovascular disease that includes stakeholders from across Canada, and a mental health commission, which is chaired by a former Liberal senator, Michael Kirby.

XXXI

And Rolling Some More ...

T he **Parliament in Ottawa** is not the only place MPs work. They also work from their constituency offices, where local matters are often, though not exclusively, the focus. For his own constituency office, Steven wanted a highly motivated staff. He wasn't looking for people seeking a nine-to-five job and he made it clear to applicants that, if they were hired, the hours would be long, the pay low, and the work hard.

When he came across Scott McFadyen, he knew he had found the right person. Young, enthusiastic and brimming with energy and commitment, McFadyen was well qualified for the job. He had majored in history and political science at the University of Manitoba, Steven's alma mater, and in the mid-'90s had been involved in student politics, both as vice-president of the students' union and as a presidential campaign manager. Student politics, Steven believes, is a good training ground for party politics.

"The University of Manitoba is the second-largest city in Manitoba, bigger than the city of Brandon," McFadyen notes. "It arguably has people that are far more radical than those who are off-campus. Manitoba students will disagree just for the sake of disagreeing, debate the negative side of every question, and ask questions as if they were in federal or provincial Question Periods. Most politicians probably wouldn't last five minutes on campus. Things can be really brutal there."

Like Steven, McFadyen was also an avid sportsman. He had led his rink to win the Canadian junior men's curling championship and participated in many other team sports. Like Steven, he understood the self-discipline required to excel in a sport at a national level and knew that such discipline spilled over into other aspects of an individual's life. Moreover, McFadyen had been reared in a family in which the word "politician" was not considered negative. With many of his relatives elected politicians and with public service honoured and respected in his family, he understood what was involved in looking after a constituency.

Though initially hired as Steven's constituency assistant, in short order McFadyen became his executive assistant, in charge of the constituency office. This position was, as Steven had forewarned, a round-the-clock, get-no-rest position. Official office hours were posted on the door, but once public hours were over for the day, the real work began. Laughs McFadyen: "I learned that the reward for hard work was more hard work!"

For accessibility for both him and constituents, Steven chose an office that was basically a large, open barn of a room, approximately 100 square metres in size. It had a front door that opened to a parking lot, a back door that opened to a lane, and washroom accommodations that could be modified to serve people confined to wheelchairs. And that was it. It had no internal walls, no phones, no computers, no furniture, no window blinds. It had nothing but four huge boxes of correspondence sitting in the middle of the floor waiting to be sorted and people lined up outside the door waiting to be seen.

Because Steven had made history by becoming the first high-level quadriplegic elected to the Canada's Parliament, he attracted a lot of attention. He received congratulations, not just from constituents and friends, but also from people all over the world who were inspired by his achievement. Steven read each letter and email, marvelling that so many people would even know of him, let alone take the time to write.

That first summer, Steven's staff consisted of McFadyen, Myrrhanda Keam (now Novak), Donna Alexander and me.

Myrrhanda Keam's family lived in the constituency. She was a cheerful young woman with boundless energy. She laughed easily and was enthusiastic about her work. Constituents coming into the office were charmed by her personality and genuine interest in others. When she returned to Carleton University in the fall to continue her journalism studies, she continued to do occasional communications work for Steven in Ottawa.

Donna Alexander and I, the two older staff members, each

worked half time. Having been around the block more than once, we were able to offer many years of experience—in fact many, many years of experience—to the mix. The younger staff members saw the things that we had done seemingly just yesterday as historical events. Remarkably, the mix worked. Steven was blessed as well with a small army of other dedicated volunteers who kept on top of the endless chores that needed to be done for the office outreach program.

The first day of work, with the constituency office not ready for occupancy, Scott and Myrrhanda worked out of Steven's house. The phone rang constantly. Within the first hour, they got a call from a woman frantic with worry and desperate for help. Her agitation, coupled with a heavy African accent, made her difficult to understand at first, but as she calmed herself, her plea became clear: She had fled war-torn Congo for Canada seeking safety for herself and her three children. She had found a job and an apartment, but she was deeply upset because her children were still in Africa, caught in immigration limbo, with a deadline quickly approaching.

It would have been entirely in order for Steven to have directed his constituent to the federal minister responsible for immigration (at that time Liberal Judy Sgro), but he knew that passing the buck would mean the file's lingering in the bureaucratic maze of the minister's office and the deadline in all likelihood passing. Further delays would be torture for the mother, who was already at her wits end trying to cope with a faceless bureaucracy. Deeply concerned over the woman's plight, Steven instructed Scott to follow up. "Bottom line here is that these kids must join their mom in Canada," he said, handing the phone over to McFadyen. So began the first team effort by the MP for Charleswood–St. James–Assiniboia and his executive assistant to solve a constituent problem. It was not yet noon on Day One, and it established the pattern of service that would become a hallmark of the Fletcher constituency office.

McFadyen followed through as instructed. After much searching, he was able to locate the children's immigration files, split between the Ivory Coast Embassies in Africa and France. With the clock ticking down, McFadyen met the deadline. One day before the children's files were to be closed, he managed to keep them open by asking for them to be updated. This was salvation at the eleventh hour, and it spared the mother the agony of having to leave her children in the Congo, while she attempted to initiate the long and difficult immigration process all over again.

After many weeks of intense contact, the children were reunited with their mother in Canada. It was a day of great celebration for the family and for Steven and his office staff when the children stopped by to say thank you. Everyone wept unabashedly as mother, children and constituency staff embraced. The children, bundled in winter jackets and scarves, their faces beaming and eyes glowing, looked incredibly happy despite the unaccustomed cold. The family will never forget the advocacy Steven initiated on their behalf and he, who truly understands how strong a mother's love can be, will never forget the relief he felt when he knew the children were finally safely in Canada with their mother.

◆ ◼ ◆ ◼ ◆

"WE set up the constituency office pretty quickly," McFadyen recalls, "and with all the activity, I didn't notice until twelve days had gone by that neither Steven nor I had taken a break. We hadn't been home except to sleep in nearly two weeks. I think it was about then that I realized that Steven doesn't take days off, period. So I started to schedule Sundays off, but still Steven didn't rest. He would go to the early service at his own church and then visit other churches in the constituency. If he knew someone was in the hospital, he would go and visit that person on a Sunday, because he felt patients in hospitals needed visitors. Despite my best efforts, I couldn't get him to just stay at home and relax, not even for a minute.

"Still, it was easy to keep the long hours, because working with Steven was an incredible experience. No matter what happened, he never complained. He was cheerful and generous, which I appreciated. I like a good laugh and Steven was always ready to laugh. I forget what we found so funny one day, but we were howling with laughter when one of our constituents came in. She promptly scolded us, pointing out that ours was a government office and we shouldn't be having fun in it. So we struggled to look serious during her visit, but after she left we started laughing again, which Steven said was okay, as long as it wasn't fun."

Working for Steven was never boring. He rose above his physical circumstances and focused so intently on the task at hand that everything else going on around him became temporarily irrelevant. He visualized the big picture, the end goal, and headed straight for it. When staff members indicated obstacles that seemed to be in the way of reaching a particular objective he would say, "Those are just details. We'll work them out." And somehow they always did. After all, if the boss dismisses details as an impediment to action, one is inclined to just get on with it and settle the details. It saves a step in the process. Ultimately, things got done because everyone in the office believed they could be done.

It didn't take long for McFadyen to realize that the man with the disability had an amazing ability—he simply didn't get physically tired. While everyone else wore out, Steven could just roll on forever. There was no physical fatigue. "There were moments", he recalls, "when I, a mere mortal, felt it would be pretty easy to become overwhelmed at the volume of work ahead of us. Yet Steven would be there at my elbow like a puppy with a ball, asking 'OK, What's next?'

"If I said there was nothing, he would say 'Why not? There's always something.' I would heave a pathetic sigh and let my shoulders sag in an exaggerated display of fatigue, but there was no sympathy. Steven would just laugh, spurring us both to action. He never took breaks of his own volition. I built up my endurance level trying to keep pace with him."

In 2006, Scott went to Ottawa to be Steven's executive assistant in his role as parliamentary secretary to the minister of Health. Almost every time Steven visited organizations, Scott got calls from cautious hosts asking for details about Steven's chair, or his food requirements or other concerns about his quadriplegia. In fact he has no unique food requirements, but the questions were appreciated because they helped make sure Steven's visits went smoothly. However they also revealed how little the public knows about spinal cord injuries. Even top health officials aren't necessarily attuned to the needs of a high-level quadriplegic. This lack of awareness is often accompanied by a sense of urgency—a fear that something will inadvertently go wrong while Steven is with them. By second visits, though, most people have relaxed.

Wherever possible, Steven circumvents the logistical problems. He travels with his own ramps and meets people in parking lots if their buildings are inaccessible. Nothing stops him. Once he was a guest at dinner at the British High Commission, where no elevator could accommodate his wheelchair. It didn't bother him, though the high commissioner felt very badly. He had a table set up for Steven on the main floor and fellow diners came to visit him there. This allowed Steven one-on-one conversations, which he particularly enjoyed. "The thing is," he says, "you have to take things as they come. The more often we do these things, the more others learn. In the meantime, it keeps me humble."

✦ ◼ ✦ ◼ ✦

IN his first week as an MP, Steven began planning regular public meetings with his constituents, which became known as Fletcher Forums. The format is simple and uncomplicated. Steven chooses a topic for discussion from a variety of sources—suggestions from constituents being foremost—then advertises it along with the time and place (though most forums take place on a Saturday morning at the constituency office). Steven frequently brings in a guest speaker with expertise on the topic of the day and issues specific invitations to groups and individuals known to have an interest in that topic. Between 2004 and 2007, sixty-five Fletcher Forums were held, with an average attendance of about thirty-five people at each. Conversations at the forums are lively, and ideas and information flow freely. Steven welcomes the input and feedback he receives through such sessions, and his constituents know that he takes their concerns seriously.

Steven was a champion of reducing wait times for patients seeking medical care. Conservative leader Stephen Harper's wait-times guarantee, announced as an election promise during the 2006 election campaign, had Steven Fletcher's fine touch all over it. Steven's constituency office was the site for the announcement and, as each province signed on, he felt a growing satisfaction. He remembered the stress of having to endure lengthy waits for care, and was eager to see the initiative to reduce wait times put into effect.

"Steven's initiatives cross many areas of interest," says Scott. "His outspoken advocacy for the needs of Canada's Armed Forces, as well as his public defence forums have helped to educate and inform the public about the importance of Canada's military. Steven's motion to allow the auditor general to audit the $9 billion given to government-related health foundations successfully passed, as he was able to persuade MPs that Canadians have the right to know how the money earmarked for health care is being used. He has a wide range of issues that keep him on the go."

Scott had plenty of opportunity to interact with office staff from other political parties, because Steven didn't hesitate to work with politicians from other parties if such cooperation would further what he considered to be worthy causes. In addition to working with NDP MP Pat Martin on the trans-fat initiative, Steven has also worked with Liberal MP Andy Scott to draft the motion for a national strategy on the treatment of persons with autism.

"Steven has a nice natural way of empowering people," Scott McFadyen says. "He doesn't take ownership of a person's problems unless or until all other options are explored. He will instead identify the steps that people should take to solve the problem themselves. He'll say 'Here's what you should do and here is how you should do it.' He'll give the person phone numbers and contacts and suggestions and ask for a report back on the progress being made. He encourages and guides people, like a good teacher. He shows people that politicians don't have magic wands to solve all problems, and that individuals can do a lot on their own, if they just know where to start. His own iron will to overcome any dilemma placed in front of him seems to be contagious in these circumstances, and he inspires others to tackle their own dilemmas. Sometimes all people need is some direction to get going on their own, and he knows how to direct them. I know Steven says that before the accident a political career would have been Choice Z on his list, but I think the fact that he has ended up as a politician is a gift from above for the people of Charleswood–St. James–Assiniboia."

Scott was keenly and emotionally aware of Steven's quadriplegia on only two occasions. One was when Steven, raised to standing position in the House of Commons by his experimental hydraulic chair, became light-headed from the rapid rise and unable to speak. The other was when Steven, determined to sign his own oath swearing him in as parliamentary secretary to the Minister of Health, used a pen held in his mouth to affix his signature to the document. This was a time when a signature stamp simply wouldn't do. Both occasions moved Scott deeply. "I had to shake my head to hold back the tears, and remind myself of a fact I usually didn't think too much about— that Steven is totally paralysed from the neck down. I was struck by the knowledge that what he was doing was amazing, absolutely amazing. I was quite overcome."

Scott was eventually offered another job opportunity, still in the political realm he loves, that would give him more experience both inside and outside of Parliament. He decided to accept the job and assumed his new duties in late 2006.

"Steven and I have shared a lot and we are close friends," he tells me, "but with our busy schedules, we don't get to spend much time together anymore. I felt a major void in my life when I left his office. It kind of surprised me to feel such a sense of loss. I miss his cheerfulness, his smile, the daily contact. Working with Steven Fletcher was a unique experience."

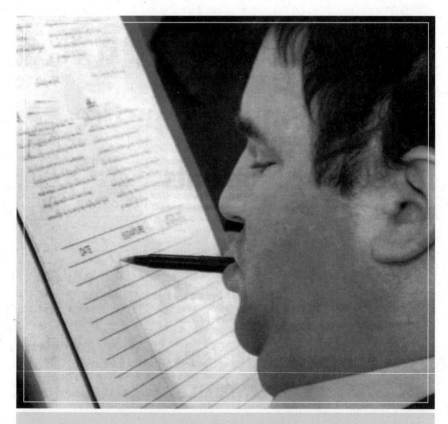

Holding his pen in his mouth, Steven signs his papers as parliamentary secretary to the minister of Health. In many other ways, he continues to make a mark in Parliament.

XXXII

Campaigning in the Cold

The 2005–2006 Canadian federal election campaign was eight weeks long, and with Christmas and New Year's Eve smack in the middle, it was a killer. Not only was the campaign long, but the weather was cold, and with the interruption of the holidays, volunteer numbers started off low. But after January 2nd, things picked up and Steven's campaign office was suddenly alive and bustling. There was a positive side to calling an election for January 23rd: January is usually a slow month for many Canadians, so volunteers had more free time to help campaign, though most sought inside duties rather than outside.

Steven's main opponent was Liberal candidate John Loewen, a high-profile figure who had served as the Progressive Conservative MLA for the southwest Winnipeg riding of Fort Whyte until he announced that he was resigning his provincial Tory seat to run federally for the Liberals. From a wealthy, well-known Manitoba family, Loewen, prior to his election to the Manitoba Legislature, had been president of Comcheq Services Ltd., a multi-million-dollar payroll cheque company founded by his uncle, Bill Loewen. The Loewens were generous patrons of the arts, especially in music and theatre, and were regarded as philanthropists in Winnipeg's cultural community.

Bill Loewen was originally a stalwart Liberal who supported Lloyd Axworthy's failed bid to lead the Liberal Party of Canada in 1990. Two years later, he jumped from the Liberals to become president of the newly formed National Party, a centre-left party that supported economic nationalism. Bill Loewen not only donated $4 million to the new National Party, he also ran as its candidate in Winnipeg South Centre—against his former friend, Lloyd Axworthy.

The National Party didn't win any seats, and after many bitter internal battles and acrimonious lawsuits, the party fell apart in 1994.

Like his uncle, John Loewen harboured political ambitions, and it was rumoured that he would eventually challenge Stuart Murray for the leadership of the provincial PC Party. The rumours ceased in September 2005 when Loewen announced his resignation from both the party and the Manitoba Legislative Assembly, and stated that he was seeking the federal Liberal candidacy for Charleswood–St. James–Assiniboia. Members of the provincial Tory party were taken completely by surprise—particularly since the country was reeling from details of the Gomery Commission, which was investigating allegations of corruption in the Chrétien government. Many Conservatives also felt that Loewen had betrayed them by jumping ship.

Nevertheless, Loewen became the Liberals' new star candidate in Manitoba. While claiming him as their own, Liberals hoped that Conservatives would be able to relate to him, too, and cast their votes accordingly. Loewen likewise believed that his loyal supporters might follow him. But many of his constituents, who had counted on Loewen to represent them in the provincial legislature, were angry that he had quit in mid-term, forcing a by-election they didn't want.

Loewen quickly learned that many voters equated his mid-term desertion with opportunism and disloyalty. He frequently advertised that he had been an MLA, but he rarely mentioned that he had been elected as a Progressive Conservative. Those who knew Loewen's background knew that he had never been elected as a Liberal. However, many who didn't know his political history assumed that he had been a Liberal MLA. Some voters were told that Loewen came from the Tory ranks, while others were left to assume he had long-time Liberal connections. Strategically, if done carefully, he could walk both sides of the street.

It was winter, however, and walking on either side of the street was difficult. But with his Trail Rider wilderness buggy, Steven can traverse almost any kind of terrain, from rocky mountain trails to winter campaign trails. During the January 2006 campaign, members of the media were astonished to see Steven and his sherpas climbing over slippery snow banks and unplowed sidewalks to go door-knocking and meet constituents. The video clips were played across the country.

The Trail Rider came in handy indoors as well, at least on one occasion. During the evenings, Steven would "door knock" through the apartment buildings in his riding. One evening, Steven and his canvassing volunteers found themselves on the top floor of a large

Winter campaigning didn't stop Steven, who relied mainly on his trusty wheelchair. But just for fun, he tackled some ski hill-sized snowbanks in his Trail Rider, with help from his campaign team.

apartment building that only had one elevator. Unfortunately for Steven, the elevator broke down while he was on the top floor. Since his wheelchair weighs nearly 250 kilograms, the stairwell was not an option. Elevator technicians were unavailable, and Steven wanted to avoid the embarrassment of contacting the fire department to be rescued. In the end, one of the volunteers went to get his Trail Rider and Steven was transferred into it. As the volunteers carefully maneuvered Steven down the stairwell, he remarked that maybe he had found his next team of sherpas to attempt the trail to the top of the Burgess Shale.

Steven also had chains made up for his wheelchair, though as it turned out, the chair proved to be quite adept at coping with snow. After the election, there was some difficulty explaining to Elections Canada about Steven's $500 expense for snow chains. One can visit the Elections Canada website and see the expense listed under "other".

Despite the mobility challenges, Steven covered large areas of his constituency each day, and made dozens of phone calls to voters each evening. Though by 2005 he had some name recognition, he knew he had to outwork Loewen. A man who thrives on competition, Steven didn't take a day off during the whole campaign, not even Christmas or New Year's Day.

Max Goldack, who had co-chaired Steven's 2004 campaign with Brian Higgins, was now president of the Charleswood–St. James–Assiniboia Conservative Association. When Max was asked to chair a campaign in the neighbouring riding of Winnipeg South Centre,

Volunteers take a break in the campaign office. From left: Scott McFadyen, Portage-Lisgar MP Brian Pallister, Emmanuel Trawon, Barbara Trawon.

Steven asked Scott McFadyen to take over as campaign co-chair for the election, with Brian Higgins on board again as co-chair. James White, a Queen's University public administration graduate, joined the group as part of the leadership team, and a wider group of volunteers formed the rest of the campaign organization. The campaign leaders set two objectives. One was to win. The second was to increase the margin of victory to strengthen the foundation of support for Steven and the Conservative Party of Canada.

The winter weather posed more problems than just slippery streets and icy beards and mustaches. Volunteers came down with the flu or caught bad colds. Stalled cars and driveways blocked with snow made people late for meetings or office assignments. Still the office was always full and there was plenty of laughter and lots of enthusiasm, good hot coffee and food. Keeping the volunteers well fed was an ongoing way of showing appreciation. Ironically, much of the delicious fare was provided by the volunteers themselves. Added to the homemade goodies was a seemingly endless supply of pizzas. "Fletcher Fare", as it was dubbed, was eagerly gobbled up by hungry helpers and the kitchen became a popular and sometimes overcrowded gathering place.

On their own, however, food, drink and fellowship were not enough to draw people to the campaign office. Their fundamental reason for dropping in was Steven Fletcher. John Alexander tells of one fellow who came in the front door one day and said, "I want to put up signs. I've never been involved in politics before, and you'll never see me again after this campaign, but I sure like your candidate, so I want to help out."

John agreed without hesitation and the volunteer was taken back to meet the sign manager, Don Pickering. He turned out to be a great help. He would drive up, jump out of his truck, run to the office, grab his sign list, load up the signs, and drive out to put them up. "Then he would come back again and repeat the whole routine," John recalls, "I never saw him when he wasn't running. And just as he said, I never saw him again after the campaign.

"That was the type of volunteer Steven attracted," John recalls. "They weren't dyed-in-the-wool partisans. They would just show up and say 'I don't know much about politics, but I like Steven. What can I do to help?'

"It was a different experience for us. Steven seems to bring these people in by the force of his personality. They're drawn to him somehow. He has a knack for making friends, especially when you meet him one on one, because he listens so closely and becomes absorbed in what people are saying.

"What I found unusual was that they often wanted to help but didn't want to get involved in politics. Almost everyone I have known in political circles has an interest they want to push forward, some sort of political interest that affects them, or that they care about, but these people just wanted to get Steven elected. They had no personal agenda or cause."

There was another unusual thing, John says. "People kept coming in to give donations. We always do fundraising between elections to build up funds to eventually run a campaign, but we do a lot of fundraising during the writ [the election campaign] period as well, to meet all the necessary expenditures. In that 2006 election campaign we did no fundraising at all. Money simply poured in the door. I've never seen anything like it. Cheques came in from all across the country, just small amounts of money. One fellow came in with a cheque that he wanted to give because Steven had helped his mother and he thought he was a great MP."

If fundraising was something that almost happened by itself, putting up signs in deep snow and frozen solid ground was a considerable challenge. The team met it with its usual aplomb. "We literally drilled holes in the frozen ground with a piercing tool that our volunteers actually made," says John. "We also had a jackhammer. We had 2,200 signs out in the end.

"Since the signs were frozen stiff, it was easier to damage them. They would crack when kicked or hit. We had repair crews going all the time. Our system was manageable and efficient and the sign crew was outstanding. But not," he jokes, "out standing in the cold."

James White adds, "We used pencils on the canvassing walks because pens often didn't work in the –25°C to –40°C temperatures. We gripped our pencils in hands that quickly became frozen into claws, and plowed our way through snow banks to get to the doors. As the campaign wore on it got colder and colder and we checked each other for frozen cheeks, noses and fingers. We had a box of toques, scarves and mittens that we kept in the office for anyone to use. People were wrapped up so completely in warm clothing that sometimes the only parts that you could see were their eyes and frost-covered eyebrows. As cold as it was, no one backed off, no one backed out."

Not everyone was happy about Steven's candidacy, however. There was the usual vandalism, and in some cases it was direct, deliberate and hostile. Once, a vulgar reference to Steven's quadriplegia was etched with acid on his glass office doors. The glass was restored and the vandalism was never mentioned publicly.

In the midst of the election campaign, Conservative leader Stephen Harper visited Winnipeg to announce that his party would guarantee patients a minimum wait time for medical treatment. As senior health critic, Steven Fletcher had played a significant role in this, and when Harper made his announcement, Steven's office was packed with members of the local and national media.

After Harper had fielded some questions on health care, a local reporter asked him if he thought the Conservative's campaign slogan, "Stand Up for Canada", was appropriate, given that one of the Conservative candidates was in a wheelchair and unable to stand. The crowd gasped audibly, but Fletcher fans liked Harper's response.

Prime Minister Stephen Harper makes his announcement on wait time guarantees in Steven's campaign office.

After pointing out that the slogan was based on a common figure of speech, Harper defended Steven Fletcher as one of the hardest working, most intelligent MPs on the Hill. "Steven Fletcher," he said, "stands up every day for his constituents."

My own political experience had begun at a time when voters were identified with recipe cards coded with coloured dots on the top right hand corners. Over the years, campaigning became more technologically advanced and exciting with the introduction of fax machines, copiers and computers, but for me, nothing was as interesting as blogging. Steven's generation talked about blogging all the time, and at first I didn't have any idea what they meant, until, that is, I saw the question, "Who should win the federal election in Charleswood–St. James–Assiniboia?" appear on someone's blog during the 2005-2006 election. Readers were invited to "Leave a comment/Enregistrer un commentaire."

What follow are some actual excerpts from responses to that question:

> GO JOHN, GO JOHN! I think he has a great shot winning the seat! Steven Fletcher seems to think that the whole damn country should change for him just because he is disabled. (Remember when he wanted them to change all of parliament for him) Its been like that historically why should it change now for one person? ... I do not want Stephen Harper as my Prime Minister! Ah, Imagine that loser running our country!!! SCARY STUFF, PEOPLE, I would advise you all to vote strategically and vote Liberal!
> Comment/commentaire by Sarah

> Fletcher gives hope to disabled people, in contrast to Liberal Star Marc Garneau's views. Fletcher will dispose of his turncoat Liberal opponent John Loewen with greater ease then he dispatched Pretty Boy Glen Murray in 2004.
> Comment/commentaire by David

> Fletcher gives so much hope to disabled? Amazingly when all three party candidates came to my school (I'm a teacher) the students were repulsed by Fletcher's attitude and senseless attacks against Loewen. It was unanimous among the staff and students that Fletcher's defense is simply knocking down the other candidates, whereas the other two had VERY positive and relevant comments about what they would do if elected. Speaking to several students who are disabled in some way (in a wheelchair, etc), they were totally shocked by his terrible attitude ... Fletcher will NOT get my vote ...
> Comment/commentaire by RJ

RJ: Let me just say—if your school is the one that the candidates were at on the 18th—then you're dead wrong about the student's impression of Steven. Steven pretty easily won the student vote afterwards (secret ballot vote) —with Liberal, Green, NDP following up in that order.

Steven's set a new example for representation here. When Harvard was my MP—I never heard from him, didn't receive so much as a letter trying to keep me up to date. With Steven —that's changed. I get fairly regular information about what is going on with the federal Government. He hosted a whole lot of forums, accepting input from everybody in the constituency, not just supporters. Add the work he has done for all Canadians ... and you have one heck of an MP.

Loewen's people were at my door the other day, saying that Fletcher costs the taxpayers a lot of money for his trans-portation—looked at the newspaper today, and they had the travel expenses for all Manitoba MPs there. Steven was second-lowest when it comes to travel expenses.
    Comment/commentaire by Greg

95% of the people (50 or so) from this riding that I've met in the past week will be voting NDP. NDP should receive your vote. I came into this election an undecided voter, and I'm now 110% convinced that NDP is the party which best represents Canadians. It's the obvious choice, do not let the polls persuade you to vote otherwise. FORGET STRATEGIC VOTING!

"FLETCHER" ... he's REFORM ... this is no longer the con-servative party ... The fact that these people are so high up in the poles is bewildering ...

"LOEWEN" ... are wse seriously going to give the liberals our vote again?" seriously????

"NDP" ... visit their site ... Look at all the issues, without any pre-conceived ideas and you will realize that the NDP is the clear choice to be made this election.
    Comment/commentaire by elle

Elle, are you serious? The only person I'm REALLY (capitals are for children) scared of is short sighted people like you that have been indoctrinated with years of liberal spin from all portions of society. I believe in a functioning democracy with viable alternatives, in this case it appears a conservative minority will pull it out (finally). I assure you the day after life will go on, Canada will not burn down, police will not come out on the streets (contrary to Martin's claim), the reformists (lol) will not build a church of intolerance on Capitol Hill. The country will function ... I'm optimistic Canada will be better than ever (we can't become much worse).
Comment/commentaire by Justin

People would go on for days, back and forth, arguing the issues, promoting their candidate and ruthlessly bashing all their opponents. Blogging, it seemed, was one more technological innovation that those in my generation were slow to understand, but which young adults were completely comfortable using. Steven and his crowd saw blogging as a natural and easy way of sharing ideas and opinions. It proved to be an effective communication tool during the election campaign, and was entertaining as well.

✦ ✖ ✦ ✖ ✦

IT was the morning of January 11, 2006, the tenth anniversary, almost to the hour, of Steven's accident. I was sitting on one of the numerous folding chairs in Steven's campaign office, at a long wooden table drinking a cup of coffee laced with far too much cream and sugar, and talking with Joanne Fletcher. We were busy at some simple task, likely folding letters or stuffing envelopes, but our minds were elsewhere. Steven was out and about on a campaign schedule too fast-paced for us to track, so we drank our coffee and tended to our work and thought about the series of events that had led us to this place.

"It's that day again," I finally said, to which Joanne replied, "Yes, it's that day, a hard day."

"But look at what he's doing now."

"And we can help him with this. We can help him win," she said, then paused, "And go on winning every battle he has to face."

The moment passed. The day went on.

✦ ◼ ✦ ◼ ✦

THERE is only one purpose to an election campaign, to get one's candidate elected. Throughout the campaign, volunteers attempt to identify their candidates' supporters, and on Election Day no effort is spared to make sure that those supporters get to the polls and vote.

Election Day, or "E-Day", is clearly the critical day in the campaign. Each party sends official observers, called scrutineers, to the polling stations to oversee the voting process and to report back to campaign headquarters on a regular basis throughout the day. Supporters are phoned and reminded to vote. Volunteers pick up and drive people who need rides to the polls. All energy is devoted to Getting Out The Vote ("GOTV").

The coordinator of E-Day activities plays a critical role in any election campaign. A candidate can have all the supporters in the world and it counts for nothing if they don't vote.

Donna Alexander was the 2006 E-Day coordinator. Early that morning, she met volunteers for breakfast at a local eatery to go over the plans for the day. Heading to the campaign office afterwards, she looked at the clock and noted the time. It was 9:02 a.m. She heaved a sigh of relief. She would be able to park on Portage Avenue, the busy street in front of the campaign office, where parking between 7 and 9 a.m. was forbidden.

At the corner of Portage Avenue and Moray Street, her car was hit by another vehicle. Scott McFadyen came upon the accident scene a few minutes later. The ambulance was already there, but Scott recognized Donna's car and stopped. "I knew it was her car the minute I saw it, even though it was all smashed up, and I knew she was hurt the second I saw the car," says Scott, "When I saw them pulling her out of the car and putting her on a striker board, I held my breath. All of us who work for Steven have a heightened awareness of spinal cord injuries. I knew Donna would be spared Steven's fate when she said that the board was cold on her back. That meant she had sensation."

Donna had several broken ribs, and was badly shaken, battered and bruised, but she was conscious and worried sick about the E-Day organization. When Steven heard Donna had been in an accident, he dropped what he was doing and went straight to the hospital. Donna couldn't believe her eyes when he rolled in. "Go back," she ordered from her bed of pain, "and win that election!" Steven did, but not until he had seen with his own eyes that she was out of jeopardy. Donna was deeply moved that on that day of all days Steven would take the time to make a personal visit to the hospital.

"It would have been completely in order for him to simply be briefed on my condition and carry on with his heavy schedule, and I know that his schedule for the day was full and that every minute was booked solid, because I had helped organize it! No one expected that he should have to come to the hospital in person." For Steven, however, not to have gone to the hospital would have been inconceivable. It was his nature, and one of the reasons he had so many loyal supporters.

That night Steven Fletcher won the election, increasing his plurality from less than 800 to 4,700 votes or forty-seven per cent of the vote. Loewen received forty-six per cent of the vote. In a first-past-the-post multi-party system, anything over forty-five per cent is considered excellent.

Election night 2006 was quite different from election night 2004. All the media outlets were there, which made operations in the campaign office confusing. Huge trailers with giant antennas were parked by the doors and cables that seemed long enough to span the English Channel were everywhere.

"It was organized bedlam," says John Alexander, "When the results came in we posted only the totals, and never lost the lead. When it became obvious that we had won, Steven came in and was covered in silver streamers by the time he got through the crowd to the door. John Loewen arrived at the same time as Fletcher and they met in a cordial fashion. The media surrounded Steven and the media coverage took place right then and there at the door, before Steven could even get in to thank everyone. Longer and more in-depth interviews took place later in the old council chambers. It looked like a crowded movie set in there, with each network's anchor person talking to their cameras while waiting to interview Steven."

The campaign team had a wonderful party in the campaign headquarters until one o'clock in the morning, and then showed up early the next morning to clean up and clear out, content in the knowledge that Steven Fletcher would continue to be their member of Parliament.

XXXIII

Never Underestimate a Man with Wheels

Steven Fletcher's wheelchair is less a chair than a machine, custom-made to fit his frame, height, and very limited head and neck movement. To operate it, he uses his head. The headrest is like a joystick—if he moves his head to the left, the chair will go left; if he pushes his head back, the chair will go forward. A small switch by Steven's left ear enables the chair to go in reverse. When the chair is stationary, Steven, again using head motions, can adjust it to recline, tilt or move the position of the legs. This is important, because it prevents pressure sores and encourages blood circulation.

Most people don't know how Steven operates his chair. For the brave who ask, Steven sometimes replies, "with brain waves."

"Really?" they respond with a momentary look of shock. Of course it's not true, but Steven's had good mileage from the joke.

And speaking of mileage, flying on a large commercial plane can be an exercise in frustration for many travellers. Politicians moving back and forth between their constituencies and the nation's capital are frequently tired, anxious to get to their destinations, and reluctant to spend any more time than necesssary in airport terminals. Waiting patiently is not something most politicians do well. Steven, of course, learned a great deal about the art of patient waiting (pardon the pun) during his long ordeal in hospital. Thus he managed to keep himself calm and composed after one memorable trip, when he landed in Ottawa in the middle of the night only to discover that the airline with which he had travelled had "lost" his 250-kilogram wheelchair en route.

Aide James Montgomery, who was travelling with Steven, directed the airport staff to move Steven from the gateway to the airport chapel, where they laid him on an air mattress with which he always travels "just in case". There he spent the rest of the night, with James sprawled across the doorway, hoping to allow him some much needed rest. When dawn came at last, a multitude of loyal Muslims arrived, answering their early morning call to prayer. Appraised of the situation, and gazing into the chapel at Steven's long recumbent body, they thoughtfully decided to pray elsewhere. Though Steven did sleep well in the quiet of the sanctuary, he would have been happy to share the chapel, and would likely have felt a certain kinship with them, as they touched their heads to the floor.

Steven had to wait until his lost chair was located (it was finally found in Toronto) and flown to Ottawa before he could complete his journey.

✦ ◼ ✦ ◼ ✦

IN 2005, Steven agreed to try out an innovative mechanized chair with an hydraulic lift that could raise people from a sitting to a standing position. This had potential to build strength in his long bones, reduce the chance of pressure sores, provide eye-to-eye contact during conversations, and give his body an opportunity to operate its digestive, respiratory and circulatory systems in a more natural position, to say nothing about getting rid of the pain in his neck that comes from having to look up all the time.

"The standing chair had a lot of benefits," says Steven, "and it may be right for me someday. But one must do a lot of preparation and practice before starting to use such a device. I discovered that I need to build a lot more bodily tolerance before I can utilize one well."

And what led to this discovery?

To begin with, he badly frightened his family, friends and staff when he stood in the House of Commons in his chair. Rising to his full body height and adding the height of the chair's base, Steven was nearly seven feet tall when the chair stopped elevating him. He was a giant, and a giant whose face had turned pale, whose eyes had glazed over and who appeared not to be breathing. He was a giant who had stood to speak, but was saying nothing.

"It was an emotional moment for me," Steven recalls, "because I hadn't stood in public for nine years. I'd practised all week, so I could look cool and suave when I rose majestically to my feet; but when the moment came, I think I went up too quickly, because I was overcome by dizziness and wasn't able to speak for the first few minutes. When I finally was able to breathe and speak again, I apologized for scaring everyone who thought I had become unconscious and I blamed my temporary speechlessness on all the hot air that was floating around the Chamber.

"I'd forgotten how tall I was! My natural body length added to the height of the wheelchair footrests seemed to place me close to the ceiling. It wasn't so, of course; but to go from sitting down and

38th Parliament

Parliamentary Role:
Senior Health Critic

Total Words Spoken in the
House of Commons: 46,734

Total Statements Made in the
House of Commons: 186

Fletcher Quotable:
"I would rather be paralyzed from the
neck down than from the neck up"

Highlight:
• Successfully brought forward a motion to
create national strategies for Cancer Control,
Heart Disease, Mental Health
and Mental Illness

Steven Fletcher, MP
Charleswood-St James-Assiniboia

www.stevenfletcher.ca

Steven was the first Member of Parliament to use trading cards as marketing tools. The card above shows Steven's standing chair. The card back features "Fletcher Quotables", as well as facts and highlights. The quote above reads: *"I would rather be paralyzed from the neck down than from the neck up."*

looking up to Liberals, to standing above them and looking down at the tops of their heads was a bit of a culture shock, as well as a physical one.

"While psychologically it was pleasure to literally look down upon them, there was much more to the experience than that. Standing again made me acutely conscious of the social significance of height, posture and body language. Various studies have shown that tall people are accorded more respect by others than those who are not tall. Tall people are judged to be healthier, make more money and attain greater heights of success (pardon the pun) than their shorter companions. Some economists go as far as to say that correlation between height and income is as dramatic as, if not more dramatic than, the correlation between gender or race and income.

"This reality is reflected in our use of language. We look up to people we admire and down on people we don't. We climb to the top of the corporate/social ladder or fall down into the gutter. When we are happy we are floating on cloud nine. When we are depressed we are down in the dumps. As a man who, pre-accident, had stood six foot, four inches tall, I was somewhat aware of this phenomenon, but since being tall was just a natural part of who I was, I had never really given it much thought. Post-accident, confined to a wheelchair, I felt the stigma of not being tall, of suffering from the same subtle slights that very short people experience. There is something about not being high enough to look another person straight in the eye that can make a man feel diminished. For me especially, unable to move, I would occasionally find myself in situations where I would heartily wish that my eye level and line of vision could be higher. Getting squeezed into an elevator, unable to turn my head and finding myself trapped eyeball to breast with a well-endowed woman, is one such situation. Very awkward, and more than a bit embarrassing.

"Before my accident I was used to looking down at most people because I was tall, and the adjustment I had to make when I ended sitting in a wheelchair looking up was traumatic. My whole view of the world literally changed. Standing after nearly a decade suddenly reversed my perspective again. It was decidedly a weird sensation."

Melissa Anderson, sitting beside Steven in the Chamber, watching his pallor and other body signals, was confident that he would be all right. "I was a bit nervous when he started to get light headed," she recalls, "but he had stood at home and in his office and I knew he'd be okay."

The standing chair gave his staff another cause for concern

during the trial period, when it refused to descend, leaving Steven in a standing position, rolling around the office for hours. While on one hand this was quite funny, it was also cause for concern, for the prolonged standing position placed undue and potentially dangerous stress on Steven's body. Everyone was greatly relieved when he was once again safely in his own chair. "I guess," he said at the time, "it will be a while before I can use this feature on a regular basis."

◆ ◼ ◆ ◼ ◆

IN the summer of 2006, Steven flew to Rio de Janeiro to attend an international public health conference. This was an exciting trip for him, since Brazil was the land of his birth and Rio de Janeiro the city in which he was born. Returning as a "politician of renown", Steven would, among other honours, be meeting with the president of Brazil. James Montgomery and Ashleigh Kraiynk attended Steven on this trip, and they, too, were excited about going to this exotic land.

The international travel arrangements for Steven, as an MP, were made by a source other than Steven's own office. For the first leg of his journey he would be travelling on a plane that was too small to accommodate his oversized chair, so it had to be shipped separately, by cargo. Montgomery and Scott McFadyen went to great lengths to ensure the safe passage of the chair, since its many specialty components make it more than just a device for getting around.

Scott and James arranged for the chair to be cleared and sent on a direct flight from Toronto to Rio. Every aspect of the shipment, including labelling, was checked and double-checked to ensure the chair's safe arrival. The chair was sent by cargo ahead of Steven's departure, so that it would arrive before him and be waiting at the airport when he disembarked in Rio. To help with whatever mobility challenges might be required while journeying, the attendants took a small push chair on Steven's plane.

The trio travelled with no difficulty from Ottawa to Washington, DC. Arriving late, and having to run as fast as they could to catch the connecting plane to São Paulo, they learned the limits of the push chair. It was hard to push and run, and they would have missed the connecting flight altogether had the plane not waited for them. A flight attendant waved them in, holding the door open as they boarded.

"I could feel the air swish behind me as the door clanged shut," said James, "It was that close. We had to maneuver our way down to the very back seats in the economy section, which were the only ones left; and we barely had time to jam Steven into one of them, belting him in as the plane began to taxi down the runway to take off for the nine-hour flight to São Paulo. It was not the most comfortable trip any of us had ever taken."

Landing in Rio on Sunday, Steven was met at the airport by the Canadian ambassador to Brazil, Guillermo Rishchynski, and his assistant, Danae Balcon. The ambassador led them to the baggage claim area, which was where the wheelchair was supposed to be waiting. It wasn't. The airport personnel suggested that they check the cargo building, a twenty-minute drive away. They drove to the cargo building. The chair wasn't there.

After much searching, with the ambassador translating, the wheelchair was located in the customs office—at the airport in São Paulo.

"Why," asked the ambassador, "is it caught up in customs?" After a lengthy conversation with officials, the ambassador turned to tell Steven that the wheelchair was being held in São Paulo because it was considered to be a dangerous good. Its big battery and the many unique and unusual accessories made the chair suspect. Authorities were reluctant to forward it to Rio without absolute confirmation that it would not pose a danger, intentional or otherwise, to Brazilians.

After much explaining and long negotiations, the São Paulo airport authorities agreed to transfer the chair to Rio, promising that it would arrive the next day. This was reassuring, until the other shoe dropped.

"We need to confirm that the chair," said the Brazilian authorities, "is being sent to Mr. Stephen Harper."

No amount of attempting to correct the name of the would-be recipient made any difference. The chair was being sent to Rio for Mr. Stephen Harper, who happened to be the prime minister of Canada.

Steven was to meet with the president of Brazil, Luiz Inácio Lula da Silva, the next day, and he was concerned that his specialized chair might not arrive in time. Not only did he need the chair for medical purposes, but he also wanted to be able to move about independently during the meeting, something that the small push chair would not allow him to do. With the promise that the big chair would be there early the next day echoing in their ears, Steven, James and Ashleigh headed for their hotel.

The chair was sent from São Paulo and did indeed arrive the next morning in Rio as promised. But by noon, it still had not arrived at the hotel. Concerned, James phoned the Canadian consulate and spoke to Danae who promptly called the airport and started the second search for the chair. It was located at the airport, but it was still waiting to be released to Stephen Harper, not Steven Fletcher. By this time it was early Monday afternoon and Steven would likely have to meet with the Brazilian president in the small push chair. The airport was a long drive away from the conference centre, and the chair, partly disassembled for shipping, would need reassembling. Since James knew how to do this, he decided to go with Danae, who spoke Portuguese, to the airport while Ashleigh laboriously pushed Steven around to events in the back-up chair. "It was kind of like driving a car a long distance with a spare tire on one of the wheels," she observed, "or like using a shopping cart with one wheel that refused to turn."

With Brazilian President Luiz Inácio Lula da Silva

When James and Danae arrived at the airport cargo stand, a clerk informed them that he could release the wheelchair, but only to the person whose name was on the crate—Mr. Stephen Harper. Tired from the previous day's travel and having had little, if any, sleep since their arrival, James could only shake his weary head in disbelief.

The two frustrated men went through six supervisors until they reached the head of the cargo department, who finally gave permission for the wheelchair to be released to their custody. They were exultant, but then the baggage workers reported that they couldn't find the crate in the cargo facility. Fortunately, the further frustration was brief. The crate had been moved to another place in the airport and was found within a half-hour.

Before leaving the airport, however, they were presented with a bill for 70 riels (about $35), a storage fee for having had the wheelchair in cargo overnight. James didn't say a word. He just paid the fee.

As for James, all that was left to do was to reassemble the various parts of the wheelchair, which he did in the rented minivan. When they arrived at the conference centre, James was able to roll the beast out in time for Steven to attend the last part of the opening ceremonies, looking splendid and in control.

✦ ◼ ✦ ◼ ✦

IT didn't take long for Steven's chair to hit the prime time spotlight. Rick Mercer wrote the following in a blog after his first meeting with Steven, in 2005: "Fletcher is one of my favorite Tories. He is ... a very funny guy and a great interview. He's also up for anything, which I love in an MP. The first time I interviewed him, we tied a rope to the back of his wheelchair, I got on a razor, and he towed me around the Parliament buildings at a very alarming speed.

"There are certain advantages when shooting a segment on Parliament Hill with a quadriplegic. Normally if I tried to use a scooter on the Hill, I'd be bounced in about three seconds. If you happen to be with a guy in a wheelchair, everyone assumes it's on the up and up. Steven is well aware of this advantage. Rumor has it that as a party trick he will intentionally run into a Liberal and then everyone gets to watch as the Liberal apologizes for being in the way."

COURETSY OF RICK MERCER

Steven, clowning for the cameras with Rick Mercer.

✦ ❚ ✦ ❚ ✦

LANGUAGE is a powerful indicator of attitude. Steven's attitude of independence is reflected in his use of language in referring to himself. His assistants, acting as an extension of him, perform the tasks that his body can not. "We are simply," one young assistant told me, "Steven's hands and feet. Steven himself is in control." That's why Steven does not say, for example, "I'll ask my assistant to drive me to your place at six o'clock so we can pick you up and then he'll drive us to the restaurant for dinner." Instead, he says, "I'll pick you up for dinner at six."

He'll say, "Let me write that down," or "Can I pour you a coffee?" With the use of such language, the rest of us are more inclined to see him as the independent person he has fought so hard to become.

There's an old pop song that includes the line: "You don't talk to me like you use to ..." People sometimes find it embarrassing to "talk like they used to" when they're in conversation with Steven. During the election campaigns, voters would sometimes ask, "Why are you running?" and then pause, flush and stammer. Others would say, "What do you stand for?" and then hastily add "ooops!"

Many words in the English language have more than one meaning. "Stand", for example, by definition has more than a dozen meanings, of which "the ability to support oneself on the feet in an upright position" (Webster) is only one. When Steven talks about what he stands for, he is using the word "stand" as a noun meaning "a strongly or agressively held position, especially on a debatable issue."

People need not worry about embarrassing or offending him by using such words. These are, after all, legitimate ways of speaking English.

XXXIV

Life is Not a Tea Party

On the eleventh anniversary of his accident, I asked Steven to
give me an assessment of how he felt about his life as a C4 quadriplegic. This is what he told me:

> "Living like this is the hardest thing I have ever had
> to cope with. No matter how well things may appear to
> outsiders looking in, believe me this is no tea party. It is
> horrendously difficult to live in this situation. To be intell-
> ectually honest and to give you a realistic assessment of my
> life, I have to tell you that it is brutal. There is a persistent,
> relentless agony that lingers in my soul after all is said and
> done, a sense of hopelessness and sorrow that never quite
> goes away. In terms of quality of life, I would have to say
> I am at the bottom of the class.
>
> "The logistics of just getting up in the morning and
> living through the day are overwhelming. The indignities
> that have to be faced every day to tend to my bodily func-
> tions have to be endured because there is no choice. I have
> learned to accept such things as necessary. I have learned to
> be grateful that there are health care attendants to perform
> these tasks for me. I have not learned, however, to enjoy
> the process.
>
> "I cannot feel my body and sometimes I wonder if it's
> really there. There are so many things about my body that I
> need to be constantly conscious of, things that can seriously

damage or kill me, like autonomic dysreflexia, heart complications, pressure sores, breathing or coughing complications, a sudden change in my body temperature, burns or cuts that could go unnoticed, problems that can occur with my digestive and circulatory systems or problems with tubing and monitoring equipment—so many things that I cannot feel—all of which could suddenly take my life. I think of Christopher Reeve, who died because of a simple pressure sore after working so hard to survive. All of the challenges of getting around and facing obstacles can be exhausting and demoralizing. You'd think you'd get used to it, but you never really do. I worry a lot about the resources I need, because keeping me alive is so expensive.

"The lack of privacy really gets to me. I cannot be left alone, and I am nervous if unattended because of all the things that could go wrong, yet sometimes I long for some privacy, some solitude, like I used to find in the wilderness. I still long for my old life, even though I know it cannot be. I look at the Ottawa River and wish I could play in the white water rapids. Those desires, unrealistic as they are, never go away. My memories of paddling are vivid. I can still name each portage I have taken and where they start and end, and how I felt, when my body was healthy and strong, carrying my canoe over those portages.

I know the potential that was mine at birth will never be fulfilled and I miss the future that could have been. I try not to say 'if only' or 'what if?' but truthfully I can't always keep such thoughts away. It's hard to be consistently positive and count my blessings. Once when I was talking about this with Liisa [a close friend and constituent] and wondering what possible purpose a life like mine could have, she told me 'Steven, your life isn't all about you or what you want. What can you do for others?' She sort of took me aback a bit, but when I thought about it, I felt she had some wisdom in her statement. Who knows what purpose a life like mine serves?

"If I get too much time on my hands I start to reflect on my situation and I become melancholy, deeply sad and feel hopeless. It gets pretty bad, and hard to talk about. I have found the way out of depression is to focus my consciousness on something other than myself. I focus on my work, my contribution to the country. My contribution is a way of mitigating the pain I feel, and knowing I am making a positive difference helps give me a solid reason for carrying on. I have a gift for being able to focus, to be able to concentrate on one thing and block other things out. That ability to compartmentalize my thoughts is imperative for me now, and has helped me in more ways than I can count.

"I have no wife, no children, so my constituents become like a family to me, and my work in Parliament is an opportunity to impact the quality of life for all Canadians. It is one reason for being. I am in to work early, and I leave later than others. This isn't just to distract me from my worries. I genuinely like what I do, and can find many moments of joy in each day, because I am decidedly open to receiving joy.

"It seems contradictory to say that my life is brutal and it's no tea party and then say I like my work and find moments of joy in each day. But I don't think it is. The poet Kahlil Gibran said, 'I would that my life be a tear and a smile ... A tear to unite me with those of a broken heart; a smile to be a sign of joy in my existence.'

"I am definitely more compassionate because of my circumstances. I can feel empathy as well as sympathy for others in distress. I want to help others because I know what agony is, and I don't want people to live in agony. But I have no patience for those who just endlessly whine about their circumstances without trying to find a way to cope. We have to live with what we're handed, like it or not, and do the best we can.

"Still, sometimes in my dreams, I am whole again. I can run like the wind and dive into lakes. I can dance and make love and paddle white water. And then I wake up to my reality and that's when tears can flow."

Appendix A

September 11, 1995

Dear Claire

I have been gone just a day and already I miss you. I enjoyed our Saturday evening walk and canoe video evening and of course our intimate Sunday Afternoon — I felt really close to you this weekend, I hope we MAKE Time in our busy schedules to continue our closeness, intimacy.

When I was driving up to Bissett last night I saw the most spectacular sight, Out of my Right window was a full moon (harvest moon) and on my left was an amazing show of Northern Lights. They swayed, trembled and swam across the sky like angels. I felt as though I was driving down a empty highway not to Bissett, but to the Yukon. The lights were like those described in a Robert Service poem — travelling to the gold mine I imagined myself travelling Through time to the gold rush of the 1880 near Dawson City. Would I meet Sam McGee?

The sense of history & time & souls travelling through the sky was reinforced today when I went into the mine vault. The mine vault is a room encased in concrete with a 12'inch steel door. This is to protect the vaults contents from the most ferocious fires. The vault contains all the mine maps, Assays, old stopes — every bit of work done in the mine since the beginning. Claire these maps go way back to the thirties. I look at them and look at see the writing as if they were written on yesterday by the mine Engineer. (ME!). All that work for all those maps *of* ore (gold) that has long since been removed done by *designed by* forgotten engineers and hand dug by nameless miners. All these perhaps thousands of people & scores of engineers are long since dead — all that is left to mark their being is a long, narrow tunnel deep beneath the earth. Perhaps, the Northern lights I saw last night is their energy, their souls looking down at their forgotten hole, looking to see if their hole will be reopened; *the hole;* remembered for a little while longer before it is forgotten forever. Those miners & engineers came from the earth, they lived to dig in the earth, the forgotten people lay to rest in the earth, the earth comes from star dust and star dust creates the northern lights. I do believe it was the forgotten people who provided me with the spiritual show of lights & angels.

I hope our lives, our dreams, our love will not become forgotten like those *people* before us. I am 23, you are 20 lets <u>live</u> !! Lets be remembered.

Love always & forever

Steve

xoxoxoxoxoxo

Appendix B

THE following article on the Manitoba Public Insurance
Corporation, by Steven Fletcher, appeared in *The Manitoban*
on January 10, 2001.

OVER the past couple of months, Manitoba Public Insurance has
received much publicity. It has enjoyed a $100-million surplus this
year, largely due to the investment income and windfall in revenue
because of new car sales.

The question for MPI now is what to do with all this money?

MPI and the provincial government decided a one-time rate
reduction for motorists and a donation of $20 million to university
infrastructure would be a great way to spend the money. This donation to post-secondary educational institutions was met with public
outrage.

Why should automobile ratepayers subsidize university infrastructure?

Many people claimed the extra money should go to the people
who pay for the insurance. The government wisely listened to the
people and MPI withdrew the donation, instead deciding to increase
the ratepayer discount. Though this may have been a wise political
decision, in my opinion it was the wrong way to go.

I believe MPI must focus on the insurance-benefits side of the
equation. If there is extra money, it should first go to improve benefits.

A large number of people who are suffering because of automobile accidents are not getting the insurance benefits they thought
they would receive when first buying their insurance.

Two of the founding principles of MPI are to restore an individual's quality of life as much as practical to the level it was before the
accident and to compensate individuals for economic loss due to the
accident.

I feel MPI fails on both counts.

Why do I care?

At the age of 23, six months after graduating from engineering,
I hit a moose with my car on the highway between Winnipeg and
Bissett, a small town three hours northeast of Winnipeg.

The accident left me paralyzed from the neck down—a high-
level quadriplegic (C4). The injury has left me with medical, social,
psychological and financial issues I still have trouble comprehending.

Since I could not come close to articulating the medical, social or psychological issues, for the purpose of this article I will focus on the financial implications of my accident.

MPI claims to compensate individuals for economic loss due to a car accident, yet this did not happen. Just about anyone involved in an accident is not compensated appropriately. This is particularly true if the accident is catastrophic in nature (i.e., spinal cord injury, brain injury) and if the victim is a young person.

A young person in a catastrophic accident sees a double-whammy effect, of which I know firsthand. My belief is that everyone should be concerned about this, since it can happen to anyone. Many who read this article have their lives affected by MPI legislation.

Even for a young person in a relatively minor accident, the financial implications can be severe. Here are a few scenarios to illustrate the points.

Economic Loss of Salary:

Scenario one—A student involved in a car accident that prevents her or him from working will be granted an income replacement based on the average industrial wage in Manitoba, which is approximately $30,000.

Therefore a medical student involved in an accident, who is one course away from completion of his/her degree, will be deemed to earn $30,000 for the rest of their life. Though that med student could probably earn a seven-digit salary soon after graduation, it does not matter.

So, any student in Manitoba, who is involved in a serious car accident and reliant on income replacement will be granted the $30,000, regardless of what they were studying, how close they were to graduation, what their goals were in life, or what they would potentially have earned in the future.

Scenario two—Say you are a recent university graduate working in an entry-level position earning $25,000 and you get into a car accident. Your salary would be frozen at 90 per cent of the level you were earning at the time of your accident. It doesn't matter that in five years you would have been earning $50,000, $75,000 or more—you will be stuck at $22,500 for the rest of your life.

Scenario three—You graduate from university and land a $100,000-a-year job, and then get into a car accident. The maximum income replacement is $55,000. If you earn more than $55,000 a year, a definite possibility as a university graduate, you will not be compensated for any amount over $55,000.

Lump sum payments:

For injuries which can "heal," like broken bones and whiplash, there is no compensation. For permanent types of injuries, there are lump sum payments. However, under the current insurance scheme the lump sum payments are inadequate.

First, there is no compensation for pain and suffering. Second, body parts are assigned an arbitrary value based on a "meat chart." For example, a finger is worth $3,000, a leg is worth $10,000, an eye is worth $25,000 and so on.

The "meat chart" equalizes the value of different body parts so that in real terms they are worth approximately the same. In other words, while the severity of an injury is exponential, it compensated on a linear scale. Using MPI logic, the worst types of injuries are worth approximately the same as much less severe injuries.

The maximum compensation for any type of injury is $100,000. There is a tremendous difference between being a quadriplegic and being a paraplegic, but the compensation is about the same over time (and regardless, both compensation levels are too low).

Interestingly, my injury wasn't even on the chart. The differences in quality of life and expenses due to different types of injuries are mind-boggling. If you experience a brain injury, are blinded, lose your hearing and are paralyzed—add any other deformity you would like—the maximum is still $100,000.

Age is not taken into consideration, either.

A 19-year-old who experiences an injury is compensated the same as a 99-year-old with the same type of injury. Obviously, the 19-year-old will experience a great deterioration in the quality of life and will incur greater economic loss due to the injury than the 99-year-old. This is particularly true with the more serious injuries. MPI does not recognize the value of youth. I don't think any of this is fair—do you?

Long-term care:

One of the most important issues an individual with a cata-strophic injury has to deal with is long-term care.

Though MPI claims to sustain the quality of life of an individual as much as practical, its long-term policies do not support this claim. A young person involved in an automobile accident is likely to end up in a long-term institutional care facility, like a nursing home.

After my accident, I faced the prospect of institutional living for the rest of my life. If you are in a similar type of accident, you will have to fight tooth-and-nail to stay in the community. How many young people have had their hopes and dreams evaporate because there is no long-term community living available?

MPI claims it covers the expenses incurred in automobile accidents. Yet this is not the case. For example, there are very low caps on things like attendant care. If your care needs exceed the $3,000 cap per month, and in catastrophic injuries they surely will—you may be institutionalized, or the provincial government may pick up the difference. (If it does, then taxpayers are subsidizing MPI's obligations.)

In both scenarios, you end up being stuck in Manitoba because the government portion is not mobile. In essence, if you incur a serious disability because of an automobile accident, you do not have the right, as every other Canadian does, to live anywhere in Canada.

It can be said that people with severe disabilities are discriminated against under the current MPI legislation.

Ironically, MPI legislation was implemented with the intent of improving benefits for people with severe disabilities caused by automobile accidents. However, the legislation does not address issues of individuals with severe disabilities. MPI can help prevent this by providing adequate funding for long-term care.

If you think ...

If you think you can sustain a serious injury and then work to offset the costs of your injury, you are wrong. MPI will call back almost every nickel you earn from your income replacement. It is actually possible to lose financially if you return to work under the current MPI scheme.

If you think the Canadian Pension Plan will save you, you are wrong. MPI calls back the CPP benefits from your income replacement as well, even though CPP is contributed to separately and is a completely independent plan.

If you think you can get private insurance as a young person to help cover the costs, you are probably wrong. Very few young people qualify or can afford to buy insurance to protect themselves from these types of accidents.

If you think you can hire a lawyer to sue MPI, you are wrong. Under the current no-fault system, you cannot sue MPI or anyone else if it is an automobile accident. (Under the previous system, which used tort law, there were many scenarios where suing wouldn't help either. But that's another story.)

If you think you can appeal decisions made by MPI, it is difficult. To appeal a decision you need a lawyer. Even if you are successful with your appeal (and I have been), you still lose money to lawyer fees, which can be substantial.

MPI will not reimburse you for lawyer expenses, even if you are successful. To make appeals even more unfair, MPI has several floors full of lawyers in their Eaton Place offices, all of them ready to fight appeals. In essence, your insurance dollars go to lawyers paid to fight against you! You are paying both for your lawyer and for their lawyers.

There are some very important positive aspects to the MPI coverage. MPI does help with vocational rehabilitation, physical rehabilitation, and medical expenses such as equipment and medication.

The no-fault system has a tremendous amount of potential, but the substantial problems with MPI coverage need to be fixed.

I have been lobbying for changes to MPI legislation and policies since my accident five years ago on January 11, 1996. My experience with MPI is what first drew me into politics.

Before my accident, I did not give much thought to these types of issues. Yet since my accident, my eyes have been opened wide and I have realized the injustices which go in our medical system and our insurance coverage.

I am determined to contribute to making MPI and other types of insurance fair and equitable.

For years I was told there wasn't enough money. My feelings of disgust resurfaced after the recent announcement by MPI of donations and rate cuts. MPI is not compensating accident victims to the level I believe Manitobans expect.

MPI policies are also particularly harsh on young people. I never thought my position as UMSU president and my experiences would intersect, but here we are.

This is why, as your student union president, I spoke out against the $20-million donation by MPI to post-secondary institutions.

This article has just touched the tip of the iceberg on the MPI issue.

I believe that if MPI is interested in helping students, it should improve benefits for young people. And if the government is serious about funding University infrastructure, then it should do so itself.

Appendix C

IT isn't possible in one short book to detail the many causes Steven Fletcher has championed, or the many organizations that he has supported or in which he has played a leadership role. The following groups, while not outlined in the text of the book itself, have nonetheless been a meaningful part of his life and it's fitting to acknowledge their importance and significance to him by listing them here.

Manitoba Recreational Canoeing Association

Manitoba Naturalists Society

University of Manitoba Board of Governors

Wilderness Access Manitoba

Alumni Association of the University of Manitoba

Disciplinary Committee of the College of Registered Nurses

Disabled Sail Manitoba

Young Associates, I. H. Asper School of Business,
  University of Manitoba

Fort Whyte Nature Centre, now known as Fort Whyte Alive

Army, Navy and Air Force Veterans Unit #286

Charleswood Legion

United Church of Canada

Rick Hansen Man-in-Motion Foundation

Awards and Recognitions
Steven has been honoured in many ways. These honours and recognitions include many presented by individuals, as well as organizations, and in all cases represent remarkable time and effort expended by volunteers. As the author of this book on Steven, I wish there was space enough in this book to tell all these stories, for each is a tale worth knowing. Moreover, Steven is deeply appreciative of all of them, from cards and plaques to major awards.

Highlighted are some of the more publicized recognitions he has been given:

- inducted into the Terry Fox Hall of Fame, 2006;

- awarded the Champions of Mental Health Award for his work in raising awareness for mental health, from the Canadian Alliance on Mental Illness and Mental Health (CAMIMH), 2006;

- recipient of the National Cancer Leadership Forum's (NCLF) inaugural Award for Outstanding Individual Leadership, 2006;

- presented with the Courage and Leadership Award from the Canadian Cancer Society, 2006;

- recipient of the King Clancy Award, for his outstanding accomplishments in helping to increase public awareness about the potential of disabled people, 2006;

- awarded the Commemorative Medal for the Golden Jubilee of Her Majesty Queen Elizabeth II for "exemplary and outstanding contribution to the community and to Canada", December 2002;

- inducted into the Shaftesbury High School Hall of Fame, Business Community category, 2005;

- awarded the Shaftesbury High School grades 10 & 11 Citizenship Awards, 1988 & 1989;

- elected as Shaftesbury High School president, 1990;

- and Manitoba kayak champion, K1, over 500, 1000 and 1500 metres, 1988 & 1989.

Glossary

alphabet board: a board with the alphabet printed on it, enabling a non-verbal paralysed individual to indicate, with a nod or blink, the letter he/she desires to have written down. As the selected letters are written, words are spelled and communication occurs.

ambient temperature: the temperature surrounding an object or individual

assisted cough maneuver, cough reflex: a physical maneuver in which pressure is applied to a patient's abdominal wall to emulate the body's normal coughing reflex and cause the patient to cough, thus removing dust, mucus and saliva from the lungs. Without this cleansing ability, infections occur, leading to pneumonia, or choking can occur, leading to death.

autism: a developmental disorder that is variable in expression but is recognized and diagnosed by impairment of the ability to form normal social relationships, by impairment of the ability to communicate with others, and by stereotyped behavior patterns, especially as exhibited by a preoccupation with repetitive activities of restricted focus. Autism spectrum disorders (ASD) range from mild to severe.

auditor general: an officer of Parliament responsible for the independent examination of the government's accounts. Reports of this examination are tabled in the House of Commons several times a year.

autonomic dysreflexia: occurs when the body reacts to a sensation but doesn't know what it is. It could be anything from a mosquito bite to a bowel blockage, an overfilled bladder or a pressure sore. The body reacts to such unidentified stimuli by increasing blood pressure dramatically. The victim experiences extreme pain, an intense, throbbing headache and excessive perspiration above his/her sensation level. Dysreflexia must be dealt with immediately or a stroke can occur, killing the individual or inflicting brain damage.

backbencher: a Member of Parliament who is not a cabinet minister, a parliamentary secretary, a house leader, a whip or an opposition critic

biofeedback: the technique of making unconscious or involuntary bodily processes (such as heartbeats or brain waves) perceptible to the senses in order to manipulate them by conscious mental control

cabinet: the executive of the government, consisting of those members and senators appointed by the governor general on the advice of the prime minister; cabinet is res-ponsible for the administration of the government and the establishment of its policy.

cabinet minister: a member of the government executive, appointed by the governor general on the advice of the prime minister. Usually chosen from among existing members and senators, ministers are responsible to Parliament for their official actions and those of the government departments they are assigned to run. Cabinet ministers are given the title "Honourable".

catheter: a tubular medical device for insertion into body cavities, usually to permit injection or withdrawal of fluids or to keep a passage open

cerebrospinal fluid (CSF): clear bodily fluid that is secreted from the blood and fills the spaces in the brain and spinal canal. CSF serves to maintain uniform pressure within the brain and spinal cord.

cervical collar (cervical orthosis): an orthopedic apparatus that encircles the neck and supports the chin, used to support and align the neck, or in treatment of injuries to the cervical spine

cervical vertebrae: the first seven vertebrae closest to the skull

collapsed lung (pneumothorax): occurs when air accumulates between the chest wall and the lung, inhibiting breathing by preventing the lung from expanding

complete quadriplegia: a complete severing of the spine which results in complete loss of function from the severed vertebra down, in contrast to a partial severing of the spinal cord which results in varying degrees of mixed function and paralysis (Steven Fletcher has complete quadriplegia at the fourth cervical vertebra)

constituency: an electoral district entitled to elect a member to Parliament to represent it in the House of Commons; also known as a riding

Crown corporation: a business, usually a monopoly, owned by the government. Crown corporations operate at arms length from government under the control of a board of directors appointed by the government, and under the authority and conditions of a government act.

decubitus ulcer, also called a pressure sore: an injury to the skin and the tissue under it which develops when the blood flow carrying essential nutrients and oxygen to the skin is cut off, causing the tissue under the skin to die. In healthy bodies, messages from nerves in the skin will be sent through the spinal cord to the brain to indicate discomfort and the need to move. The brain then issues a command for the body to shift positions, even while sleeping. A person with a spinal cord injury, however, will not be aware that his/her tissue is beginning to break down, since the messages are blocked at the level of injury and never reach the brain. Heavy immobile weight is then left to lie on the skin, stopping the blood flow. If the wound is on one of the body's pressure points—such as the buttocks—the wound will expand and get worse throughout the day, spreading quickly and eating through to the bone, eventually causing infection which in turn can lead to serious medical complications and death.

E-Day: election day in any election campaign

electro-stimulation: electrical stimulation of body tissues

extubation: the removal of a tube which has been placed into an opening in a body

floor of the House: the part of the Chamber of the House of Commons reserved for members of Parliament and officials of the House

front benches: the first few rows of seats in the House of Commons, which on the government side are occupied by the prime minister and the cabinet ministers, and on the opposition side by the leaders of the recognized opposition parties and their principal spokespersons

GOTV: Get Out The Vote, refers to the activities of volunteers making sure their candidate's supporters remember to vote on election day. Activities can include phoning to remind people where and when to vote, and driving people to the voting station

governor general (GG): appointed by the Queen on the recommendation of the prime minister, the governor general represents the Queen in the nation for an unspecified term, which by tradition is usually about five years. The governor general's functions are largely ceremonial and include the reading of the Throne Speech and the dissolution of Parliament at the request of the prime minster.

Hansard, the Official Report of Debates: the verbatim recording of all speeches, questions, statements and debates made by MPs in the House and in Committee of the Whole. Identified as "Hansard", which was the name of the British family originally responsible for the official reporting of debates in the British House of Commons

health care attendant: one who cares for the ongoing medical needs of patients unable to care for themselves

hematuria: the presence of blood or blood cells in the urine

heterotropic ossification: formation of bone in extraskeletal soft tissue, especially in connective or muscle tissue

high level quadriplegia: quadriplegia caused by damage to the brain itself, or damage high up on the spinal cord. If the injury is extremely high up on the spine, for example at the first cervical vertebra (C1), the individual will lose all body function. If the injury is a little lower, but still high on the spine, for example at the seventh cervical vertebra (C7), the individual will likely be paralysed from the chest down, but may still retain some use of the arms and hands.

hospital ER: hospital emergency room where medical emergencies are handled. The emergency room is often actually a series of rooms with equipment and medical staff that provide immediate first treatment to patients experiencing medical trauma. The purpose of the emergency room is to stabilize a patient for further treatment or release.

House of Commons (also called the Lower House): the most representative of the three components of Parliament is the House of Commons; its 308 members are chosen directly by the people of Canada, through their votes. Those elected to the House of Commons carry the title Member of Parliament or MP. Only the House of Commons is constitutionally authorized to introduce legislation concerned with the raising or spending of funds.

Hoyer sling: a cloth sling, frequently made of polyester mesh, in which handicapped individuals can be seated in order to be lifted and moved. The sling, with the person in it, is suspended from a metal lifting device for the lifting and moving action.

hypothermia: occurs when body temperature falls below that required for normal body functioning

indwelling catheter: a long tube inserted into the bladder through the urethra, which drains urine from the body into an external bladder bag taped to the body. The indwelling catheter remains in the body, held in the bladder by a small saline-filled balloon.

intensive care unit, ICU: a specialized unit within a hospital that provides intensive care for patients who are in critical condition, with constant monitoring of patients and round-the-clock treatment

intubation: the introduction of a tube into a hollow bodily organ, such as the trachea. Tracheal intubation is the insertion of a flexible plastic tube down into the trachea to protect a patient's airway and provide a means of mechanical ventilation

leader of the official opposition: the leader of the party holding the second greatest number of seats in the House of Commons

lieutenant governor (LG): appointed by the Queen on the recommendation of the prime minister, the LG represents the Queen in the province to which he/she has been appointed, usually for a five-year term

loss of sensation: the inability to feel external stimuli. Victims will be unaware of cuts, burns, severe frostbite or other injury unless or until the consequences are noticed by someone else. Serious complications can result from lack of attention to such injuries, even if they are small.

magnetic resonance imaging (MRI) machine: a large scanning machine, using a magnetic field and radio waves, which can provide detailed images of the inside of the body in any plane. MRI involves placing the individual to be imaged within a strong magnetic field, usually within a cylindrical shaped unit. Images obtained through MRI are more detailed than most other scanning technologies.

Manitoba Public Insurance (MPI): compulsory vehicle insurance operated under the control of a government appointed board, MPI is a Crown corporation monopoly in the province of Manitoba, Canada

Member of Parliament (MP): an individual, usually a political party's candidate, elected in a local constituency (also called a "riding") to represent that constituency in the federal government

neuron: electrically active cells in the body's nervous system that process and transmit information; also known as a nerve cell

neurosurgeon: a surgeon who specializes in performing surgery involving the nervous system (nerves, brain and spinal cord)

Official Opposition: the party or coalition of parties holding the second largest number of seats in the House of Commons. It is accorded certain financial and procedural advantages over other parties in opposition.

Opposition critic: a member of a party in opposition, responsible for presenting that party's policies in a given area and commenting on those of the government in the same area

osteoporosis: a decrease in bone mass with decreased density and enlargement of bone spaces, producing undesired bone porosity and fragility

Ottawa: the capital city of Canada, located in the province of Ontario, near its border with Québec

paraplegic: one affected with paralysis of the lower half of the body with involvement of both legs

Parliament of Canada: The Canadian Parliament has three components—the Queen, the Senate and the House of Commons. Through these three components, the work of governing Canada is accomplished.

parliamentary secretary: a member of the government party named to assist a minister. A parliamentary secretary may table documents or answer questions on the minister's behalf.

party leader: The person chosen by a political party to provide leadership in Parliament and during election campaigns. Those so chosen are either already members of Parliament or are expected to seek a seat in the House of Commons as soon as possible.

party nomination: the process by which a member of a political party becomes the official candidate for that party for the next election

party president: the person elected by members of a political party to serve as the presiding officer over all aspects of the internal running of the party

physiatrist: a physician who specializes in physical medicine and rehabilitation

physiotherapy (PT): the management of medical problems that cause pain or limit the ability to move. PT also works to restore body functions and develop management plans to help patients achieve healthy lifestyles

plurality: a simple majority

post-traumatic myelomalacia: the softening of the spinal cord after trauma

Precambrian Shield, also called the Canadian Shield: a vast area of bedrock covered with a thin layer of soil that stretches north from the Great Lakes to the Arctic Ocean, and from Labrador to Alberta. The underlying rock structure includes Hudson Bay and the submerged area between North America and Greenland. When Greenland is included, the Shield covers approximately eight million square miles or about twenty million square kilometres. The base rocks are mainly from the Precambrian era (between 4.5 billion and 540 million years ago). The area is covered by boreal forests in the south and tundra in the north, and is one of the world's richest areas in terms of mineral ores.

pressure sore: see decubitus ulcer

prime minister: the leader of the government who is ordinarily the leader of the party having the greatest number of seats in the House of Commons. Appointed by the governor general, the prime minister selects the other members of the cabinet and, along with them, is responsible to the House for the administration of public affairs.

quadriplegic: one affected with paralysis of both arms and legs: (quadra from the Greek, meaning four, and plegia meaning paralysis)

Question Period (officially "Oral Questions"): occurs each day while the Parliament of Canada is sitting. During the forty-five minute Question Period, members of Parliament are able to ask questions of the prime minister and cabinet ministers in order to hold them accountable to the public. Time limits are set for the questioning, and simultaneous translation is provided since questions may be asked or answered in either English or French.

riding: see constituency

Royal Canadian Mounted Police (RCMP): Canada's national police force, it serves as the provincial police in Western Canada and as the municipal police in many small communities

scribe: in this book, the reference to an individual who takes written dictation from another

self-managed care program: home health care in which the patient, under an authorized health care program, hires and instructs his/her own staff and makes decisions regarding equipment and other budgetary items, within the terms of reference of the health care program

Senate: the Canadian Senate consists of 105 individuals appointed by the prime minister to serve until age seventy-five. The Senate reviews bills passed by the House of Commons.

septicemia: an infection in the blood

session of Parliament (parliamentary session): one of the fundamental time periods into which a Parliament is divided, usually consisting of a number of separate sittings. Sessions are begun by a Speech from the Throne and are ended by prorogation or dissolution of the Parliament.

shadow cabinet: the group of members in each opposition party, especially the official opposition, chosen to act as party critics for each of the government's cabinet ministers

Sherpa: a member of an ethnic group from the most mountainous region of Nepal, famous for its expert mountaineering skill. The word "sherpa" has now come to refer to elite mountain guides and porters, having outstanding physical endurance and strength.

sip-and-puff technology: used to send signals to a specific device, using air pressure by sipping and puffing on a straw-like instrument. It's used most often by people who are unable to use their hands to manipulate various mechanisms.

spasm: an involuntary and abnormal muscular contraction

Speaker of the House: a Member of Parliament (MP) who is the presiding officer of the House of Commons, elected at the beginning of each session by fellow MPs. He or she controls the House, chairs debates, manages the House of Commons and supervises its staff. The Speaker, according to the constitution, cannot vote unless his or her vote would break a tie, in which case convention dictates that he or she must vote so as to maintain the status quo.

spinal column: also called the backbone, a column of an articulated series of bones called vertebrae which extend down the back from the neck to the tailbone, which enclose and protect the spinal canal and spinal cord

spinal cord: a thin, tubular bundle of nerves that extends from the brain lengthwise along the back inside the vertebral canal, which carries impulses to and from the brain, and has thirty-one pairs of spinal nerves that leave the cord to transmit neurons to and from the body muscles and trunk

standing board: a flat surface to which a bedridden or wheelchair confined patient is strapped and which is tilted almost to a vertical position, enabling the patient's muscles and bones to maintain capacity and strength through weight bearing activity

supply day: a day in a parliamentary session reserved for the discussion of the business of supply, the actual topic of debate being chosen by a member in opposition, called a supply day motion. There are twenty-two allotted days in each calendar year, which are divided among the opposition parties in proportion to their representation in the House. All motions are put to a vote unless the sponsor of the motion specifies that there will be no vote.

syrinx, syringomyelia, post-traumatic syringomyelia: a known complication of traumatic spinal cord injury. When this occurs a cyst, known as a syrinx, can develop within the injured spinal cord. The term syringomyelia is reserved for cysts that are larger and may be associated with loss of neurological function.

Terry Fox Hall of Fame: Terry Fox (1958-1981) lost one leg to cancer and undertook to run across Canada to raise money for cancer research. Fox ran a marathon every day with a prosthetic leg, and died of his cancer when he was halfway across the country. His "Marathon of Hope" and engaging personality won the hearts of Canadians. Every September the Terry Fox Run takes place and it has become one of the world's largest one-day fundraisers for cancer research. The Terry Fox Hall of Fame was established to recognize others who display similar qualities of character and achievement.

tetraplegia: another name for quadriplegia, (tetra from the Latin referring to four)

Throne Speech: a speech prepared by the government outlining its plans for the upcoming parliamentary session, which is read by the monarch or the monarch's representative to the members of Parliament at the beginning of each Canadian parliamentary session. The Throne Speech content is debated and voted upon by all members, and defeat of the Throne Speech signals a federal election.

tilt board: an apparatus that is used to rotate a person from horizontal, vertical, oblique position in order to test perception of bodily perception, also called a tilt table

Tory: a Conservative politician

trach cuff: a soft balloon around the far end of a tracheostomy tube that can be inflated to allow for mechanical ventilation in patients with respiratory failure

tracheotomy or tracheostomy: a surgical operation that involves cutting into the trachea (windpipe) through the neck in order to open a direct airway into the body. This opening can be permanent or temporary; also called a "trach".

trans-fats: of unsaturated fat with trans isomer fatty acid(s). Trans-fats may be monounsaturated or polyunsaturated. Most trans-fats consumed today are industrially created by partially hydrogenating plant oils—a process developed in the early 1900s that extends the shelf life of unsaturated fats. It was first commercialized as Crisco in 1911. Unlike other dietary fats, trans-fats are neither required nor beneficial for health. Eating trans-fats increases the risk of coronary heart disease.

University of Manitoba Students' Union (UMSU): the campus student association for Manitoba's largest university, not a labour union

vertebrae: the thirty-three bones that make up the spinal column. Each of the series of small bones is called a vertebra.

vertebral canal: a canal that contains the spinal cord; also called the spinal canal

whip: a Member of Parliament who has the responsibility of ensuring his/her elected party members are in the House of Commons to vote

Whiteshell Provincial Park: a provincial park along the eastern border of Manitoba, next to Ontario. Located in the Canadian Shield, the Whiteshell has many rivers and remote lakes, and a large wilderness back country covered in boreal forest.

Index

Bold numbers indicate illustrations

Photo identification for colour pages

First colour page: Steven Fletcher, MP, in front of the Library of Parliament, overlooking the Ottawa River on Parliament Hill.

Second colour page, spiralling clockwise from centre:
+ Steven, with father David, on graduating from engineering in 1995;
+ on the beach with Claire Vivier the same year;
+ with sister Julia on an outing in Assiniboine Forest in the fall of 1996, during his year-long stay in hospital.
+ ready for rowing in Pinawa 1995;
+ aged 19, chopping wood near the Manitoba Naturalists Society Mantario cabin in 1992;
+ posing in front of Bissett's San Antonio gold mine in 1995;
+ Steven (at left) with sister Julia and brother Gordon at a kayaking regatta;
+ working as a canoe instructor at Camp Stephens on Lake of the Woods;
+ photographed during a campaign with (from left) Colleen Bready, Béla Czifra and brother Gordon Fletcher during a campaign at the University of Manitoba;
+ ready for a game of street hockey at 24 Sussex with MPs and Ben Harper (in red);
+ enjoying the summer sun at the Assiniboine Park Pavilion with Claire Vivier and Jen Paterson;
+ with Gary Filmon, then premier of Manitoba;
+ speaking during a student protest in front of the Manitoba Legislative Building in 2000, with Gordon holding the mic,
+ a portrait of Steven at age 20;
+ (top of page) clowning with a canoe paddle at a regatta in Selkirk;
+ field mapping near Flin Flon in the summer of 1994;
+ and as a boy, elegantly attired.

First back colour page, spiralling clockwise from centre:
+ in front of the House of Commons with his parents, Joanne and David Fletcher;
+ with siblings Julia and Gordon on the Whiteshell River.
+ with MP Rona Ambrose soon after his first election to Parliament;
+ sailing in Victoria Harbour during the 2001 Mobility Cup;
+ at a rally with then Opposition Leader Stephen Harper during the 2006 election campaign;

+ bundled for a mountain trek in Yoho National Park;
+ with Stephen Harper at the Caboto Centre in 2005;
+ posing with Grand Chief Phil Fontaine;
+ campaigning in 2004;
+ a breathless moment—standing to speak in the Commons;
+ (across the top, left to right) with Sam Sullivan, then mayor of
   Vancouver;
+ David Fletcher, Steven's father, posting campaign signs in
   January 2006;
+ and with constituents at his constituency office.

Last colour page, clockwise from top left:
+ with the Dalai Lama;
+ Steven's Christmas photo, 2007;
+ chatting in the hallway of Ottawa General Hospital with Prime
   Minister Stephen Harper and disability activist Rick Hansen
   moments before an announcement of the government's $20
   million investment in the Rick Hansen Man-in-Motion
   Foundation for Spinal Cord Research;
+ meeting California Governor Arnold Schwarzenegger;
+ with former Olympian and noted speaker Silken Laumann;
+ meeting Afghan President Hamid Karzai;
+ being introduced to the then Australian Prime Minister
   John Howard;
+ with Environment Minister John Baird in front of a campaign-
   ready van at The Forks in Winnipeg;
+ chatting with Defence Minister Peter McKay,
+ celebrating the 2007 Winnipeg Blue Bombers with Manitoba MPs
   Joy Smith, James Bezan and Rod Bruinooge;
+ and at centre: motoring around Parliament with aide Kristy
   Osmond.

As complex as his life may seem, Steven Fletcher lives by a simple
creed: "The best way to prove people wrong is just to go ahead and
do the things they say you aren't able to do."

Linda McIntosh

LINDA McIntosh is a writer and artist who lives with her husband Don on the shores of beautiful Lake Agimak in the boreal forests of Northwestern Ontario, in the township of Ignace. The McIntoshes have two adult children.

During the 1980s and 1990s, Linda was a politician in Manitoba, Canada, first elected as a school trustee and then as a Member of the Legislative Assembly, where she served as Treasury Board minister, Education minister and minister responsible for the Manitoba Public Insurance Corporation in Premier Gary Filmon's Progressive Conservative government.

Says the author, "I first met Steven when he came to see me during my tenure as a cabinet minister. Steven had been out of the hospital for a relatively short time, and he wanted the government to make some changes to its policies in order for him to realize greater independence. I liked him immediately. I liked the logic of his presentation and the way he articulated his case. I liked the way he had screwed up his courage and managed to get himself into the minister's office to make his pitch. He acted as if his life depended on it. And to a degree, it did.

"Eventually a deep and lasting friendship formed between us, a relationship that has always had as its hallmark a direct and honest dialogue."

Linda has been Steven Fletcher's close friend and mentor for many years.

Recycled

**Supporting responsible use
of forest resources**

www.fsc.org Cert no. SW-COC-1271
© 1996 Forest Stewardship Council

FSC

100%

ENVIRONMENTAL BENEFITS STATEMENT

Heartland Associates Inc saved the following
resources by printing the pages of this book on
chlorine free paper made with 100% post-consumer
waste.

TREES	WATER	ENERGY	SOLID WASTE	GREENHOUSE GASES
73	26,539	51	3,408	6,394
FULLY GROWN	GALLONS	MILLION BTUs	POUNDS	POUNDS

Calculations based on research by Environmental Defense and the Paper Task Force.
Manufactured at Friesens Corporation

More information on Steven Fletcher and the causes he
champions can be found at www.thestevenfletcherstory.ca

"This is not how I envisioned my life. If I could go back and avoid the accident I would in a second. But that is not an option. I will never get used to my physical situation nor will I ever feel comfortable with this reality. However, as challenging as it is, I have to deal with it. I am blessed with a wonderful family, and the opportunity to further my education and integrate into society. The people of Manitoba have allowed me to give back to the community that has given me so much. I am very grateful for the support of all those who have touched my life and helped me along the way. I particularly thank the residents of Charleswood–St. James–Assiniboia for their support. It has been a long and difficult journey from a ditch in northern Manitoba to Parliament Hill, but this journey is probably only possible in this great country of Canada." — *Steven Fletcher*